Signals from the Hill

Signals from the Hill

Congressional Oversight and the Challenge of Social Regulation

Christopher H. Foreman, Jr.

Yale University Press
New Haven and London

Designed by Nancy Ovedovitz and set in Baskerville type by Rainsford Type. Printed in the United States of America by BookCrafters, Inc., Chelsea, Michigan.

Library of Congress Cataloging-in-Publication Data

Foreman, Christopher H.
  Signals from the hill.
  Bibliography: p.
  Includes index.
  1. Legislative oversight—United States. 2. Trade regulation—Political aspects—United States. I. Title.
JK585.F68   1988   328.73′07456   88–17434
ISBN 0–300–04410–0

The paper in this book meets the guidelines for permanence and durability of the Committee on Production Guidelines for Book Longevity of the Council on Library Resources.

10   9   8   7   6   5   4   3   2   1

For My Father

Contents

Acknowledgments

I had no idea when I began this book just how many people would ultimately play important roles in helping me to complete it. The seeds were planted in June 1983 in Washington, D.C., at an Urban Institute conference on the Reagan administration regulatory relief effort. George C. Eads and Michael Fix invited me to participate and unwittingly set me thinking about undertaking a project of my own. The comments of conference participants Paul Quirk and Patrick McLain were especially helpful.

Shortly thereafter my work began in earnest under the generous auspices of the Twentieth Century Fund. In particular, I wish to thank James A. Smith, Steve Andors, Jeffrey Laurenti, Marcia Bystryn, Beverly Goldberg, Wendy Mercer, and, of course, the late M. J. Rossant for their support, patience, and helpful prodding at various stages of the project. Edward D. Berkowitz suggested my name to the Fund and later offered advice and encouragement. The Fund also retained Alex Holzman, who not only contributed a superior job of text editing but also challenged arguments or characterizations he thought questionable. The book improved considerably in his hands.

At different times I also enjoyed the services of two very capable research assistants. Early on, Cindy Burack performed considerable exploratory research that helped clarify my thinking. Later, Michel McQueen, then at the *Washington Post* and currently at the *Wall Street Journal*, put at my disposal the skill and energy of a superb professional journalist. I am indebted to the *Post* for granting the sabbatical that made her available for work on this book.

The various drafts of the manuscript also benefited from careful and insightful scrutiny by Gary Bryner, Paul Light, Paul Quirk, Clarence Stone, James Q. Wilson, and several anonymous readers. Laura Jones Dooley provided a swift and sure-handed final editing for the Yale University Press.

I cannot, for reasons set forth in the Appendix, name all the seventy persons in Congress, the federal bureaucracy, and elsewhere who gave me their time and insights. I know, however, that this book would have been impossible but for their generosity.

My wife, Lena Zezulin, provided unwavering support, even in the difficult months after the appearance of our son, Alexander, as the project moved toward completion. My mother, Thelma P. Foreman, kept asking, "How's the book coming?"

Much as I might like to blame any or all of the above for such errors as remain, the responsibility for these is mine alone.

Introduction

Risk seems to be everywhere. That inescapable message is delivered daily to millions of Americans via television, newspapers, and magazines. Whether by street crime, shoddy financial investments, or environmental pollution, we are increasingly made aware of ourselves as a nation of potential victims.

Much of this perceived risk originates in modern technology. Innovation has proved to be a double-edged sword, steadily improving our quality of life while creating risks heretofore unknown. Industries produce useful chemicals that may also threaten workers, consumers, and future generations. Drugs intended to alleviate pain, supplement diets, or fight disease may be misused or may induce harmful (and unpredictable) reactions in some persons. Firms may make unsubstantiated or misleading claims for their products or market goods they know to be either defective or worthless for their prescribed uses. In short, the blessings of modern industry and technology come freighted with a variety of potential misapplications, abuses, side effects, and unforeseen consequences.

The political response to such seemingly ubiquitous risk has been considerable. In this century (and especially since the late 1960s) the United States has given several federal agencies vast responsibility for assessing and managing such risks. These agencies include: the Environmental Protection Agency (EPA); the Occupational Safety and Health Administration (OSHA); the Food and Drug Administration (FDA); the Consumer Product

Safety Commission (CPSC); the National Highway Traffic Safety Administration (NHTSA); and the Federal Trade Commission (FTC). It is a list by now familiar to anyone even moderately attentive to public affairs.

But the proliferation of these agencies, the staggering scope and complexity of the tasks they perform, and the generally high degree of administrative discretion they appear to enjoy raise questions about how effectively and to what ends elected officials supervise their work. Scholars and journalists often suggest that government bureaucracies, especially the kinds of regulatory agencies listed above, are less subject to meaningful and coherent influence from Congress and the president than they should be. Some persons would contend, moreover, that existing influence is excessively focused on serving narrow constituencies.

One institutional focus of this book is the United States Congress, that great mirror and blender of public demands and sentiments. More precisely, I will probe several of the formal tools that Congress employs to oversee administration, the uses to which these tools are put, and the implications of that use. (The term *oversight* is given various and sometimes misleading meanings. My own definition follows in chapter 1.)

My second institutional focus is the national bureaucracy to which Congress and the president have jointly ceded operating responsibility for the statutes and programs they have created. No nation can rightfully claim to be "democratic" unless the unelected career experts of the bureaucracy and their appointed superiors are somehow formally and routinely constrained by the preferences and powers of "the people" or their freely elected representatives. Though truly indispensable to large-scale governance, bureaucracy becomes compatible with democracy only when held in check by popular will.

Political scientists commonly regard congressional oversight (whether of regulation or of anything else) as highly problem-ridden. The weakness and inadequacy of its program supervision has become a routine criticism of the institution. Political scientists have observed that congressional authorizations—the laws that create and continue programs, specifying agency powers and procedures—are generally quite vague, the result of limited expertise on the part of legislators (who then need to delegate to experts) and of Congress's chronic inability to reconcile competing policy perspectives in more precise language. In essence, Congress throws up its hands and instructs the agency to "handle the situation." And once the laws have been enacted, subsequent congressional supervision of administrative behavior and policymaking tends to be episodic or nonexistent. Both scholarly and popular treatments of Congress generally suggest a legislature that, except for the occasional instance when oversight offers concrete political rewards, remains far more interested in claiming credit for new programs than in the tedious review of old ones. As one critical journalist put it:

Congress as the legislative branch of our government has to a large extent abdicated its role and its responsibilities for monitoring and controlling the vast bureaucracy it has so painstakingly created layer by layer over many decades. Not only does Congress lack the time, the interest, or the desire to regularly conduct its myriad oversight functions, but there is a serious question of whether with all its resources, it has the capacity adequately to survey and control everything under its vast legislative domain.[1]

Analysts often portray Congress as too distant from the wheels of administration and too preoccupied with a plethora of other matters—especially legislation, reelection, and constituency service—to supervise agencies closely.[2] A natural

1. Donald Lambro, "Congressional Oversights," *Policy Review* (Spring 1981): 116. Lambro, a journalist, elaborates on his general condemnation of congressional oversight in *Washington—City of Scandals: Investigating Congress and Other Big Spenders* (New York: Little, Brown, 1984), chap. 2. In a more academic vein see also Robert E. Litan and William D. Nordhaus, *Reforming Federal Regulation* (New Haven and London: Yale University Press, 1983), chap. 4; Seymour Scher, "Conditions for Legislative Control," *Journal of Politics* 25 (August 1963): 526–51; and Lawrence C. Dodd and Richard Schott, *Congress and the Administrative State* (New York: John Wiley and Sons, 1979).

2. See, e.g., David E. Price, "The Impact of Reform: The House Commerce Subcommittee on Oversight and Investigations," in *Legislative Reform: The Policy Impact*, ed. Leroy N. Rieselbach (Lexington, Mass.: Lexington Books, 1978), pp. 133–78. See also David R. Mayhew, *Congress: The Electoral Connection* (New Haven and London: Yale University Press, 1974), p. 122.

corollary of the "oversight-incapable" or "oversight-indifferent" Congress is the unresponsive, self-possessed bureaucracy. It is an image with much inherent appeal. Politicians have long appreciated that bureaucracy makes a wonderful foil. It can be made to seem (depending on the particular horror or abuse one is conjuring) inept and slothful or imperialistic and rigid.

It is striking and, I believe, quite telling that the image of legislative weakness has arisen alongside a far different one: the fearsome congressional potentate able to bludgeon or scare agencies into doing his bidding with scarcely the batting of an eyelash. Journalists have gotten considerable mileage out of chronicling Washington's power brokers. Academic commentators, if perhaps less breathless in their assessments, have likewise generally acknowledged the special prerogatives of committee and subcommittee chairmen—and, increasingly, of their staffs. No secretary of agriculture dares make an important innovative move, we are told, without consulting Democrat Jamie Whitten of Mississippi, chairman of the House Appropriations Committee and, nearly continually since 1949, head of its subcommittee on agriculture.[3] Through another Appropriations subcommittee chairmanship, Democrat John Rooney of New York wielded profound influence over the State Department during the 1960s.[4] Congressional democratization in the mid-1970s caused subcommittee chairmanships to increase significantly, with even relatively junior members getting a piece of the action. Today committee ties to the agencies and bureaus within departments are reputedly so strong, jurisdictional prerogatives so jealously guarded, and committee meddling in administrative and policy detail so pervasive and unpredictable that coordinated, responsible governance is less a prospect than ever before.[5]

    3. Nick Kotz, *Let Them Eat Promises: The Politics of Hunger in America* (Englewood Cliffs, N.J.: Prentice-Hall, 1969), chap. 6.
    4. Donald P. Warwick, *A Theory of Public Bureaucracy: Politics, Personality, and Organization in the State Department* (Cambridge, Mass.: Harvard University Press, 1975), pp. 73–76, 160.
    5. Harold Seidman, *Politics, Position, and Power: The Dynamics of Federal Organization*, 3d ed. (New York: Oxford University Press, 1980), chap. 2.

These contrasting impressions of Congress are not logically inconsistent. Power may be exercised for quite narrow purposes by a select few, whereas important administrative and policy-making activities—perhaps more significant to the broader public in the long run—go unreviewed. Or the power of individual members may come at the expense of Congress as an institution. Any fair-minded student of legislative-executive relations must remain sensitive to such complexities. One must also take a fresh look at stereotypes. I have concluded that perceptions of congressional power—and thus debate over remedies—have often been subject to serious and frequently deliberate distortion, especially at the hands of politicians anxious to expand the scope of conflict on particular issues or to highlight the usefulness of favored "reforms."

Nowhere has this been truer than for social regulation, one of the most contentious realms in American politics.[6] In this book I do not focus on oversight and administration of the entire bureaucracy but on the relationship between congressional power and the agencies that protect citizens from the misrepresentations and hazards that innumerable products and processes might pose. I reach beyond resources and formal powers toward applications and responses. The emphasis here is not on what, in a textbook sense, congressional overseers *can* do but on what they *actually* accomplish—and how, if at all, things might be made to work more effectively.

Politicians and ordinary citizens have a considerable stake in having an accurate picture of legislative power over such programs. Politicians and activists engaged in battle over the future of institutions and policies need intelligent guidance on the implications of the choices available to them. As for the rest of us—

6. The scope of the term *social regulation* has varied somewhat. I use it here in a fairly restrictive sense, as a catchall for programs intended to produce protective impacts in three arenas: the environment, consumer protection, and worker health and safety. For usage akin to mine, see Lester B. Lave, *The Strategy of Social Regulation: Decision Frameworks for Policy* (Washington, D.C.: Brookings Institution, 1981); Lawrence J. White, *Reforming Regulation: Processes and Problems* (Englewood Cliffs, N.J.: Prentice-Hall, 1981); and William Lilley III and James C. Miller III, "The New 'Social Regulation,'" *Public Interest* 47 (Spring 1977): 49–61.

we must live, ultimately, with both the successes and the damage wrought by public choices. The policies in question—pollution control, product safety, and the like—rank high on the national political agenda and often impose considerable burdens. They are neither obscure nor insignificant, and they must be treated with as much care as society can muster. To the extent that they are problematic, part of the blame—and hope for improvement—may lie with the very Congress that created them. And, as I will discuss, an ongoing debate about regulatory reform hinges on the question of what Congress can and should do through its oversight tools. Assessing the direction that reform can and should take requires that we grapple with a fair amount of recent history, sorting out myth from reality, the important from the trivial. I seek to contribute to this important task.

The Argument

I pursue two related questions and embrace three major themes here. What, as a practical matter, does Congress achieve, or fail to achieve, through regulatory oversight? And what are the prospects for improving congressional performance? The themes emphasized are: (1) political uncertainty, extending long past the enactment of regulatory legislation; (2) the great distance between regulatory protective goals and the mostly means-focused supervision Congress nearly always undertakes; and (3) the ironic, and therefore easily misperceived, nature of an oversight system that works largely by appearing to have failed. Oversight emerges as a sometimes painful, inevitably self-interested process of consultation and second-guessing that reasonably well keeps administration sensitive to the concerns of persons and groups affected by or attentive to regulatory policy. As a system for monitoring agency decision making and adherence to approved procedure—that is, as a set of mechanisms for enforcing accountability regarding agency behavior and policy choice—oversight succeeds. For this purpose, Congress has evolved an oversight system of commendable redundancy and aggressiveness.[7] The various committees and subcommittees and

7. A provocative defense of redundancy in policymaking is Martin Landau,

congressional staff agencies collectively comprise an intricate and impressive system of screens or "fire alarms."[8] I believe that the major problem bedeviling the oversight of social regulation is neither the inherent autonomy of regulators nor the lack of incentive to supervise them. In my view, chronic uncertainty and conflict among political authorities, and the limited horizons of those same authorities, represent far more substantial challenges. The very contentiousness of policy formulation and implementation suggests that politicians are paying attention and that they will have continuing incentive to do so.

Regulatory programs of the type I will discuss in this book are exceedingly unlikely to move far toward major decisions (or even many minor ones) without Congress discovering the change and objecting to anything seemingly out of hand. The rhetoric of runaway bureaucracy—of regulators able to undertake and enforce policies in the face of a Congress too weak or indifferent to stop them—is both false and dangerously misleading. I regard this impression as *dangerously* misleading because the result may be an unnecessarily alarmed public and thus misallocation of reformist energy and scarce political capital. The image exists at least partly because of a campaign of deliberate misrepresentation in the 1970s by elements of the business community. But oversight consists of a quite effective if nevertheless disheveled and politically charged set of tools that can constrain agency behavior and shape the agendas of regulatory bureaucracy, executives, and managers.

What Congress lacks, however, is a stable and shared understanding of what, and how much, regulators ought to do. Given the nature of the tasks assigned to them, regulators will often stand accused of either doing too little or going too far—frequently on the same issue and in the same breath. Disagreement among attentive interests, within Congress, or between Congress and the president is inevitable. Moreover,

---

"Redundancy, Rationality, and the Problem of Duplication and Overlap," *Public Administration Review* 29 (July-August 1969): 346–58.

8. Mathew D. McCubbins and Thomas Schwartz, "Congressional Oversight Overlooked: Police Patrols versus Fire Alarms," *American Journal of Political Science* 28 (February 1984): 165–79.

those who embrace one point of view quite easily see oversight as having failed when the competing perspective is ascendant. Those who think an agency has gone too far will cry out for congressional restraint; those who think an agency has done too little (including, most prominently, Democrats on the key authorization committees) will see Congress as having failed to prod the bureaucracy with sufficient vigor. There is no easy way either Congress or the regulatory bureaucracies can escape this dilemma, upon which the usefulness and acceptability of any profound oversight reform necessarily hinges. But this is entirely different from asserting that an agency is out of control, a claim belied by the evident robustness of congressional inquiry and direction, especially when it comes to policing an agency apparently bent on doing unwanted things. The FTC and OSHA were two of the most frequently cited villains of regulatory overkill during the years preceding the Reagan presidency. A controversial and abortive inquiry into the television advertising of sugared cereals to children, along with other ventures in regulatory aggressiveness, fueled charges that the FTC was an overregulating "national nanny." OSHA likewise found a reputation as the quintessentially intrusive and insensitive regulatory bureaucracy. Mere mention of its name conjured a stereotype: a rule-bound and possibly rude inspector citing a well-meaning employer for some picayune infraction. OSHA allegedly cared more about the heights of toilet seats and the positions of fire extinguishers than about real protection, especially in health issues. But although both OSHA and the FTC may have been cast as rogue bureaucracies, Congress had been instrumental in starting the agencies down these ill-fated paths and, later, in trimming their sails.

Though reasonably effective at monitoring agency behavior, influencing leadership priorities, and restraining perceived "excesses," congressional oversight has been invariably weak at facilitating the achievement of protective impacts. As we shall see through repeated examples in important oversight arenas, congressional supervision is remarkably detached from the question of whether the citizenry will be rendered healthier or safer.

Indeed, for reasons summarized in chapter 5, regulatory goals are likely to prove largely immune to congressional supervision. One important reason (aside from the complexity inherent in regulatory tasks) is that for issue after issue overseers have incentives to concentrate their fire on *means rather than ends*, in part because political uncertainty and conflict make it hard for Congress to know what its ends are. With genuine safety and health impacts but distant blurs on the policy horizon, overseers focus more shortsightedly on immediately placating constituencies and policing procedures—a preoccupation with means related only imperfectly, if at all, to policy effectiveness. Agency executives and managers are thus sensitized, but within a framework that remains remarkably indifferent or irrelevant to whether the public is substantively better off.

It would not be surprising to find a relative indifference to protective impacts among those overseers who, on a given regulatory question, adopt a going-too-far stance. It is perhaps more disheartening that such indifference and goal resistance applies even to persons who adopt a consistently, even zealously, proregulation posture. When House Democrats during the early Reagan era took aim against the various manifestations of White House-inspired regulatory relief, they proved far more interested in short-run political victories, in catering to favored economic and ideological constituencies, and in defending favored regulatory tools than in the ultimate goals toward which their efforts were ostensibly directed. For officeholders of all political stripes, regulatory means—rules, inspection practices, enforcement statistics, funding levels, instances of procedural malefaction or apparent waste—are far more concrete and intriguing than fuzzy impacts. Politicians have strong incentives to defend, attack, or provoke adjustment in these tools on behalf of constituencies who find this behavior attractive. But the resulting agency attempts to placate overseers may well be of dubious benefit to the public. This does not imply, however, that agencies would be better off without congressional oversight.

This means orientation suggests that change aimed primarily at endowing Congress with more power over agencies is

less important by far than reform promising greater coherence, discipline, and farsightedness. Where the occasional
case of bureaucratic overreaching might occur, Congress has
shown itself well armed to cope with the challenge. Regulators can be, and have been, reined in; the tools for doing
this exist and are effectively employed. The more significant
challenges to reformers are larger, more subtle, and far
harder to address successfully.

In undertaking reform, moreover, we must remain alert to a
basic irony of congressional oversight: it works by seeming to
have failed. Bureaucracies are often effectively sensitized and
inhibited by members of Congress using strident, even extreme,
language; an inherent attribute of the system is to sound the
alarm when agencies make debatable choices. But even though
the agency in question may be effectively impeded from unde-
sired actions, or propelled toward desired ones, the very alarmist
tone of the rhetoric essential to the system may add to a perception of ineffective supervision. Hence, in an important respect, it is easy to make the oversight system appear worse than
it actually is.

I draw on the recent oversight histories of six major social
regulatory agencies: the EPA, OSHA, the FDA, the CPSC,
NHTSA, and the FTC. In no sense do I provide, however, a
comprehensive history of congressional supervision of these
agencies. In some instances I refer to particular targets of
congressional oversight as "horror stories." While I believe this
to be a fair description of the kinds of troubles that often rivet
congressional attention, the reader should not infer an unin-
tended cynicism. Only in rare circumstances might a regulatory
issue flow from a genuinely illusory problem, though overseers
(my catchall term for members of Congress and staff assistants
engaged in regulatory oversight) sometimes focus on relatively
insignificant aspects of agency behavior. Overseers will highlight
tragedy, but they do not manufacture it—nor should observers
trivialize it.

Chapter 1
The Framework for Regulatory Oversight

What is oversight? This question has bedeviled all inquiry into the subject, a quandary well stated by political scientist Morris Ogul:

Assessment of oversight is conditioned... by one's perception of what oversight is. If oversight is defined only in terms of formal powers, different conclusions emerge about its adequacy than if informal relationships are taken into account. Those who view oversight as simply an attempt to influence the implementation of legislation through post-statutory investigations will reach different conclusions than will those who are sensitive to oversight performed latently.

How one defines oversight affects what oversight one finds. Writers assess oversight differently at times because they are not talking about the same thing. These differences are mirrored in vocabulary. Thus the words scrutiny, review, inspection, control, command, supervision, watchfulness, and influence each carry connotations about what is expected.[1]

Discussions of congressional power traditionally proceed from potentially misleading distinctions among the various formal mechanisms through which the institution makes or influences

---

1. *Congress Oversees the Bureaucracy: Studies in Legislative Supervision* (Pittsburgh: University of Pittsburgh Press, 1976), pp. 6–7.

policy. In many textbook accounts of Congress, one finds three activities highlighted: authorizations, appropriations, and investigations-oversight. These reflect a roughly three-part, committee-based structure for doing business. Authorization committees in both houses consider bills to create or continue programs and establish (authorize) maximum permissible agency spending levels for a given year. Appropriations committees in each house—or, more accurately, their subcommittees—allocate the actual amounts that may be spent, in a process wholly separate from authorizing committees. Two standing committees, the House Committee on Government Operations and the Senate Committee on Governmental Affairs, roam more or less freely across the spectrum of federal programs, inquiring into the economy and efficiency with which they are run.

But this formal structure can be misleading in at least two respects. First, it encourages the nonsensical perception that oversight is something that happens entirely apart from the other two processes. Second, it probably biases discussion toward an underestimation of cumulative congressional influence. The lack of formal oversight should not be taken (though it often is) as indicative of congressional inattention or impotence. A wealth of informal monitoring and bargaining constantly fleshes out the structural bones of both the congressional division of labor and the legislative-executive relationship.

The complexity and controversy engendered by regulatory implementation translates into recurring pressures for change in the thrust of a program's authorization or appropriation. Debate over those changes necessarily involves oversight in the narrow and conventional sense of reviewing recent past administrative performance, and such oversight may, in turn, provide political impetus for legislative change. Hence, Congress's "legislative" and "oversight" roles tend to merge.[2] The truth is that what we conventionally tend to think of as postenactment oversight is in many respects simply a continuation of preenactment politics.

2. Lawrence D. Brown, *New Policies, New Politics: Government's Response to Government's Growth* (Washington, D.C.: Brookings Institution, 1983), p. 33.

The particular angst generated by regulation aside, congressional efforts to review and influence implementation may emerge from almost anywhere on Capitol Hill, and one is hard-pressed to say that oversight, in any sense, emanates from one place and not another. Appropriations and authorizing committees surely conduct a kind of oversight. The questions asked at reauthorization hearings, the preparatory work undertaken by committee and agency, and the clarifying language contained in committee reports all constitute supervision apart from whatever statutory text finally emerges. No rule bars, say, the House Energy and Commerce subcommittee on health and the environment—technically an authorization subcommittee—from staging a hearing, launching a staff inquiry, or attempting to signal agencies informally as to the chairman's preferences. Such activity occurs constantly within the myriad subcommittees that are so much the basic operating units of the contemporary Congress. Some authorizing committees have also evolved specialized oversight subcommittees, whose staffs devote themselves more or less exclusively to investigations and inquiry rather than formal lawmaking. What can be said if hearings staged by the Energy and Commerce subcommittee on oversight and investigations help to propel a law? Where does "oversight" stop and "legislation" commence? In the face of such overlap and confusion, it might be tempting to take refuge in Supreme Court Justice Potter Stewart's famous epigram on pornography: "I can't define it but I know it when I see it."

This messiness need not cripple understanding. In light of the preceding discussion, I will construe congressional oversight broadly, adopting *oversight* as an essentially commonsense synonym for *supervision*. With either term, I refer to two interlocking congressional processes: the efforts to *gather information* about what agencies are doing and to *dictate or signal to* agencies regarding the preferred behavior or policy. The formal authorization process takes center stage only occasionally, for it is but a fraction, and often a small one, of the political contest that is congressional supervision. It is necessary to look well beyond the narrowest interpretation of oversight as formal fact-finding and evaluation. Otherwise the richness of the congressional supervisory effort and the politics that generally underlie it can be missed, as can the critical, if elusive, question of *influence*.

It is also important to keep in mind that the legislative-executive struggle is not the sole arena of regulatory conflict. The judiciary also plays a critical role. When some person or group wants to contest administrative performance or decisions in a direct or forceful way, they regularly go to court—the case law in environmental protection is voluminous and far-reaching.[3] For interest groups lacking the budgets or grass-roots memberships that are especially useful in lobbying Congress, the judiciary may be a far more attractive forum. And a judicial opinion or order may be as potent as any statute.

Policy Entrepreneurship

Congressional oversight often involves a fair measure of policy entrepreneurship. An entrepreneur is a creator. Outside government, organizational entrepreneurs start firms or voluntary associations.[4] In government, they have been known to lead large bureaucracies and possess, on occasion, an almost frightening degree of autonomy.[5]

The congressional policy entrepreneur seeks to create issues and to mold opinion through the judicious and creative use of available resources. Membership in each house confers a distinct advantage in this regard. The far larger size of the House means that its members can more easily specialize in a given policy area. Multiple committee assignments more severely tax the ability of the average senator to focus his or her energies. On the other hand, the greater prestige and visibility accorded a senator may be quite helpful. For both the House and Senate entrepreneur, however, the objective is to promote support for broad new legislation or to pressure the executive branch into modifying

3. R. Shep Melnick, *Regulation and the Courts: The Case of the Clean Air Act* (Washington, D.C.: Brookings Institution, 1983).

4. James Q. Wilson, *Political Organizations* (New York: Basic Books, 1973), chap. 10.

5. Eugene Lewis, *Public Entrepreneurship: Toward a Theory of Bureaucratic Political Power—The Organizational Lives of Hyman Rickover, J. Edgar Hoover, and Robert Moses* (Bloomington: Indiana University Press, 1980).

its policies. Massachusetts Sen. Edward M. Kennedy's successful push for airline deregulation in the 1970s (like his unsuccessful promotion of national health insurance) is an example of policy entrepreneurship.[6]

The mass media helps make formal oversight a vastly different enterprise than it was in the early days of the Republic. Public, and thus congressional, indignation can be a formidable weapon, and press coverage, especially television, helps create both. Congress may often lack interest in administrative supervision, but the exposé is good politics. A claim of slovenly regulatory practice concerning public health or safety issues is bound to attract the attention of a press that gravitates to stories about victims. Victims may be geographically concentrated, as at Love Canal or Times Beach, or as broadly defined as "buyers of automobiles" or "breathers of air." Some have suffered real harm, but the intended audience is the millions of ordinary citizens who are potential victims. Victims create drama (or, in the language of journalism, "human interest") that can elevate agency behavior above the mundane realm of interagency memos and *Federal Register* notices. This tactic can also be used by antiregulation entrepreneurs, who argue that the bureaucracy has created its own victims.

Much oversight, then, involves attempts at entrepreneurial political communication, that is, efforts to highlight unsatisfactory performance—and, not incidentally, to become recognized for doing so. During the first Reagan term, Representatives John Dingell (D-Michigan) and Albert Gore, Jr. (D-Tennessee), were two of the most conspicuously aggressive such entrepreneurs in the House. On such regulatory issues as hazardous waste enforcement, medical device safety, and FTC performance, Dingell and Gore displayed remarkable tenacity and dexterity. Motivated by genuine concern for the public interest and for their own political careers, congressional-policy entrepreneurs find the press indispensable.

But most members of Congress are only episodically interested

6. Bradley Behrman, "Civil Aeronautics Board," in *The Politics of Regulation*, ed. James Q. Wilson (New York: Basic Books, 1980), pp. 99–100.

in social regulation and are unlikely to emulate such behavior in any sustained way. Some conceive their role as members differently. Others lack necessary resources; and access to energetic staff assistance is essential to oversight. Congressional staff assistants themselves suggest that many members lack a "taste for detail work," or "the ability to ask follow-up questions" at a hearing, or the "stomach" for playing a role that is inherently "not nice." The skills and tastes of members vary widely.

Staff Assistance

Members of Congress are not the only ones who matter in the legislative supervision of agencies. Members vote, ask questions at hearings, and make remarks for the record. They occupy the public, sometimes even glamorous, side of congressional life. But between World War II and the advent of the Reagan administration, a larger and more complex program agenda helped push Congress to enlarge its capability for coping with its political and policy challenges. A larger staff, which today does most of its day-to-day work, was the unavoidable result. The increase came in three areas: the congressional staff agencies, personal staffs, and committee staffs.

The four staff agencies include: the Congressional Research Service (CRS), the General Accounting Office (GAO), the Office of Technology Assessment (OTA), and the Congressional Budget Office (CBO). All—but especially the first three—perform work relevant to social regulation, but the GAO is most directly significant. Created in 1921 as part of larger budget reforms, the GAO is today by far the largest staff agency. Its 5,100 employees produce and distribute dozens of studies that scrutinize regulatory programs each year. GAO findings regularly constitute the basis for congressional hearings or press accounts that focus on regulatory agency failings.

Personal and committee staffs have also exploded. The combined House and Senate personal staffs grew from 1,150 in 1930 to 10,679 by the end of the 1970s. Committee staffs swelled from a mere 275 persons to over 3,000 in the same period.[7] Personal

---

7. Data on congressional staff are contained in Michael J. Malbin, *Unelected Rep-*

staffs write legislative proposals, track their progress through the Congress, and manage each member's office as well as his or her relations with constituents and the press. Generally speaking, personal staffs contribute much less than committee staffs toward sustained regulatory oversight. In interviews, the personal staffs of members holding seats on the House Energy and Commerce Committee routinely seemed nearly as overwhelmed as their bosses by the committee's vast legislative agenda.[8]

Outside the staff agencies, committee staffs constitute the core of regulatory oversight staff resources. In the House, key subcommittees of six standing committees maintain the major oversight jurisdiction and staff for social regulation: Energy and Commerce, Science and Technology, Public Works and Transportation, Education and Labor, Government Operations, and Appropriations. The Senate is similarly arranged.

Like most organizations, subcommittees are hardly collections of equals; some persons matter far more than others. For regulatory oversight, the staff director, other professional staff with ongoing assignments, and the chairman are where the action is. Everyone else is generally peripheral or irrelevant. On a continuing basis, a staff's judgment and activities are critical; the staff serves as the eyes and ears of the subcommittee, as its principal collector and sifter of the reams of information passed on by agencies, outside groups, disgruntled bureaucrats, and other sources.

The inertia generated by the separate agendas of individual staffers profoundly influences the allocation of resources. "You tend to look into things you already know about," said a veteran member of Representative Dingell's oversight staff. Previous inquiries in one area lead to new ones in that same area because the staff person has expertise and contacts there. Moreover, he or she knows that the staff director and the chairman already consider the subject important enough to merit some investment of time. This is important, because staff must always be able to

---

resentatives: Congressional Staff and the Future of Representative Government (New York: Basic Books, 1980), appendixes.

8. Personal interviews.

justify any new project to their superiors or it will be displaced by something else. As reasonable (or inevitable) as this orientation may be, it is also symptomatic of the difficulty that Congress has in addressing genuine protective impacts. After all, there is no reason to believe that the continuation of an existing staff agenda will have any ameliorative relationship to such impacts.

Minority party staff on a subcommittee play a far different and diminished role. They neither set the oversight agenda nor initiate and execute investigations. Sometimes they will be kept largely in the dark about what the majority staff is up to, especially if an inquiry seems likely to arouse partisan sensitivities. "As minority counsel," said one, "your job is to guard the political flanks of your members. By the time you attend the hearings, read the documents and brief your members, you're out of time."

Selectivity

Finally, oversight is not, need not be, and cannot be, omniscient. Much escapes attention. After the 1976 enactment of the Medical Device Amendments to the Food, Drug and Cosmetic Act, for example, five years elapsed before significant congressional attention was paid to their implementation. Neither committees nor their staffs nor the Congress as a whole undertakes anything like comprehensive inquiry into, or assessment of, the programs and policies pursued by an agency. Limited resources and contrary incentives make this impossible. In grappling with the whole, committees lose sight of and leverage over the particular. And an agency's defensiveness is of no small significance. One House staff aide who had spent several years scrutinizing regulatory agencies laughed at the idea of comprehensive oversight: "If you tried to do oversight like that the agency would overwhelm you with bullshit."[9] Although Congress regularly pays lip service to the *idea* of extensive and systematic oversight, defined in the Legislative Reorganization Act of 1946 as "continuous watchfulness" by committees over everything done by an agency

---

9. Personal interview with staff aide on the House Committee on Energy and Commerce, subcommittee on oversight and investigations.

within its jurisdiction, this aspiration is bound to remain unfulfilled.[10]

Most of what agencies do, at the level of the myriad individual actions that comprise the daily life of any department or agency, is simply not knowable by Congress. Indeed, it is not understood even by those who run agencies. With some 1,200 health and safety inspectors in OSHA, the assistant secretary of labor for occupational safety and health must rest content with only the broadest indications of what is going on in the field. Members of Congress, at far greater remove from agency operations, will almost certainly know much less, no matter how interested they are in following agency behavior. For the most part, the status of major initiatives, the general thrust of administration policy, some sense of how these compare with earlier efforts, and the opinions of affected interests constitute the limits of what even a reasonably attentive member will grasp. These are what Congress, collectively, digests in its treatment of regulatory programs.

Layers of Controversy

The debates about regulatory reform and oversight are closely linked, comprising a complex of concerns originating partly in constitutional structure, partly in ideological and economic cleavage, and partly in institutional history. The primary *political* tensions run along two axes.

---

10. Ogul, *Congress Oversees the Bureaucracy*, p. 5. Yet lack of comprehensiveness need not undermine the generation of substantial oversight. As Mathew D. McCubbins and Thomas Schwartz have argued, Congress generally opts for "fire-alarm" oversight instead of the "police-patrol" variety. The latter is proactive, congressionally initiated sampling of agency activity. The former is reactive to constituency triggering of congressional attention through "a system of rules, procedures, and informal practices that enable individual citizens and organized interest groups to examine decisions (sometimes in prospect), to charge executive agencies with violating congressional goals, and to seek remedies from agencies, courts, and Congress itself" ("Congressional Oversight Overlooked: Police Patrols versus Fire Alarms," *American Journal of Political Science* 28 [February 1984]: 165–79, quotation on p. 166).

First is the *clash of policy interests* discussed in the introduction. Social regulation covers a broad scope, is budgeted limited resources in the face of gargantuan tasks, and inspires competing economic and ideological passions—hence the high likelihood that any policy or innovation will dissatisfy someone. Even when the political forces line up more or less unanimously, the consensus extends only to a given issue in that particular context. The same issue framed differently can generate different political alignments.

For example, the existence of the EPA is not controversial. But the agency may be accused of doing too little to protect citizens from the threat of hazardous waste, dealing with only a small portion of known sites of such material. At the same time, industries or firms that bear the burden of these policies either through taxes or by complying with disposal regulations are inclined to perceive the agency as having gone too far. Similarly, the agency, in the view of environmentalists, has made too little progress in the fight against air pollution. But it may go too far or too fast to suit some state governments in pushing for the creation of costly inspection and maintenance programs to reduce automobile emissions. Similarly, if a newly marketed drug produces serious unforeseen side effects in some patients or if nutritionally deficient infant formula reaches the market, the FDA may seem to have done too little. But when the agency moved in 1977 to ban saccharin, even though the law gave it little choice, a storm of protest erupted; the FDA had gone too far. In general, the proponents of regulatory stringency have tended to hold the upper hand within the key authorization committees, thus channeling most oversight energies toward support for regulation. Yet controversy and congressional opposition always loom just over the horizon when the costs of stringency become apparent to those who must bear them.

Some spheres of policy simply do not create this sort of conflict, at least for considerable periods of time. Relations among the players are relatively harmonious, invisible, and closed to all but a small coterie. The relevant bureaucracies, congressional committees, and interest groups enjoying such a state of affairs are often described as "subgovernments" or "iron triangles."[11] In other words, policy debate is persistently dominated by a single advocacy coalition. Veterans affairs, at least during the 1950s and 1960s, was a prime example. Veterans groups, the Veterans Administration, and the congressional veterans affairs committees have constituted, in general, politically symbiotic elements of a distinct policy subsystem.[12] That excludes most others, such as members of Congress not on the relevant committees; they have little incentive to join in. The same has traditionally been true of much economic regulation through which agencies control prices or the ability of firms to enter the marketplace. Typically, few persons besides those directly benefiting care deeply about occupational licensing, freight rates, or maritime subsidies.[13]

It is impossible to speak of policy triangles or neat networks when discussing social regulation—there are simply too many competing participants. Symbolism, ideology, and media attention run high, for these are vital to the very creation of programs destined to impose severe costs upon narrow but well-organized interests.[14] Regulatory policy and decisions are often fiercely contested; relationships among players are hardly cozy. Groups like the Environmental Defense Fund or the Natural Resources Defense Council approach EPA's mission with ideological zeal. The Chamber of Commerce and the Chemical Manufacturers Association, meanwhile, embrace the perspective of those on whom regulatory costs fall most directly.

Environmental and consumer protection issues also attract press attention, in large measure because the players regularly pose the issues in dramatic terms of conflict and victimization that make good copy. Players with strong "proregulation" views

11. J. Leiper Freeman, *The Political Process* (New York: Random House, 1965).
12. Gilbert Y. Steiner, *The State of Welfare* (Washington, D.C.: Brookings Institution, 1971), chap. 7.
13. See, e.g., Edward Mansfield, "Federal Maritime Commission," in *Politics of Regulation*, ed. Wilson, pp. 42–74. For an intriguing account of how and why this can change, see Martha Derthick and Paul J. Quirk, *The Politics of Deregulation* (Washington, D.C.: Brookings Institution, 1985).
14. Wilson, *Politics of Regulation*, pp. 370–71.

retain a powerful incentive to berate the opposition publicly, thus galvanizing public and congressional opinion favorable to their cause.

Environmental policy also involves state and local governments that must frequently carry out mandates defined and dictated by Washington; often they have different priorities or find federal initiatives burdensome or unresponsive to their needs. In short, because social regulation imposes direct costs on some while purporting to safeguard the lives and health of others or of the community at large, it is inherently controversial—and controversy is the enemy of the policy triangle.[15]

Overlaying and interacting with these policy tensions is a *clash of institutional interests*. Much of this is rooted in the American constitutional framework of "separated institutions *sharing* powers."[16] Legislative supervision as practiced in the United States is unique; in Great Britain, for example, the House of Commons enacts laws and supervises their execution through the prime minister and the cabinet. Individual members of Parliament are nearly impotent in comparison with their American counterparts. The American House member or senator controls a sizable staff that may number from fifteen to about thirty persons, uses membership on committees to achieve considerable familiarity with selected policies, and keeps his or her seat only by remaining personally popular among the voters of a district or state. A rise to a subcommittee or full-committee chairmanship brings still more visibility and staff assistance, increasing opportunities for all manner of independence and policy entrepreneurship. By contrast, the typical member of Commons has little staff assistance, scant access to power through committees, and advances mainly by pleasing party superiors. Members of Parliament have, as one observer has put it, "more bark than bite."[17] Traditionally,

15. For an example of an "iron triangle" that dissolved into controversy see James R. Temples, "The Politics of Nuclear Power: A Subgovernment in Transition," *Political Science Quarterly* 95 (Summer 1980): 239–60.

16. Richard E. Neustadt, *Presidential Power: The Politics of Leadership* (New York: John Wiley and Sons, 1960), p. 33. Emphasis in original.

17. Richard Rose, "British MPs: More Bark than Bite," in *Parliaments and Parliamentarians in Democratic Politics*, ed. Ezra N. Suleiman (New York: Holmes

one of the most striking differences between Congress and the House of Commons has been the latter's substantive incompetence on policy details.[18]

By design, the U.S. Constitution does not erect such firm boundaries around legislative and executive domains. Instead, as James Sundquist notes, it "put two combattants into the ring and sounded the bell that sent them into endless battle." But as to precisely who has power over what, the document is "either silent, or *ambiguous*."[19] Resolving such ambiguity is an endless process. Weak presidents may cede power to Congress, as was the case in the late nineteenth century. Stronger ones may recapture it. But in a legislature elected independently of the president, where party ties are relatively tenuous and reelection a function of every member's resourcefulness, it can be hard either to predict where dissent will erupt or to keep it within desired limits once it has arisen.

Even below the presidential level, where the vast majority of legislative-executive relations are conducted, Congress does not simply dictate to the bureaucracy. The bureaucracy possesses considerable resources—especially expertise and allies among interest groups and within other levels of government—that may be turned to explicitly political purposes. A naive reading of the Constitution may suggest that the Congress commands and the bureaucracy listens, but in reality these relations take on the flavor of bargaining. Committee chairmen cannot spend all their time lashing out at an

and Meier, 1986), pp. 8–40. Legislative committees in Britain have been far weaker than their counterparts in the United States largely because the former have been created on an ad hoc basis to review legislation and because members of the Commons tend to dislike the work. See S. A. Walkland, "Committees in the British House of Commons," in *Committees in Legislatures: A Comparative Analysis*, ed. John D. Lees and Malcolm Shaw (Durham: Duke University Press, 1979), pp. 253–57.

18. Geoffrey Smith and Nelson Polsby, *British Government and Its Discontents* (New York: Basic Books, 1981). The authors state that the "institutionalized capacity for Parliament is to chart its own ends, to develop a rounded sense of any policy whatever is virtually nil" (p. 128).

19. *The Decline and Resurgence of Congress* (Washington, D.C.: Brookings Institution, 1981), p. 16. Emphasis added.

agency or its leadership; they must go on to other things. Agencies may also stonewall, especially if they perceive that their position is likely to be sustained should the scope of conflict expand to include other players. One committee chairman may be opposed by others. Or the press may be enlisted to spread the word regarding the kinds of demands being made of the agency in the hope that opposition will mobilize. Congress is powerful but not omnipotent. Agencies take their primary guidance from the legislature, but they are hardly impotent.

Personal and institutional maintenance needs are highly significant in charting the course congressional oversight will take. Over the years, the opposing themes of overregulation and regulatory negligence have proved to be good fodder for both. President Reagan and innumerable Republican candidates for the House and Senate have blamed regulators for stifling productivity and harassing solid citizens. Congressional Democrats in the mid-1980s embraced the safety issue with renewed vigor; it played well with a Middle America that admired Reagan but craved protection against all manner of unseen or potential hazards.[20] Policy conflict nurtures institutional and partisan combat, which in turn propels still more policy debate and cleavage.

Much of the tension between Congress and the executive over regulation is exacerbated by institutional developments unanticipated by the Constitution. I have already alluded to two: the rise of political parties and, more recently, congressional democratization and the resulting proliferation of subcommittees. Committee chairmen no longer have the power to select subcommittee chairmen. Nor does a rule of strict seniority any longer assure that mere longevity places one in command of a standing committee. With power and resources more widely scattered, relatively junior members, many of whom are committed to the relentless pressing of favored issues, have a public pres-

20. Steven V. Roberts, "Democrats Press the 'Safety' Issue," *New York Times*, June 3, 1986, p. B6; and David Broder, "Tony Coelho: The Triumph of the Democrats," *Washington Post*, June 8, 1986, p. F7.

ence that would have been inconceivable as recently as a generation ago.

Additional factors contribute to current controversies over social regulation. For decades, Congress and the executive have episodically debated and skirmished over the independent regulatory commissions—agencies that fall outside the executive departments. The FTC and the CPSC, created in 1914 and 1972, respectively, are the two commissions with which I deal here. Secretarial-level appointees in charge of departmental agencies, once past the hurdle of confirmation, serve entirely at the pleasure of the president; he may ask for their resignations at his whim or involve himself in their decision making. Members of multimember independent regulatory commissions, by contrast, are more distant from the long arm of the White House once confirmed. The president may designate the chairman and fill other posts with supportive commissioners as vacancies occur, but once installed in their jobs, these appointees generally may stay until their terms expire. The courts have long maintained that these persons cannot have their appointments terminated on grounds of political incompatibility with the president.[21] Indeed, the independent regulatory commissions have traditionally been deemed, at least on Capitol Hill, "arms of the Congress"—a warning to prospective commissioners to consult fully with their legislative overseers and to keep a prudent distance between themselves and the White House. The commissions are relatively, not absolutely, independent, and were never intended to be otherwise.

More recently, and particularly relevant to social regulation, the Office of Management and Budget (OMB) has become far more prominent in the war for influence over programs and policies. Created in 1921 as the Bureau of the Budget and identified for decades thereafter mainly as a tool for coordinating executive-branch budget requests, the agency received a far more overt managerial (and partisan) role through a 1970 re-

---

21. See the Supreme Court decision in *Humphrey's Executor v. United States* (1935).

organization sponsored by President Nixon.[22] President Reagan later issued two executive orders that accorded OMB even more extensive powers to review proposed regulations before public discussion, a change that sparked a fire storm of disagreement on Capitol Hill, where Democrats vehemently objected that OMB was being used as a kind of nefarious "black hole" from which important regulatory proposals might never emerge. Indeed, the Reagan initiative, a dramatic departure from previous presidential efforts, promptly triggered a long and acrimonious struggle that cut to the very heart of how regulation ought to proceed.

This history reflects an enduring dilemma of legislative-executive relations. Congress *wants* the executive to have power sufficient to cope with challenges basic to the national interest and to carry out chores for which the legislature may be ill-equipped. It was Congress that clamored for order to be brought to the annual submission of departmental budget requests. But Congress also wants to restrain the executive. Powers and resources granted under one set of circumstances may easily evolve in ways that were not intended or foreseen when first conferred. The Congress of the 1920s could scarcely have envisioned that half a century later its successors would draft the Budget and Impoundment Control Act of 1974 to make the legislative role in budgetmaking more competitive with the president's. Nor could Congress have foreseen in 1980 that it would, in 1986, consider stripping *all* funding from the unit within OMB responsible for regulatory review, the Office of Information and Regulatory Affairs (OIRA). Ironically, Congress had *created* OIRA to implement the Paperwork Reduction Act of 1980. Such are the turns possible within a system where Congress may demand that the president lead, only to see leadership take an unexpected course.

Gradually, Congress has acted to fill in the blanks left by the Constitution but implied by the framework it created and the tasks at hand. The enterprise has been relentlessly partisan. And

22. Larry Berman, *The Office of Management and Budget and the Presidency, 1921–1979* (Princeton: Princeton University Press, 1979).

because in recent years it has appeared ever more likely that the president's party may differ from that controlling either the Senate, the House of Representatives, or both—a division that only increases the prospects for a power fight over program implementation—the opportunity and incentive for congressional inquiry have been enhanced.

The first formal congressional inquiry, launched a scant three years after the states ratified the Constitution, clearly foreshadowed the partisanship that would characterize later endeavors. Early 1792 saw a Congress shaken by the resounding defeat of Gen. Arthur St. Clair in his expedition against the Indian tribes of the Northwest Territory. The House passed a resolution creating a seven-member special investigating committee. A key justification for the investigation, and one employed ever since, was "that an inquiry into the expenditure of all public money was the indispensible duty of this House," since the Constitution placed primary responsibility for revenue bills in that chamber. The committee ultimately absolved the general, instead citing War Department inefficiency and mismanagement.[23] The report was never acted on, however, since Federalists deemed it an embarrassment.

Congress also created specialized committees to handle the legislative workload—and these, too, became forums for partisan competition. In the 1860s, Congress opted to separate its taxing and spending function into separate committees. Appropriations bills became potent vehicles for legislative proposals; rules allowed the attachment of substantive riders so long as the provisions reduced rather than increased expenditures. Riders give opponents an effective means to stop an agency from continuing some action or to preclude funding for one merely proposed (see chapter 3). The power of the purse has generally been Congress's most potent instrument for directing policy, competing with the president, and playing out the partisan and ideological struggles that infuse regulatory policy.

23. Joseph P. Harris, *Congressional Control of Administration* (Washington, D.C.: Brookings Institution, 1964), p. 251.

Regulatory Oversight: Recent Issues

Although Congress has long possessed tools to influence and evaluate administration, major debate and concern about oversight has arisen since the early 1970s. One reason has been increased suspicion of the executive, brought about at least in part by the Vietnam War and the Watergate scandal.[24] Fears of an imperial presidency grew from 1967 to 1974, and congressional Democrats in charge of both houses mistrusted a Republican White House that seemed bent on tilting the institutional balance even further toward the president.

A second factor in the increased concern about Congress's oversight role was the strong impulse toward institutional reform that swept through Congress, especially the House, in the early and mid-1970s. Part of the impulse was directed, as noted earlier, at democratizing Congress. The Democratic Caucus decided that no member of the House could chair more than one legislative subcommittee and made the subcommittee assignment process more equitable.[25] Such changes naturally gave junior members more power. Many members were also dissatisfied with the way Congress went about its oversight task. Reformers urged standing committees to establish oversight subcommittees.[26] The rationale was to institutionalize, and thus strengthen, a committee-level oversight capability deemed insufficient.

A third reason for the increased attention to oversight was the advent of a new era of social regulation. From 1966 to 1976 Congress enacted a series of laws that created or enhanced the

24. Joel D. Aberbach, "Changes in Congressional Oversight," *American Behavioral Scientist* 22 (May-June 1979): 512.

25. Roger H. Davison and Walter J. Oleszek, *Congress and Its Members* (Washington, D.C.: Congressional Quarterly Press, 1981), p. 226.

26. A 1977 Senate study makes the following observation: "Last session the House adopted a rule which requires the committees with more than 15 members to establish oversight subcommittees or carry out their oversight functions in another way. It was thought that establishing separate oversight subcommittees would create an oversight capacity that is lacking in many committees" (*Study on Federal Regulation*, Vol. 2: *Congressional Oversight of Regulatory Agencies*, 95th Cong., 1st sess., 1977, p. 110).

federal commitment to the environment, to occupational safety and health, and to consumer protection. These included the National Highway Traffic and Motor Vehicle Safety Act (1966); the first major Clean Air Act amendments (1970); the National Environmental Policy Act (1970); the Occupational Safety and Health Act (1970); the Consumer Product Safety Act (1972); the Federal Water Pollution Control Act (1972); the Safe Drinking Water Act (1974); the Toxic Substances Control Act (1976); and the Resource Conservation and Recovery Act (1976). Along with the new laws came new agencies to implement them: NHTSA, EPA, OSHA, and the CPSC. Older agencies, such as the FDA and the FTC, were given additional responsibility for protecting the public.[27]

The growth of such regulation helped raise nagging questions about congressional oversight and influence. Both houses began to generate and debate a variety of reform proposals just as the newer initiatives in social regulation had settled firmly onto the national policy agenda. Congress was clearly uneasy with the programs it had created, despite their strongly bipartisan origins. Liberals feared that business influence would weaken the programs, whereas conservatives anticipated and perceived bureaucratic excess. Academic criticism of both economic and social regulation fueled the concerns; legal scholars, economists, and political scientists produced a flood of commentary challenging both the basic regulatory approach and the adequacy of political control. As regulatory burdens became more apparent, the business community became increasingly vocal, attacking particular programs or decisions while sometimes endorsing broad-scale reforms such as mandatory cost-benefit analysis that might inhibit overregulation.[28]

27. Under the Magnuson-Moss Act of 1974, the FTC received broad authority to promulgate industrywide consumer protection regulations. In 1976 Congress enacted the Medical Device Amendments, giving the FDA explicit responsibility for a wide range of products.

28. See Richard N. L. Andrews, "Economics and Environmental Decisions, Past and Present," in *Environmental Policy under Reagan's Executive Order: The Role of Benefit-Cost Analysis*, ed. V. Kerry Smith (Chapel Hill: University of North Carolina Press, 1984), esp. pp. 57–70.

Critics both in and out of Congress saw greater use of the legislative veto, a requirement that executive-branch actions be formally cleared with Congress before becoming effective, as a means to help assure more effective oversight. For its strongest disciples, the legislative veto became a sine qua non for "government by the people" in a bureaucratic age. Some thought that requiring the automatic termination of agencies unless affirmatively reauthorized (known as sunset legislation) would force congressional attentiveness to regulatory programs and thereby strengthen the institution's role. As will become clear, the list of ideas about how to reform the regulatory state grew quite long but produced little actual payoff. Meanwhile, the creation of successively more elaborate White House oversight processes under Presidents Nixon, Ford, Carter, and Reagan highlighted the perceived need for both coordination and enhanced direction of agencies by Congress and the president.[29]

This growing White House role in oversight also sparked clashes with the legislative branch. White House review generally aimed to enhance cost-sensitivity among mission-focused agencies, which irritated congressional advocates determined to safeguard programs and suspicious of economic critiques that sounded to them too much like endorsements of laxity.

Conflict became all the more direct when the Reagan administration's push for "regulatory relief" seemed to threaten years of congressional handiwork, enervating agencies that were just beginning to find their footing in a treacherous policy terrain. Executive order number 12291, issued barely a month after Reagan's inauguration, made clear the administration's determination to subject major regulatory proposals to a searching cost-effectiveness review inside OMB (by OIRA) before releasing them for public comment. The Carter administration's regulatory program had taken pains to avoid even the appearance that regulations must meet a cost-benefit test, had been decentralized among multiple offices, and had been conducted with the ethic of open government firmly in mind. The Reagan program, by

29. George C. Eads and Michael Fix, *Relief or Reform? Reagan's Regulatory Dilemma* (Washington, D.C.: Urban Institute Press, 1984), chaps. 3, 6.

contrast, insisted on a cost-benefit test, centralized authority in OMB, offered less opportunity for public scrutiny of White House involvement, and appeared to embrace off-the-record contacts with industry and agencies as acceptable.[30] In addition, the Reagan administration wanted less stringent rule-making and enforcement for major regulatory programs. Through such measures and through the appointment and budget processes, the Reagan administration aimed toward what it deemed a more balanced approach. Such a posture predictably provoked intense opposition among public interest groups and their allies on Capitol Hill, resulting in an episodic, multifront counterattack.

30. Andrews, "Economics and Environmental Decisions," p. 70, and Eads and Fix, *Relief or Reform?*, chap. 6.

Chapter 2
The Influence
of Inquiry

If the agenda looks promising, the first to arrive are the technicians with their cameras, control panels, and bundles of cable. Spectators gradually fill the public seating—lobbyists, agency officials, congressional staff, relatives and personal associates of scheduled witnesses, tourists, and curiosity-seekers. A table at the side or rear of the room has been set aside for the working press. Key staff members take seats near the chairman's; others position themselves quietly along the back wall. The bureaucrats, lobbyists, and reporters are often well acquainted with these staffers, but to the uninitiated they are all but invisible.

As the clock nears 9:30 or 10:00 A.M. the star player arrives: the subcommittee chairman. He—it is nearly always a "he," because there are so few women in Congress—moves comfortably to his post at the center of the panel, surveys the attendance, nods smilingly to select individuals around the room, perhaps shares a quick joke with the staff or with another member. The chairs around the witness table have filled with agency heads, their deputies and assistants, company executives, more lobbyists, technical experts, or ordinary citizens whose paths happen to have crossed, perhaps in misfortune, those of the officials and businessmen. Still photographers crouch between the table and the dais, snapping away.

A single loud crack of the gavel announces the start of the hearing. The chairman welcomes everyone and states the business of the day—an unfortunate accident, perhaps, or some questionable agency practice. Can the agency justify its performance? What were its motives? What was the relationship between agency officials and representatives of a regulated industry? Is the agency compromising the public safety? Is it unduly injuring innocent firms? The chairman poses such questions, but *not* out of ignorance. He more or less knows what answers he will get and what position he will take; he is merely warming up his audience.

After the chairman has introduced the issue of the day, he offers the floor to other members of the committee for their remarks. Then the witnesses get their turns. They read from formal statements while members, staff, and spectators—provided with advance copies—read right along with them. If the witness list is crowded and time short, some may be asked to summarize their remarks. The tone of the questioning is mostly polite but sometimes partisan and adversarial. Some questions attempt to lead a witness, perhaps toward conclusions he or she finds embarrassing or invalid. "I think the White House should have done it differently, don't you?" one questioner may offer. Another may wonder whether "the Secretary tried to get you to water down that regulation." Other questions will be more benign, even perfunctory. As all this goes on, members of Congress will drift in and out of the room. Some enter, listen briefly, and depart without having said a word. Others grill witnesses aggressively, even theatrically. If a floor action is imminent, the proceedings may grind to a temporary halt while the committee members hurry off to vote.

Staff aides are always close by. Inevitably, one or two such aides will have done all the important legwork to set up the hearing: contacting and questioning agency officials formally or informally; culling through stacks of documents for days or weeks at a time; arranging for interest-group representatives, agency officials, or private citizens to testify. But all that is done behind the scenes; nowhere is the dependency of members upon staff more publicly apparent than at the hearing itself. The chairman and other members confer quietly with assistants about which questions to ask, about witness answers, or about the proper interpretation of documents under discussion. If a member enters late, perhaps unfamiliar with the details of the day's topic, a staff aide may approach to offer a quick, whispered briefing.

Little, if anything, of substance is resolved on the spot, for such an encounter is but one stage in the life of most issues. Major surprises are unlikely since the entire exercise has been carefully planned from the start to the typical early-afternoon finish that allows attending journalists to meet their deadlines.

Hearings are a Washington ritual. Participants and sophisticated observers understand that the exercise, however well motivated, is largely staged to get media attention, especially television. Hearings are also, in a sense, the tip of an iceberg, since a vast amount of congressional inquiry and comment occurs either informally or less publicly through telephone exchanges, letters, and private discussions between agency officials and overseers.

What do these efforts achieve? Congressional inquiry into regulatory programs generally pursues two broad, often simultaneous, themes that are impressed with mixed results on the higher levels of regulatory bureaucracy. These are concern for *constituency sensitivity* and for *procedural integrity*.

By constituency sensitivity, I refer to the assorted concerns and preferences of economic and ideological interests: states, congressional districts, farmers, environmentalists, consumer groups, business firms, and unions. By procedural integrity, I refer to a focus on whether the behavior of officials constitutes lawful, ethical, and administratively sensible procedure. Note that these descriptions say nothing about fidelity to regulatory policy goals or about the protective impact of regulation. That is because overseers do not focus on such matters; they do not, despite their rhetoric, pursue "health and safety" or "consumer protection." Instead, overseers focus on means, directing their energies to constituency and process, where they possess both the incentive and the capability to make a mark. Within this framework, congressional inquiry functions effectively to sensitize agency executives and managers to a plethora of issues, sometimes with spectacular concrete results. As a result of oversight, an agency may either move more aggressively into an area, may terminate proceedings that some organized and vocal interest finds offensive, or may speed up some action it had planned to take anyway. Officials may find themselves disciplined, even, on rare occasions, dismissed. But they may also find themselves strategically applauded by their allies within Congress.

Whatever the particular aim, the most common impact of congressional scrutiny is to raise a given issue, whether significant or trivial, as a priority for those who run regulatory programs. Congressional scrutiny is an exercise in manipulating the political environment in which programs and issues are considered. It attempts or threatens to expand the scope of political conflict, so as to encourage, if not compel, some preferred administrative or policy choice. Of course, how an issue plays out—that is, the precise nature of an agency's response—depends on many factors both inside and outside of Congress. Agencies necessarily filter the demands that overseers put forth.[1]

Congress is often intensely divided over both broad programmatic direction and specific regulatory decisions. Because of these intense conflicts, oversight is not merely a process of professional, disinterested monitoring. Rather, scrutiny is a *weapon* used by persons and groups with all sorts of personal, institutional, and political agendas, which is patent in the congressional inquiry and comment directed at four agencies: the Environmental Protection Agency, the Food and Drug Administration, the Occupational Safety and Health Administration, and the Consumer Product Safety Commission.

These agencies differ as to task and structure. Each has its separate regulatory domain. OSHA and the FDA are large agencies nestled within far larger executive departments. The CPSC, as a small, independent regulatory commission, is outside any

1. Paul J. Quirk, "Comments," in *The Reagan Regulatory Strategy: An Assessment*, ed. George C. Eads and Michael Fix (Washington, D.C.: Urban Institute Press, 1984), pp. 218–22.

department and headed by five presidential appointees. The EPA, like the CPSC, is also independent of any department but is far larger and more complex, headed by a single administrator, and responsible for an appropriation 120 times as large.

In spite of these differences, the congressional scrutiny directed at the agencies and the dynamics affecting the *impact* of such scrutiny share important elements. For all the apparent differences, it is the similarities that merit the most attention.

Constituency and Procedure: Inquiry in Action

The Environmental Protection Agency

The Environmental Protection Agency seems to draw more intense and contentious scrutiny and comment on Capitol Hill than any other regulatory agency. Its activities are so varied, so important, and so potentially costly to various interests that environmental protection consistently ranks among the more important domestic policy concerns of both the White House and the Congress. *Everyone* wants clean air and water—poll results show remarkably consistent and overwhelming public support for tough environmental regulation—but the price can be *very* steep for some, and the technology extremely uncertain.[2] For example, in 1977 the EPA estimated the cost of achieving clean air and water by 1986 at $360 billion, and the Clean Air Act alone was thought to soak up well over $20 billion per year.[3] Farmers and ranchers must cope with potentially costly restric-

2. See William Schneider, "The Environment: The Public Wants More Protection, Not Less," *National Journal*, Mar. 26, 1983, pp. 676–77. See also Laura M. Lake, "The Environmental Mandate: Activists and the Electorate," *Political Science Quarterly* 98 (Summer 1983): 215–33. More generally see Seymour Martin Lipset and William Schneider, *The Confidence Gap: Business, Labor, and Government in the Public Mind* (New York: Free Press, 1983).

3. George C. Eads and Michael Fix, *Relief or Reform? Reagan's Regulatory Dilemma* (Washington, D.C.: Urban Institute Press, 1984), p. 89. See also David Harrison, Jr., and Paul R. Portney, "Making Ready for the Clean Air Act," *Regulation* (March-April 1981): 26.

tions on poisons, pesticides, and herbicides.[4] Localities are constrained to abide by the Safe Drinking Water Act.

Because the agency makes such "big bucks" decisions, the EPA offices are constantly being pressured by powerful economic interests such as utilities, heavy industry, agriculture, mining, and organized labor. These groups exert similar pressures on members of Congress. The fundamental political dilemma at the EPA is that on any given issue some businesses and governmental jurisdictions will want to fend off "excessive" regulation, while environmentalists, other firms, and other jurisdictions will seek continued or greater regulatory stringency.

Business firms do *not* inevitably champion reduced regulatory burdens. Existing firms can become accustomed to the regulatory status quo and fear "unfair" competition if newer firms are not required to invest in the equipment necessary to meet tougher standards.[5] In addition, firms in one region could hardly be expected to rally to any version of deregulation that threatened to enhance the economy of other regions at their expense. And, for obvious reasons, those that market pollution-control technology have a stake in seeing regulation maintained, not eliminated.[6]

Nor are labor unions reliably pro- or antiregulation. Organized labor has held tenaciously to a prostringency orientation in worker health and safety. But such concern melts away when nonworkplace regulation appears to threaten jobs. Hence the United Auto Workers made common cause with auto manufacturers and dealers in seeking to delay the introduction of tougher air-quality emissions standards for "mobile sources." By contrast, lobbyists for the United Mine Workers sought to *retain* require-

4. See, e.g., Cynthia Gorney, "Banning a Weedkiller: No Middle Ground," *Washington Post*, Aug. 3, 1987, pp. A1, A10.
5. Robert A. Leone, *Who Profits: Winners, Losers, and Government Regulation* (New York: Basic Books, 1986).
6. Such a group is the Manufacturers of Emissions Controls Association (Roger G. Noll and Bruce M. Owen, *The Political Economy of Deregulation: Interest Groups in the Regulatory Process* [Washington, D.C.: American Enterprise Institute, 1983], p. 18).

ments for expensive scrubber technology on coal-fired power plants in the belief that doing so would save jobs in the Eastern and Midwestern states; eliminating scrubbing was thought to favor Western mines, whose product is far lower in the sulfur responsible for sulfur dioxide emissions and thus acid rain.[7]

Environmental groups are fairly consistent in seeking tough regulation. The Sierra Club, the Natural Resources Defense Council, and the Environmental Defense Fund have excelled at publicizing various environmental crises and scandals, at defending continued statutory stringency in Congress, and at using litigation to compel aggressive implementation to the greatest extent possible.

Interest groups actively promote congressional scrutiny that helps their own causes and to do so nurture alliances within a large universe of congressional participants. The result is an agency constantly under fire from institutions and individuals having quite narrow perspectives—former EPA administrator Douglas Costle once complained of having to report to forty-four committees and subcommittees of Congress.[8] Congressional inquiry and comment spring readily from the problematic implementation (marked by crisis, scandal, conflict, and slow decision making) so common in social regulation. The 1984 revelation that a researcher retained by both the FDA and EPA had falsified data in work for the former led House Energy and Commerce Chairman John Dingell to stage a hearing in which he extracted a promise from the EPA administrator that the researcher's work would not be used in setting a carbon monoxide standard.[9] The catastrophic leak of methyl isocyanate gas

7. Bruce A. Ackerman and William T. Hassler, *Clean Coal/Dirty Air* (New Haven and London: Yale University Press, 1981). See also Robert W. Crandall, "Air Pollution, Environmentalists, and the Coal Lobby," in Noll and Owen, *Political Economy of Deregulation*, pp. 84–96.

8. Douglas M. Costle, "A Regulator's Path Isn't a Rose Garden," *New York Times*, Apr. 24, 1983, p. E21.

9. Morton Mintz, "Pollution Standard Has a Murky Past, Hearing Indicates," *Washington Post*, Oct. 2, 1984, p. A17. Earlier, Dingell had urged the GAO to look into the matter, resulting in a report embarrassing to the EPA. See General

at a Union Carbide plant at Bhopal, India, that resulted in over two thousand deaths prompted Henry Waxman (D-California), chairman of the House subcommittee on health and the environment, to conduct hearings questioning apparent administration foot-dragging in the war against hazardous pollutants.[10] Oversight, however motivated by sincere concern for public protection, often feeds on public misfortune. Overseers will be strategic and opportunistic even in pursuit of public-spirited ends.

Oversight and hazardous waste. Congressional scrutiny of the EPA's effort to deal with the hazardous waste problem exemplifies the most conspicuous uses of oversight. Overseers have been effective at highlighting slow administrative process, mismanagement, imminent regulatory decisions that appear unjustified, and the perceived needs of particular congressional constituencies. As impressive as this list is, one must keep in mind that it indicates a focus on regulatory means (and how those means are regarded by affected parties) rather than on the ostensible protective ends of regulation.

The problem of hazardous waste disposal first captured public attention in the late 1970s and has never been long out of the news. Stories of communities threatened by dangerous dump sites are by now depressingly common, and the scope of the problem, though not precisely known, is surely enormous. A 1985 GAO report noted that the EPA had about 19,400 hazardous waste sites in its official inventory but that no complete inventory existed.[11] The actual number of such sites is far larger, reaching perhaps into the hundreds of thousands. For com-

---

Accounting Office, *Status of EPA's Air Quality Standards for Carbon Monoxide* (GAO/RCED–84–201), Sept. 27, 1984.

10. The hearing was staged at Institute, W.Va., site of another Union Carbide plant producing the substance. See House Committee on Energy and Commerce, *Hazardous Air Pollutants* (hearing before the subcommittee on health and the environment), 98th Cong., 2d sess., Dec. 14, 1984.

11. General Accounting Office, *EPA's Inventory of Political Hazardous Waste Sites Is Incomplete* (GAO/RCED–85–75), Mar. 26, 1985.

munities dependent on threatened water supplies, the situation is potentially catastrophic.

The regulatory effort to deal with the problem hinges on two statutes. The 1976 Resource Conservation and Recovery Act (RCRA) provides that regulators create a comprehensive scheme of "cradle-to-grave" waste management. The widely reported contamination at Love Canal, near Niagara Falls, led Congress to enact the Comprehensive Environmental Response, Compensation, and Liability Act—popularly known as Superfund. Through Superfund, the federal government took on the massive technical and political challenge of leading the cleanup effort at existing sites.

Unfortunately, program implementation has suffered delays stemming from the technical, administrative, and political complexity inherent in the regulatory challenge.[12] Landfill disposal is relatively inexpensive but perilous, since such sites can never be made impervious to leakage. Such alternatives as incineration or deep-well injection are more costly and create their own hazards. Politics enters into waste disposal simply because, though everyone wants access to a disposal facility, few want to live near one. States have been late in gearing up for their share of the regulatory effort, often, they would contend, because the federal government was slow to disburse promised funds. At the federal level, the RCRA waste-disposal program has been said to lack resources. According to one observer, the Office of Solid Wastes has been "chronically understaffed and underfunded, even compared to other EPA program offices."[13]

Congressional oversight has provided a continuing forum for both EPA critics and supporters. Dramatic results are evident in two kinds of situations. Sometimes particular implementation actions can trigger an avalanche of criticism inside and outside Congress, creating a decision-making environment in which

---

12. Richard Riley, "Toxic Substances, Hazardous Wastes, and Public Policy: Problems in Implementation," and Harvey Lieber, "Federalism and Hazardous Waste Policy," in *The Politics of Hazardous Waste Management*, ed. James P. Lester and Ann O'M. Bowman (Durham: Duke University Press, 1983), chaps. 2, 4.

13. Lieber, "Federalism and Hazardous Waste Policy," p. 71.

reassessment quickly becomes attractive as an exercise in political damage control. In October 1981, for example, the EPA decided that some ten thousand waste-disposal facilities would not have to obtain liability insurance. But following public outcry, the agency reversed itself six months later. In February 1982, the agency proposed to suspend temporarily pending rules prohibiting the burying of drums filled with liquid waste. Again, an immediate, massive outcry from environmentalist forces, in Congress and beyond, caused the EPA to back down three weeks later.[14]

A second scenario that stimulated implementation action involved accusations of deliberate, politically motivated maladministration and attempts to undermine the course of a congressional investigation. The scandal and political crisis that erupted at the EPA in late 1982 and early 1983 gave environmental enthusiasts, who abhorred the Reagan administration from the beginning, the opportunity to raise for a time the issue of environmental program implementation near the top of the nation's (and the president's) domestic policy agenda.

In autumn 1982 Chairman Dingell's oversight subcommittee was already months deep into an ongoing means-focused probe of the EPA, especially the hazardous waste program. Along with the chairman of the Public Works and Transportation subcommittee on investigations and oversight, Elliott Levitas of Georgia, Dingell had negotiated with the EPA for the delivery of documents pertaining to various aspects of agency program implementation. When the administration stalled and finally declined to provide these documents, Dingell's subcommittee subpoenaed Administrator Anne Gorsuch to appear, documents in hand. An administration claim of executive privilege only whetted Dingell's appetite. These and other subcommittees received frequent doses of leaked material from within the agency, pointing to serious abuse, including the attempted political manipulation of the Superfund program by Assistant Administrator Rita Lavelle. The Levitas subcommittee issued Gorsuch a subpoena. When Gorsuch refused to honor it, the full committee, and then the

---

14. Riley, "Toxic Substances," 39–40.

entire House, voted to hold her in contempt. At about this time, a Midwestern flood spread deadly dioxin (a contaminant in waste oil that had been sprayed on local roads years earlier) throughout the Missouri town of Times Beach. The resulting media attention further increased pressure on the EPA.

The attention only intensified in early 1983. When Lavelle was asked to resign but refused, President Reagan fired her. In the end, Gorsuch herself, along with many other top officials, had to depart, their positions having become politically untenable. Though Lavelle was the only person actually indicted and convicted of a crime—perjury before a congressional committee—the Reagan administration had to launch a major political damage-control effort, bringing back respected former EPA Administrator William Ruckelshaus, to demonstrate its commitment to the environment.[15]

Naturally, members of Congress are also interested in getting attention for threats of particular interest to their electoral constituencies. Representative James Florio's ceaseless pursuit of stronger hazardous waste enforcement is most conspicuous in this regard. During one seven-week period in 1984, the General Accounting Office issued six studies dealing with toxic substances and hazardous waste that had been initiated at Florio's request. Florio's state, New Jersey, produces more toxic and hazardous material than any other. Focused efforts directed at particular dump sites are quite common. If the threat of such waste looms large enough, even members of Congress who might not see themselves as especially environmentalist find themselves drawn in. In some cases, especially where a member happens to have the right committee assignment, oversight can look virtually indistinguishable from constituency service.

The congressman and the creek. Take, for example, the case of Tar Creek in Oklahoma. When twenty-eight-year-old Mike Synar arrived as the freshman Democratic representative from

15. A reasonably thorough, if strongly adversarial, recounting of the EPA scandal is Jonathan Lash, Katherine Gillman, and David Sheridan, *A Season of Spoils: The Story of the Reagan Administration's Attack on the Environment* (New York: Pantheon Books, 1984), chap. 1.

Oklahoma's second district in 1979, he did not intend to stress environmental issues. Colleagues warned him not to: "tree-hugging" would get him into trouble in a conservative, energy-producing state. Synar had decided to make economic development for the district his office's top priority.

But all that soon changed. By 1979 water tainted with poisonous residue from abandoned iron and zinc mines had begun to contaminate Tar Creek in eastern Oklahoma, killing fish and threatening underground aquifers.

Soon after the creation of Superfund, Oklahoma began lobbying for federal money to study and clean up the Tar Creek site. Because of the severity of the threat, Tar Creek was at the top of the EPA's national priority list. But questions arose over whether the Superfund could be used to clean up mining waste. Agency lawyers viewed the statute as ambiguous. The Chemical Manufacturers Association resisted the idea that its members pay Superfund taxes for another industry's mess.

Tar Creek quickly became the top priority for Synar's office. He approached the issue essentially as a problem in constituent casework and the EPA as a source of necessary funds. He cultivated EPA officials, used oversight hearings, and had the good fortune of powerful allies. In March 1982 Synar and his state allies won $435,000 of EPA money to evaluate the Tar Creek problem. James Florio supported Oklahoma's position on mining wastes and in June collaborated on a hearing in Tulsa that allowed Synar to stress his district's problems.[16] The following November, at another hearing, Synar pressured Assistant Administrator Lavelle into stating that she "had not precluded" making a greater funding commitment.[17]

Synar's effort apparently received a considerable boost from an unlikely source. Republican Sen. Barry Goldwater of Arizona

16. House Committee on Energy and Commerce, *Tar Creek: Implementation of Superfund* (hearing before the subcommittee on commerce, transportation, and tourism), 97th Cong., 2d sess., June 14, 1982.

17. House Committee on Energy and Commerce, *PCB and Dioxin Cases* (hearing before the subcommittee on oversight and investigations), 97th Cong., 2d sess., Nov. 19, 1982.

was also after the EPA to include mining waste under Superfund in order to help a community in his state. An EPA official recalled later that the political climate seemed to point in only one direction: "Nobody [at the EPA] wanted to take the political heat for saying, 'we're not going to address the problems with the mines. . . .' Here's a mining site that cried out for action. . . . So you had this conservative Republican putting pressure and the agency just had to back off its position."[18]

Oklahoma got the assistance it sought. The issue also gave Synar positive visibility back home; through tenacity and good fortune he emerged as a slayer of the bureaucractic dragon. Not surprisingly, Synar later stressed the effectiveness of his efforts: "I'll admit it. One of the things we did . . . was to keep the media attention. What I couldn't accomplish through media, I could accomplish through oversight. I can make their lives miserable. Agencies don't like to be on the front pages of newspapers."[19]

Of course, not all such attempts at entrepreneurship are quite so successful. With so many communities clamoring for assistance and action, while resources are limited and technology uncertain, some must be disappointed. Moreover, a committed cadre of political appointees can in some ways resist congressional efforts at supervision and policy direction. I would stress, however, that this is evidence of conflict between institutions, not the anonymous decision-making power of faceless bureaucrats. House Democrats may have had their difficulties with Reagan's EPA, but one problem they did *not* have was keeping track of what and how the agency was doing and what decisions it was considering and making. Regulatory agencies may not always respond as some particular set of critics might wish, but given formal and informal monitoring tools, the agencies are almost endlessly permeable. Scrutiny of the hazardous waste program exemplifies the political disagreements and technical impediments that bedevil regulation, as well as the resourcefulness of

18. Personal interview.
19. This account is based largely on congressional and agency interviews conducted by Michel McQueen.

which congressional overseers are capable when their interest has been truly piqued.

The Food and Drug Administration

Next to the EPA, the Food and Drug Administration draws more congressional attention than any other agency discussed here. Throughout Congress, several subcommittees have sufficient jurisdictional claim to examine or attempt to constrain agency practices. The collective demand for information is substantial; agency officials testify on Capitol Hill as often as fifty times each year. Written correspondence and informal and preparatory interactions amount to thousands more contacts between the agency and the Hill.

Scrutiny naturally embraces two competing perspectives. On one hand, some congressional overseers, bolstered by advocacy organizations like the Ralph Nader-sponsored Health Research Group, have often proclaimed the FDA insufficiently vigilant on behalf of consumers, branding it solicitous toward industry, especially pharmaceutical manufacturers. From this point of view, the agency approves the marketing of products that are more dangerous or less effective than they should be, is slow to act on evidence of harmful effects that appear only after approval, inadequately oversees the quality of industry-sponsored research, and does less than it should to promote consumer awareness.

But to some, the FDA overregulates. It allegedly keeps much-needed drugs off the market with its ponderous review procedures.[20] Sometimes it issues proposals that energize opposition

20. For rare congressional attempts to elevate this perspective, see House Committee on Science and Technology, *Oversight: The Food and Drug Administration's Process for Approving New Drugs* (hearings before the subcommittee on science, research, and technology), 96th Cong., 1st sess., June 19, 21, July 11, 1979. See also House Committee on Science and Technology, *Drug Lag* (hearing before the subcommittee on natural resources, agricultural research, and the environment), 97th Cong., 1st sess., Sept. 16, 1981. The first of these was, according to former FDA Chief Counsel Peter Barton Hutt, "the first hearings in the history of the FDA that were designed to show that the agency was overly cautious, rather than not cautious enough, in regulating new drugs." See his

from distinct economic constituencies. For example, the agency's move to revise labeling requirements for baked goods provoked the ire of the House Small Business Committee.[21] Agricultural interests were similarly anxious to fend off calls for restrictions on the use of antibiotics in animal feed—a practice that produces larger and more profitable cattle and poultry.[22] Hence, congressional oversight of the FDA does not reinforce a clear, preestablished "legislative intent." Rather, oversight represents a continuing struggle over precisely what acceptable policy is to be.

The most likely catalyst to formal congressional inquiry and comment, especially through public hearings, is a product associated with demonstrable harm. Unlike most other regulatory agencies, the FDA is charged with *approving* products before marketing and can thus be held accountable, along with a manufacturer, for any misfortune that attends product use. An approval or failure to catch an unapproved product can easily spark criticism if reported side effects capture media and congressional attention. Yet approval decisions on drugs and medical devices must often be made with ambiguous information; the agency must balance risks against benefits. Any difference of opinion among agency review personnel can later be highlighted in a way that calls into question the agency's commitment to protecting the consumer. As one veteran congressional staff aide put it: "No member of Congress will ever get in trouble by asking the [FDA] why it didn't study something a little bit longer."

But slow process is the great continuing frustration of all those attentive to the agency's activities, regardless of the particular agenda. Manufacturers want their products approved more rapidly. Consumer groups want speed, too—on such things as warning labels, implementing regulations, and reassessment of

---

"Investigations and Reports Respecting FDA Regulation of New Drugs (Part II)," *Clinical Pharmacology and Therapeutics* 33 (1983): 578.

21. A summary of this issue is contained in U.S. Department of Health, Education and Welfare, Food and Drug Administration, *Food and Drug Administration and the Ninety-fifth Congress—January 1, 1977–December 31, 1978*, pp. 173–75.

22. Ibid., pp. 109–13.

over-the-counter drugs. The pressures for speed and care are constantly at war.

In recent years, the most aggressive practitioner of what might be dubbed "horror-story product" oversight has been New York City Democrat Ted Weiss, chairman of the House Government Operations subcommittee on intergovernmental relations and human resources. A combative liberal from Manhattan's West Side, Weiss took over the subcommittee in 1983 from the retired North Carolinian L. H. Fountain, who had, over many years, earned a substantial reputation for close scrutiny of FDA activities. In tandem with Daniel Sigelman, an energetic subcommittee staff aide who had worked for the Health Research Group before coming to the Hill, Weiss soon established a solid reputation for consumer-oriented criticism of FDA management. In a 1983 report, Weiss took the agency to task for deficiencies in its review of Oraflex, a prescription painkiller associated with several deaths.[23] Weiss held similar hearings and issued reports on Zomax, another painkiller associated with severe reactions, and E-Ferol, an intravenous vitamin supplement responsible for several infant deaths early in 1984. Each, for Weiss, represented an instance of "bureaucractic blundering."[24]

Representative Weiss is not alone. In the case of infant formula, a harmful product led to legislation and later provided ammunition in the war by House Democrats against President Reagan's policy of regulatory relief.[25] In 1979, a pediatric ne-

23. House Committee on Government Operations, *The Regulation of New Drugs by the Food and Drug Administration: The New Drug Process* (hearings before the subcommittee on intergovernmental relations and human resources), 97th Cong., 2d sess., Aug. 3, 4, 1982. The ensuing report is *Deficiencies in FDA's Regulation of the New Drug "Oraflex,"* House Report 98–511, 98th Cong., 1st sess., 1983.

24. The prolific Daniel Sigelman wrote reports for Weiss on both subjects in the wake of hearings. See House Committee on Government Operations, *FDA's Regulation of Zomax*, House Report 98–584, 98th Cong., 1st sess., 1983. On E-Ferol, see *Deficiencies in FDA's Regulation of the Marketing of Unapproved New Drugs: The Case of E-Ferol*, House Report 98–1168, 98th Cong., 2d sess., 1984.

25. House Committee on Interstate and Foreign Commerce, *Infant Formula* (hearing before the subcommittee on oversight and investigations), 96th Cong., 1st sess., Nov. 1, 1979.

phrologist in Memphis, Tennessee, noticed that infants consuming two soy-based infant formulas had developed metabolic alkalosis, a condition associated with appetite loss and other problems. This happened because the formulas were chloride deficient. When a subsequent recall proved incomplete—the formulas could still be found on some store shelves weeks later—a Washington, D.C., television station broke the story, attracting the attention of House Democrats Albert Gore, Jr., of Tennessee and Ron Mottl of Ohio.

Though legislative change was arguably unnecessary—both the FDA and some congressional staff involved were skeptical—the political momentum proved irresistible. Industry lobbies are notably chary of rushing to defend a lone firm accused of a serious preventable mishap; other firms share an obvious stake in being perceived as safe operators. And few policy issues are so instantly compelling as the possibility of a direct threat to the lives and health of children. An aroused Congress passed the Infant Formula Act of 1980, mandating new recall and quality-control requirements (and explicitly listing minimum acceptable levels of several formula nutrients) less than a year after the television story that started it all had aired.

When a batch of vitamin B6–deficient formula surfaced in early 1982, Gore and Mottl used it as an opportunity to flog the Reagan administration publicly on regulatory relief. Why, they wanted to know, had the quality control and recall regulations implementing the new statute not been effected? Was this not a further example of OMB-sponsored regulatory relief at public expense? FDA Commissioner Arthur Hull Hayes was forced to concede that "the proposed regulations would have, if followed by the firm, prevented" the deficient formula from reaching the market.[26] The regulations were promptly issued.[27]

The preceding examples of horror-story product oversight suggest that congressional scrutiny of the FDA, like that for the EPA, is especially aggressive and effective when particular de-

26. House Committee on Energy and Commerce, *Infant Formula: The Present Danger* (hearing before the subcommittee on oversight and investigations), 97th Cong., 2d sess., Mar. 11, 1982, p. 11.

27. Ibid., p. 7. See also *HHS News* (press release), Apr. 5, 1982.

cisions or mishaps expose an agency's failings. Overseers use individual cases to suggest and dramatize wider patterns of failure or wrongheaded policy. Congressional Democrats anxious to show that President Reagan's executive order number 12291 has had deleterious effects on agency efforts to protect the public naturally gravitated to examples that turned an abstract management issue into one of life and death.

Congressional inquiry has rarely stressed the possibility that excessive *caution* rather than laxity might characterize approval decisions, even though such caution could easily be as damaging to public protection as regulatory laxity. As chairman of a House Science and Technology subcommittee, New York Democrat James Scheuer attempted to highlight the problem of possible regulation-induced drug lag during the late 1970s and early 1980s.[28] But this has not proved a broadly attractive posture, given the relative invisibility of the persons thus victimized. Should such persons emerge as a distinct class, however, matters may differ vastly. To relieve the visible plight of those suffering from illnesses too rare to make drug development and marketing profitable, Congress, with the enthusiastic support of consumerist liberals like Weiss, enacted the 1983 Orphan Drug Act, giving companies special incentives to serve that constituency. And in the mid-1980s elements of the organized gay community harshly criticized the FDA for alleged foot-dragging in the approval of medications to treat Acquired Immune Deficiency Syndrome (AIDS).

Constituent anger and specific product horrors are not the only forces that inspire oversight. A concrete threat to the very integrity of the regulatory process, stemming from the purported influence of regulated interests over agency decisions, has been a major theme of inquiry.[29] This posture has proved

28. House Committee on Science and Technology, *Pharmaceutical Innovation— Promises and Problems* (hearing before the subcommittee on natural resources, agricultural research, and environment), 97th Cong., 1st sess., Apr. 27, 1981. See also General Accounting Office, *FDA Approval—A Lengthy Process that Delays the Availability of Important New Drugs* (HRD–80–64), May 28, 1980.

29. During the mid-1970s Sen. Edward Kennedy (D-Massachusetts), acting as chair of two subcommittees, charged that the FDA was unduly influenced by the drug companies. Testimony by agency employees appeared to corroborate

remarkably durable; in exposing villainous behavior, legislators establish national reputations as defenders of the public good and cement useful alliances with consumer groups. There is little incentive to appear evenhanded. As political scientist Paul Quirk has observed, "Such behavior simply reflects the necessity for congressmen to decide who will be their friends and who their enemies—an attitude of judicious moderation is likely to gain the support of no one."[30]

As in other agencies, the concrete instance of procedural male-faction is always an attractive oversight target. It is directed at behavior that no one can endorse and places members and staff, many of whom are lawyers, on familiar ground—playing cops and robbers rather than science and numbers. In 1980–81, for example, the House Energy and Commerce oversight subcommittee examined allegations that two FDA employees had maintained an improper relationship with a pharmaceutical company that resulted in the approval of its product and the removal of cheaper competing ones.[31] Early in 1985, Government Operations subcommittee Chairman Weiss got the GAO and the departmental inspector general to ask whether the new deputy commissioner

---

this claim. Indeed, a major theme of oversight efforts extending back to the 1960s was the belief that the agency must do ever more to challenge the voice of manufacturers in drug regulation. See Senate Committee on Labor and Public Welfare and Committee on the Judiciary, *Examination of the Pharmaceutical Industry, 1973–74—Part 7* (joint hearings before the subcommittee on health and the subcommittee on administrative practice and procedure), 93d Cong., 2d sess., Aug. 15, 16, 1974. See also *Regulation of New Drug R. and D. by the Food and Drug Administration, 1974* (joint hearings before the subcommittee on health and the subcommittee on administrative practice and procedure), 93d Cong., 2d sess., Sept. 25, 27, 1974.

30. "Food and Drug Administration," in *The Politics of Regulation*, ed. James Q. Wilson (New York: Basic Books, 1980), p. 216.

31. House Committee on Interstate and Foreign Commerce, *Soft Contact Lens Solutions: Oversight of FDA* (hearing before the subcommittee on oversight and investigations), 96th Cong., 2d sess., July 1, 1980; *FDA Regulation of Soft Contact Lenses* (hearing before the subcommittee on oversight and investigations), 96th Cong., 2d sess., Dec. 12, 1980; House Committee on Energy and Commerce, *FDA Mismanagement: Regulation of Soft Contact Lenses* (hearings before the subcommittee on oversight and investigations), 97th Cong., 1st sess., May 29, June 2, 1981.

had, immediately before joining the agency, been paid consulting fees and awarded contracts in violation of federal rules.[32]

Medical Devices

Like lawmaking, a single oversight effort may be built on a foundation of multiple motives. Investigations not only are a means to highlight or correct particular problems but can also serve as a vehicle for a broader partisan competition and debate. It is even possible to pursue the contrasting themes of too much and too little in a single inquiry, provided those who embrace each posture do not clash directly and immediately.

Scrutiny of the Medical Device Amendments by the House Energy and Commerce oversight subcommittee exemplifies these possibilities. The amendments give the FDA authority over a vast, heterogeneous family of products, including the state-of-the-art surgical appliances and diagnostic aids. Collectively, they represent a regulatory challenge of mammoth proportions.[33]

At the heart of the amendments lies a three-tiered classification scheme. The agency ranks a product according to the degree of regulatory control thought necessary. So-called general controls (designated class I) include prohibitions against adulteration and misbranding, mandatory notification before a device is marketed, and "good manufacturing processes." Tougher class II requirements mandate more explicit "performance standards," defining how the device should function under given conditions of use. Most stringently regulated are class III devices, which directly sustain life, prevent impaired health, or carry a risk of illness or injury, such as kidney dialysis machines and heart pacemakers. Class III devices, like new drugs, require premarket approval.

In 1982 several findings suggested to overseers that the agency

32. Howard Kurtz, "Questions Raised about FDA Deputy," *Washington Post*, June 18, 1985, p. A13.

33. For a detailed review of the medical device industry and the problems associated with regulating it, see: Office of Technology Assessment, *Federal Policies and the Medical Device Industry* (OTA–H–230), October 1984, esp. chap. 5, and General Accounting Office, *Federal Regulation of Medical Devices—Problems Still to Be Overcome* (GAO/HRD–83–53), Sept. 30, 1983.

was off course; no performance standard had been issued for any of the thousand or so class II devices then marketed.[34] Furthermore, the agency had largely ignored class III devices already on the market when the amendments were passed; although the law applied to both old and new products, resources were directed mainly at post-1976 devices. A regulation requiring manufacturers to report instances of "adverse experience" with their devices had been delayed, it seemed, by OMB review. Subcommittee overseers argued that the FDA simply was not enforcing the law.

Subcommittee chairman John Dingell and colleague Albert Gore, Jr., held a hearing, demanding explanations for the delays. Asked Gore: "Is this another example of measures designed to protect the public disappearing in a black hole of Reaganomics because companies have found a way to jigger the system and prevent the Government from doing anything that displeases them?" Dingell and Gore were joined by Republican Bob Whittaker of Kansas, who focused his attention on the FDA's handling of contact lenses. Whittaker, an optometrist, wanted the agency to act favorably on petitions filed by the Contact Lens Manufacturers Association (CLMA) to reclassify certain contact lens materials from class III to class II, but the manufacturers had not submitted the required data. The agency lacked the resources to gather its own data quickly and fulfill its other obligations in the eye care–device field.

Unlike Dingell and Gore, Whittaker was not interested in at-

---

34. In this account I rely on interviews with Patrick McLain and Benjamin Fisherow of the Dingell subcommittee staff and with agency officials and on the following reports of the House Committee on Energy and Commerce: *FDA Oversight: Medical Devices* (hearing before the subcommittee on oversight and investigations), 97th Cong., 2d sess., July 16, 1982; *Medical Device Regulation: The FDA's Neglected Child*, Committee Print 98–F, 98th Cong., 1st sess., 1983; *Health and the Environment: Miscellaneous—Part 2* (hearings before the subcommittee on health and the environment), 98th Cong., 2d sess., 1984, pp. 273–435; *Failed Pacemaker Leads* (hearing before the subcommittee on oversight and investigations), 98th Cong., 2d sess., Mar. 13, 1984; and *Anesthesia Machine Failures* (hearing before the subcommittee on oversight and investigations), 98th Cong., 2d sess., Sept. 26, 1984.

tacking a popular Republican president; his primary concern was regulatory relief for an industry about which he was intensely concerned. But the subcommittee's majority leadership and staff found that they could accommodate Whittaker's concerns without much practical difficulty and could achieve the added benefit of an oversight report bearing some measure of bipartisan coloration. Thus, in a single hearing, the FDA was criticized *simultaneously* for being both too lax and too stringent in enforcing the law.

All of this ultimately persuaded FDA management that "something" had to be done. "As far as I'm concerned," James Benson, deputy director of the agency's Center for Devices and Radiological Health, later remarked, "this whole process of introspection got underway in 1982 with the first oversight hearings.... [That effort] along with other investigations that followed, stimulated us to engage in comprehensive analysis."[35]

Although oversight helped generate concrete results, there were points of resistance. To some extent, this was a matter of sheer regulatory capacity; the agency could not possibly establish performance standards promptly for all class II devices, something the subcommittee well understood. Indeed, one high agency official suggested that many devices had been given class II status mainly because reviewers sought middle ground rather than because the public safety demanded it.[36]

The adverse-experience reporting regulation was another

35. "An Analysis of Device Problems: A Look at FDA's Medical Device Program—An Opportunity for Reform," speech delivered by James S. Benson, deputy director, Center for Devices and Radiological Health, before the Food and Drug Law Institute, June 13, 1984.

In May 1983 the agency released for public comment an adverse-experience reporting regulation. In the next two months, the FDA announced its intention to develop performance standards for 11 high-priority devices of the 1,100 then in class II. These were followed, in September, by a formal call for the first premarket approval application for a pre-1976 class III device and by the identification of 12 additional preamendments products that would be similarly reviewed in the near future. By March 1984 the agency had created ten task forces to examine various long-range problems associated with implementing the device amendments.

36. Personal interview with FDA official.

sticking point, but the prospect of further public hearings helped speed its promulgation. The final regulation had still not been issued by summer 1984. It sat, unsigned, in the office of Health and Human Services Secretary Margaret Heckler. Then Chairman Dingell announced a hearing in the wake of deaths caused by improperly functioning anesthesia machines. In a letter to Secretary Heckler, Dingell indicated his intention to have her explain the delay publicly. Within a few days, Heckler signed the regulation.[37]

The political conflict over a particular regulatory issue always plays a huge role in how it is resolved—if, indeed, it *is* resolved. For some FDA regulations, harmony reigns both within Congress and between the legislative and executive branches. In that case, if the agency can placate overseers with some straightforward action, then the oversight triggers the most obvious and direct adjustment.

A good example in the FDA involves the so-called man-in-the-plant practice.[38] By the late 1970s, name-brand drug manufacturers commonly entered into agreements with generic firms to market a kind of hybrid: a so-called branded-generic. Under such an agreement, the drug would be manufactured by a generic company but distributed by a brand-name firm. In some cases, the brand-name company might place a representative on a generic firm's premises, ostensibly to assure quality control. Based on the presence of its man-in-the-plant at the generic facility, the brand-name firm would label drugs as if made in-house. In 1978 this practice caught the attention of Democrat John Moss of California, then chair of the House Interstate and Foreign Commerce Committee's oversight subcommittee, which Dingell would later head. Moss and his staff found the man-in-the-plant a "false and misleading practice" and succeeded in getting the FDA to issue regulations constraining the practice.

37. *Anesthesia Machine Failures.*
38. House Committee on Interstate and Foreign Commerce, *Man-in-the-Plant—FDA's Failure to Regulate Deceptive Drug Labeling*, Committee Print 95–7, 95th Cong., 2d sess., 1978.

The political environment for such action was favorable in critical ways. The agency itself was not at all interested in defending the practice; an earlier memo by agency counsel Peter B. Hutt had already urged its termination. The agency had, however, given low priority to issuing a regulation; congressional interest simply bumped the process forward. The economic stakes were manageable, political pressures were relatively unilateral, and sufficient agency resources were available for fairly quick resolution.

Chairman Moss confronted a far different situation when investigating antibiotics in animal feed.[39] In this case, a public health concern that antibiotics fed to cattle and poultry could assist the spread of drug-resistant disease ran squarely counter to an economic one, that livestock interests would have to forgo the increased yields, and profits, resulting from drug-fed animals. Through agriculture committees on the Hill, farm interests mustered opposition, attempting in testimony to cast doubt on the harm that might stem from antibiotic use and to emphasize the economic pain a ban would cause.[40] The FDA leadership and the Moss subcommittee wanted to end the practice, but Congress and the agency ultimately retreated into the "more study" position common for intense product controversies. A decade after the first Moss subcommittee inquiry, neither Congress nor the agency had yet decided the issue. The outcome of subcommittee-agency relations thus can differ dramatically depending on the broader political context of an issue.

The Occupational Safety and Health Administration

Persistent political conflict and an obsession with process and constituency gratification are also the central themes in congres-

39. House Committee on Interstate and Foreign Commerce, *Antibiotics in Animal Feeds* (hearing before the subcommittee on oversight and investigations), 95th Cong., 1st sess., Sept. 19, 23, 1977.

40. House Committee on Agriculture, *Impact of Chemicals and Related Drug Products and Regulatory Processes* (hearing before the subcommittee on dairy and poultry), 95th Cong., 1st sess., May 23–25, 1977. See also Senate Committee on Agriculture, Nutrition, and Forestry, *Food Safety and Quality, Parts 1 and 2* (hearings before the subcommittee on agricultural research and general legislation), June 30, July 19, Sept. 21, 22, 1977.

sional oversight of OSHA. A look at the agency's relations with Congress demonstrates three general points. First, oversight may be a vehicle for strategically applauding agency performance. Second, Congress can be a useful forum for helping to incite concrete change in agency behavior. And finally, even with the White House and Senate committees in conservative Republican hands, congressional Democrats would still have ample resources to monitor and challenge agency performance—especially the activities of agency leadership.

By the time Jimmy Carter entered the White House, OSHA had become an agency besieged. Policy-oriented economists in particular assailed it as insensitive to the costs its rules imposed on society and as generally ineffective, particularly in addressing the "health" portion of its mandate.[41] Employers complained of rude and inflexible inspectors, the expense of complying with agency standards, and a proliferation of nit-picking safety rules. One OSHA standard provided that "each water closet shall occupy a separate compartment with a door and walls or partitions between fixtures sufficiently high to assure privacy." Another prescribed the maximum height for wall-mounted fire extinguishers. Such nuisance rules originated in industry consensus standards that had existed, often as unenforced guidelines, well before OSHA. But by promulgating 4,400 legally binding safety standards shortly after the Occupational Safety and Health Act became effective in 1971, the agency unwittingly made itself responsible for a plethora of rigidities, minutiae, obsolete provisions, and outright mistakes. Tough enforcement of such standards could only lead to trouble.

As the years went by, the agency's critics would forget that OSHA had taken this action pursuant to a statutory requirement. Within two years of the act's effective date, the Department of Labor, which includes OSHA, had been required to promulgate any extant federal or consensus standards as agency rules unless they "would not result in improved safety or health for specifically designated employees." In retrospect, the quick mass adop-

41. See, e.g., Albert L. Nichols and Richard Zeckhauser, "Government Comes to the Workplace: An Assessment of OSHA," *Public Interest* 49 (Fall 1977): 39–69.

tion, with twenty-three months left until the legal deadline, seems foolish. Yet, in the short term at least, it was an understandable, even rational, response to the agency's contentious political environment. The action helped forestall attacks and disenchantment from unions and other elements of the proregulation left. At the same time, business lobbyists had for strategic reasons largely soft-pedaled any problems they had with the standards during debate on the law. As the late Rep. William Steiger (R-Wisconsin), a key architect of the law, told John Mendeloff: "We were misinformed by industry, which kept telling us that these standards were widely used and generally accepted. That simply turned out not to be true."[42]

The agency's other major sphere of responsibility, health, also proved frustrating, but for different reasons. At the advent of the Carter administration, OSHA's normal rule-making procedures had yielded just four permanent health standards, a pace that seemed dishearteningly slow to organized labor, the agency's primary constituency. Increasingly, the perceived excesses of regulatory programs in general were being highlighted, with OSHA serving as a prime example and target. Barely five years after opening its doors, OSHA had become a kind of pariah bureaucracy to business. Its ill-considered safety standards and insensitive field enforcement had allegedly gone too far for business and done too little to satisfy labor concerns about workplace carcinogens and other chronic health hazards.

Despite this dissatisfaction, however, no proposal to amend the statutory authorization has, at this writing, ever been enacted. Organized labor and its congressional allies, who largely dominate the key committees that would consider such changes, have generally feared that amendments would weaken the law. Until the Reagan administration, when partisan control of the Senate shifted to the Republicans, the leadership of the key subcommittees in both houses had been characterized by an unwavering support for what might be called a "labor view" of OSHA policymaking. This perspective emphasized the agency's responsi-

42. John Mendeloff, *Regulating Safety: An Economic and Political Analysis of Occupational Safety and Health Policy* (Cambridge, Mass.: MIT Press, 1979), pp. 37–38.

bility to push forcefully toward stringent standard setting—
despite the often huge gaps in information and opposition from
business that slowed things down—and vigorous field enforcement. Such novel policy approaches as injury taxes, negotiated
settlements with employers, reliance on personal protection devices rather than more expensive engineering controls, and the
introduction of formal cost-benefit analysis into agency decision
making were either ignored by congressional overseers or
strongly opposed; labor interests interpreted them as opportunities for unwarranted leniency toward employers. Once again,
the means used to implement a regulatory program seemed to
get far more attention than the question of whether protective
impacts were being enhanced or diminished.

This perspective imparted a distinctly *protective* cast to most
oversight, especially in the pre-Reagan years. Policy analyst John
Mendeloff observed in the late 1970s that "business lobbyists
complain that the oversight hearings are held only to stiffen
OSHA's spine and make it tougher in its enforcement."[43] During
the Carter years, House Education and Labor Committee and
Senate Labor and Human Resources Committee inquiries largely
constituted an effort to highlight the agency's good work in the
face of difficult tasks and strenuous business opposition. The
committees generally supported the agency rather than attacked
it. Prolabor forces were only too well aware of the agency's public
image and of attempts by such groups as the American Conservative Union's STOP OSHA Project to exploit it.[44] But when
Reagan appointees later sought to alter the regulatory framework administratively, scrutiny by the House subcommittees attentive to OSHA turned frankly hostile.

Before Reagan, the bipartisan team of Harrison Williams (D-
New Jersey) and Jacob Javits (R-New York) kept the Senate
subcommittee on labor, through which any legislation to amend
the act would have to move, a safe haven for the AFL-CIO. A
former Senate staff aide recalls that

43. Ibid., p. 31.
44. On the STOP OSHA Project, see Bureau of National Affairs, *Occupational
Safety and Health Reporter*, Nov. 24, 1977, p. 877. See also ibid., May 10, 1979,
p. 1749; May 31, 1979, p. 1001.

the strategy that developed was that nothing would happen. All the bills would be bottled up [in committee] and they would just tough it out. The committee did virtually everything by consensus. Williams and Javits always went together. The Republicans on the committee tended to be liberal Republicans. The Democrats on the committee were so firmly in control and were so clearly liberal, no Republican would go on that committee who wasn't pro-labor because you'd be embarrassed.[45]

And like the FDA, OSHA had a permanent authorization; it did not come up for periodic renewal. This worked to the advantage of the agency's congressional defenders.

Williams and Javits used formal oversight more to defend the agency than to change it. In October 1978, for example, they staged three days of hearings explicitly designed to show that the agency and its patrons could keep their own house in order. Noting that the agency was "under very concentrated attack," Javits added that "the light of truth is what's needed . . . and the wisdom of strong and sound administration. . . . Now [Assistant Secretary of Labor] Eula Bingham has done a great job in that regard."[46] At one point in the hearing, Javits openly invited Bingham to issue a fact sheet that would give the agency's congressional patrons more ammunition.[47] Sixteen months later, Javits and Williams went through the exercise once more, Williams noting that he was "struck by the fact that so much of the criticism of the OSHA enforcement program has been centered on past practices of the agency, and on the program as it might have been, but not necessarily on the program as it is now."[48]

In the House Education and Labor Committee, a similar sit-

45. Personal interview.

46. Senate Committee on Human Resources, *Oversight on the Administration of the Occupational Safety and Health Act, 1978* (hearings before the subcommittee on labor), 95th Cong., 2d sess., Oct. 3–5, 1978, p. 34. Chairman Harrison Williams later confirmed that getting favorable commentary about OSHA onto the record was a major impetus for the oversight effort. See Bureau of National Affairs, *Occupational Safety and Health Reporter*, Oct. 26, 1978, p. 703.

47. *Oversight on Administration of Occupational Safety and Health Act*, p. 45.

48. Senate Committee on Labor and Human Resources, *Oversight on Administration of the Occupational Safety and Health Act, 1980—Part 1* (hearings before the committee), 96th Cong., 2d sess., Mar. 18, 21, 28, 1980, p. 1.

uation prevailed, led by health and safety subcommittee chairman Joseph Gaydos (D-Pennsylvania). Frequent oversight has allowed Gaydos an ideal platform to espouse prolabor policies. His is a strong labor state, and his congressional district (Pennsylvania's twentieth) is solid labor territory where the steelworkers' union is "the dominant political influence."[49] Control of the subcommittee has also given Gaydos and his labor allies a way to stress the need for continued regulatory vigilance. The resulting oversight has been, on occasion, strikingly benign. A 1979 field hearing was one long paean to OSHA orchestrated by Gaydos, his staff, and twenty-two witnesses, all but one of whom had some direct affiliation with labor. Witnesses asserted that "had it not been for OSHA we would still be exposed to excessive noise," that "OSHA is our only appeal mechanism for these long-term developing illnesses," and that "the unfair attacks on OSHA come from greedy interests who put profits above the safety and health of workers and the people in our neighborhoods." Even the lone employer to testify called his working relationship with the agency "excellent," adding that his firm had found OSHA personnel to be "competent, understanding, no problem at all."[50]

For all of this, however, congressional criticism outside the principal oversight committees could not be contained or ignored. That, of course, was the main reason that Senators Williams and Javits felt compelled to defend OSHA. Outside the labor committees, Congress constantly agitated for change. At the beginning of the Carter administration, for example, two House subcommittees submitted reports critical of OSHA. The manpower and housing subcommittee of Government Operations judged OSHA slow both at boosting its output of health standards *and* at eliminating the nuisance standards.[51] A sub-

49. Alan Ehrenhalt, ed., *Politics in America: Members of Congress in Washington and at Home* (Washington, D.C.: Congressional Quarterly, 1984), p. 1334. In fact, in 1979 the health and safety subcommittee was informally dubbed "the Keystone Committee" since *all four* Democrats on it hailed from the Keystone State—Pennsylvania.

50. House Committee on Education and Labor, *Oversight on the Occupational Safety and Health Act* (hearing before the subcommittee on health and safety), 96th Cong., 1st sess., May 18, 1979, pp. 12, 21, 81, 123.

51. House Committee on Government Operations, *Failure to Meet Commitments*

committee of the Small Business Committee endorsed expanded on-site consultation and advocated a less punitive approach to enforcement generally.[52] And, as we shall see in the next chapter, OSHA's critics successfully constrained the agency's enforcement practices by targeting its appropriations on the House and Senate floors.

By the time Eula Bingham became head of OSHA under President Carter in 1977, congressional advocacy had helped produce a distinct, if uncomfortable, political climate full of defensive labor-oriented friends and embittered, cynical adversaries. Given this confrontational atmosphere, Bingham and other agency leaders quickly grasped the need for an approach that would appeal to labor while addressing OSHA's most obvious points of vulnerability within the business community.

Labor and its allies wanted more health standards, including more frequent use of the power to issue an emergency temporary standard (ETS), and Bingham promised to deliver.[53] But she also wanted to deal with business complaints about overzealousness and an unnecessarily confrontational attitude on the part of OSHA's inspectors.

Sure enough, in the eight months between April 1977 and January 1978, OSHA issued three ETSs. Only four such standards had been produced during the agency's preceding six years of existence. Under Bingham, OSHA also added five permanent health standards, two of which developed from ETSs, and completed its Standards Revocation project, an effort to weed out the unnecessary safety rules that had so damaged the agency's public image.[54] With a formal mandate from Appro-

---

Made in the *Occupational Safety and Health Act*, House Report 95–710, 95th Cong., 1st sess., 1977.

52. House Committee on Small Business, *Impact of the Administration of the Occupational Safety and Health Act on Small Business*, House Report 95–757, 95th Cong., 1st sess., 1977.

53. House Committee on Government Operations, *Performance of the Occupational Safety and Health Administration* (hearings before a subcommittee), 95th Cong., 1st sess., 1977.

54. Before the Carter administration, new permanent standards had been set for asbestos, a collection of fourteen carcinogens, vinyl chloride, and coke oven emissions.

priations Committee overseers set forth in the agency's fiscal 1977 spending bill, OSHA announced plans to eliminate over 1,100 standards that would, pending final revocation, be subject to minimal enforcement. Although some labor leaders resisted, by autumn 1978 OSHA announced the mass revocation of 928 rules (or parts thereof) judged unnecessary.[55] It is interesting that the screams of pain and protest, both inside and outside Congress, had a discernible impact on agency management and policy. Assertions that the agency was "out of control" were critical to the very process by which control was exercised.

There were other initiatives; the agency enhanced its on-site consultation program, which had developed in response to long-term congressional prompting. Shortly after OSHA's creation, the House Small Business Committee had begun urging the agency to provide for some sort of consultative arrangement that would enable firms to discover and correct violations without exposing themselves to citations and fines. This would serve regulatory policy goals while limiting the pain for a vocal constituency. By the end of the Carter administration, consultation had been well established. The program served the political ends both of OSHA's business critics, for whom it meant a measure of regulatory relief, and of its supporters, who could cite it as evidence of greater agency reasonableness.[56]

55. On the proposed and final revocation actions, see: 42 *Federal Register* 62734 (Dec. 13, 1977); ibid., 62892 (Dec. 13, 1977); 43 *Federal Register* 49726 (Oct. 24, 1978); and ibid., 49751 (Oct. 24, 1978).

56. See *Impact of the Administration . . . Small Business*, p. 5, and Bureau of National Affairs, *Occupational Safety and Health Reporter*, Nov. 3, 1977, p. 774.

Although another Bingham initiative, the New Directions Grants, seems not to have been pushed by Congress, it certainly took root in soil made fertile by congressional criticism and also served political as well as policy ends. On the assumption that greater knowledge among workers and firms would enhance workplace safety and health, OSHA began to subsidize education and training programs offered under the auspices of unions, employer associations, schools, and nonprofit organizations. By the end of fiscal year 1984, the program, begun in 1978, had awarded $65 million to 188 grantees. Like on-site consultation, the program had clear political appeal; it gave evidence of increased agency creativity and sensitivity and provided material support to distinct beneficiaries. General Accounting Office, *How OSHA Monitors and Controls Its New Directions Program*

During the Reagan administration, the congressional dynamics of OSHA oversight changed considerably. In the Senate, the team of Williams and Javits was disbanded; Javits was defeated for reelection and Williams's chairmanship ended when conservative Republican Orrin Hatch of Utah took the helm. But the committee did not immediately launch a wave of critical or probusiness inquiry; instead, it probably paid the agency less formal attention than ever before. With OSHA's leadership perceived to be in friendly hands, committee Republicans had little incentive to pursue such scrutiny. At the sole Senate oversight hearing during Reagan's first term, conservatives castigated the agency's prior reputation for mindless inspections and harassment of business. Assistant Secretary of Labor Thorne Auchter assured them that matters would be turned around—although, to a large degree, they already had been.[57] Asked by an interviewer why his Senate subcommittee had not held more hearings on OSHA under Reagan, a Republican staff aide hesitantly responded that the majority was essentially pleased: "It's a very uncomfortable question for me. . . . The easy answer is, the agency does seem to be on track. . . . The main thing is, I don't know what would come out of hearings like that. No one has ever asked for a hearing."[58]

Soon after coming to power, the Reagan administration blocked an OSHA regulation long sought by labor establishing what employees would have to be told about the substances they worked with. Thereafter the pace of regulation seemed to slow considerably. Auchter also redirected enforcement policy, reducing the number of inspections (turning many of them into records inspections only), focusing on high-hazard industries, and emphasizing informal settlements with employers found in violation of rules. The administration said that the new policies

---

(GAO/HRD–85–29), Dec. 31, 1984. See also Bureau of National Affairs, *Occupational Safety and Health Reporter*, Apr. 20, 1978, pp. 1699–1700, 1718–20.

57. Senate, *Oversight on the Administration of the Occupational Safety and Health Act, 1981* (joint hearing before the subcommittee on investigations and general oversight and the subcommittee on labor), 97th Cong., 1st sess., Sept. 23, 1981.

58. Personal interview.

would make regulation less "confrontational" and more effective; scarce resources would be better used. By avoiding the legal
battles of contested citations through informal settlements (a
policy initiated in the Carter administration), OSHA hoped to
expedite the correction of violations. Such activity would provide
little grist for a conservative oversight mill.

Meanwhile, the House subcommittees, which remained in
Democrat hands, emerged as hotbeds of opposition to administration policy. Labor viewed the Reagan policies as nothing less
than "a systematic assault upon the job safety and health pro-
tections" the law was supposed to guarantee. Ironically, perhaps
the least confrontational was the Gaydos subcommittee, a reflection, some alleged, of the chairman's personal style. For whatever reason, agency civil servants opposed to administration
policy and practice tended to view Gaydos as having been
shunted into the background. Other Democrats were far less
reticent. From the Appropriations subcommittee responsible for
OSHA's budget, Democrat David Obey of Wisconsin lashed out
repeatedly and harshly against the administration. After taking
over the manpower and housing subcommittee of Government
Operations in 1983, Democrat Barney Frank of Massachusetts
proved a particularly aggressive critic, chiding the administration
on a number of fronts, including OMB interference in OSHA
rule-making and slowness in moving to tighten the regulation
of asbestos.[59] Frank also requested a GAO review of OSHA's
settlements policy.[60] A recurring theme of Frank's was that much
had been made of regulatory costs but little of "the cost of *not*
regulating." Others likewise alleged agency inaction as caving in
to business. Relations grew no more amicable with Auchter's
departure in spring 1984.[61]

59. House Committee on Government Operations, *OMB Interference with
OSHA Rulemaking*, House Report 98–583, 98th Cong., 1st sess., 1983. See also
House Committee on Government Operations, *The Failure to Regulate—Asbestos:
A Lethal Legacy* (hearing before the subcommittee on manpower and housing),
98th Cong., 1st sess., June 28, 1983.

60. General Accounting Office, *Informal Settlement of OSHA Citations: Comments
on the Legal Basis and Other Selected Issues* (GAO/HRD–85–11), Oct. 26, 1984.

61. In the weeks immediately preceding his own resignation in 1985, Auch-

Though attentiveness by House Democrats was responsible
for few concrete changes in agency policy—political appointees
simply took their cues more from the White House and an ethos
of deregulation than from congressional liberals—there is no
doubting the defensiveness it engendered among the agency's
top officials. Reagan appointees knew they faced an enemy
within: career bureaucrats opposed to the administration who
would not hesitate to leak damaging information to the press
and to congressional committees. In an interview, one such official openly acknowledged having tipped off a subcommittee
about alleged threats to career civil servants to toe the line or
face retribution. As noted earlier, access to such persons is one
of Congress's strongest informal assets. A House staff aide on
Barney Frank's subcommittee remarked that "this administration doesn't write a lot down on paper, I think, for fear of
embarrassment."[62] A Reagan political appointee at OSHA rue-
fully agreed:

We have had, I think it's fair to say, strong opposition from some of
the career people. Obey has better contacts in the agency than we do.
He's in a position to find out about things that are in the planning stages
that other people don't even know about. The people on that subcommittee know more about what's going on in the department than the
secretary does. . . .
    This place is sieve. That's one reason why we don't write a lot of
things down on paper. Even things that you are just looking at in an
exploratory way, something you just want to think about, get out. If
you write it down, it's going to turn up in Pete Early's column [in the
Washington Post]. I tell people we are prisoners in our own kingdom.[63]

---

ter's successor, Texas lawyer Robert Rowland: (1) was roundly criticized for
deciding not to issue a proposed field sanitation standard for which farm workers
had clamored since the agency's inception; (2) endured conflict-of-interest
charges raised by Chairman of Education and Labor Augustus Hawkins (D-
California); and (3) found himself hauled before yet another House subcommittee to answer allegations that Reagan appointees had "created an atmosphere
of fear and intimidation" by threatening OSHA employees who dissented from
agency policy.
    62. Personal interview.
    63. Ibid.

The Consumer Product Safety Commission

Since the Consumer Product Safety Commission's creation in 1972, the strongest themes of congressional inquiry and comment have been condemnation for ineffectiveness and insufficient aggressiveness and dissatisfaction with a helter-skelter setting of priorities. There has been a somewhat contradictory focus on particular product horrors and much personal animosity toward a beleaguered chairman. Occasionally, economic interests with a stake in a given product have campaigned in Congress but generally with nothing like the stridency or tenacity described earlier. A long-standing agency emphasis on voluntary action and negotiation partly accounts for this, and, unlike the act that created OSHA, the requirement that the Consumer Product Safety Act be reconsidered periodically has given business an outlet in the authorization process.[64]

Most importantly, the CPSC's jurisdiction—though it potentially encompasses many thousands of products—does not activate such potent economic lobbies as oil and gas, utilities, the coal industry, automobile manufacturers, agriculture, and the like. Rather, the CPSC's responsibilities tend to pit it against smaller industries (often individual companies) and concern discrete product lines rather than entire production processes. As former EPA Administrator Douglas Costle stated: "The CPSC had to decide what kind of lawnmower you are going to allow. We had to decide [in writing air pollution regulations for new stationary sources in the late 1970s] how you are going to generate electric power in the country."[65] Mary Ellen Fise, product safety director for the Consumer Federation of America, a major consumer lobby, put it more tersely: "It's just not as many dollars."[66]

CPSC oversight has clearly displayed the shifting congressional political winds. Criticized as inept and "ineffective" during the

---

64. As noted earlier, OSHA and the FDA both enjoy permanent authorizations.
65. Personal interview.
66. Ibid.

middle and late 1970s, the agency's termination was briefly considered by the Carter administration.[67] Yet, by the beginning of the Reagan era, the agency was being coddled by the same committees that had once stoned it. As usual, the frustrations of politicians and consumer lobbies stemmed from a mammoth task and a convoluted process imposed by a Congress that attempted to please everyone. The commission must protect the public against "unreasonable risks of injury" associated with the use of virtually any consumer product not explicitly assigned to another agency. The magnitude of such a task virtually assured that the agency would have to struggle mightily both to define and to implement its priorities.

Until 1981 the safety act burdened the agency with an unusually cumbersome procedure—the offeror process. Through this mechanism, the commission would proclaim its intention to develop a product standard and invite an outside party to step forward within 30 days to write it. The "offeror" selected would then craft a proposal for agency review, amendment, and promulgation. Congressional guidelines envisioned the whole process taking about 330 days. Although portrayed as a way to elicit "meaningful participation" from both consumers and industry, variations in offeror capacity and in the complexity of the standard-writing challenge overwhelmed the guidelines. The agency was likely to have to rewrite the final offeror product. The first three standards—the *only* three issued under "normal" procedures during the agency's first five years—took 570, 954, and 979 days, respectively.[68]

Yet in the 1970s the agency faced its toughest political challenge not on such broad procedural matters but because of a single class of products that aroused tremendous public and constituency fear: synthetic fabrics treated to reduce flammability. These fabrics had been laced with Tris, a chemical flame retardant. Evidence began to suggest that Tris could produce

67. "Abolition of Consumer Product Agency Considered," *National Journal*, March 4, 1978, p. 359.

68. General Accounting Office, *The Consumer Product Safety Commission Needs to Issue Safety Standards Faster* (HRD–78–3), Dec. 12, 1977.

genetic mutations and might cause cancer. The Environmental Defense Fund (EDF), a nonprofit public interest lobby, petitioned the agency to require a label warning that a Tris-treated garment "should be washed at least three times prior to wearing." With the National Cancer Institute announcement, early in 1977, that Tris caused tumors in rodents, the EDF promptly requested a *ban* on the sale of all Tris-laden garments. The agency hesitated, and the EDF, believing that firms were trying to dump the tainted material on an unsuspecting public, went to court to force the agency's hand.[69]

Congressional overseers also became involved. Subcommittees helped to elevate dramatically the issue of chronic hazards as a commission priority and to raise serious questions about the quality of agency leadership. The Tris issue reverberated more broadly than most oversight efforts. The House Government Operations subcommittee on commerce, consumer, and monetary affairs, chaired by a consumerist liberal, Benjamin Rosenthal (D-New York), was the first off the mark. Rosenthal found inexcusable both the agency's hesitancy and its lack of a defined policy for dealing expeditiously with hazardous substances. Based on data compiled by the National Cancer Institute, Rosenthal charged that Tris was "a potent carcinogen that could expose up to 45 million children to the enormously serious risks of developing cancer."[70] Of particular concern for him and others in Congress was the quality of Tris-treated children's sleepwear on the market. In effect, the EDF was contending that parents would unwittingly expose their children to a potent carcinogen merely by dressing them for bed. Supported by EDF and other testimony, Rosenthal relentlessly pressed the CPSC and especially commission chairman John Byington, a Ford administration appointee, to ban Tris. CPSC critics hammered away at one theme: that the agency had shown itself insufficiently alert and overly slow to respond to a deadly carcinogen. Byington, in turn,

69. House Committee on Government Operations, *Consumer Product Safety Commission's Ban on Tris* (hearing before the subcommittee on commerce, consumer, and monetary affairs), 95th Cong., 1st sess., Apr. 4, May 17, 1977.

70. Ibid., p. 1.

pleaded limited resources and ambiguous or incomplete information.

The Rosenthal effort was merely the opening salvo in an extended congressional barrage. The Senate Commerce subcommittee for consumers, chaired by Wendell Ford, launched its own probe, calling on many of the same critics that had gone before Rosenthal.[71] Ford, a Kentucky Democrat who had come to Commerce largely to defend his state's business interests, especially tobacco, was no one's idea of a consumerist zealot, though public interest groups occasionally found him approachable.[72] Ford tended to purvey the image of an agency adrift, unsure of its course. Like Rosenthal, he too was critical of Byington's leadership.

After the commission voted to ban Tris-treated sleepwear in April 1977, there arose in Congress nagging questions of thoroughness and fairness. Both were manifested in proceedings before Congress. For weeks after the commission's action, spot checks continued to turn up Tris-treated garments in stores, a fact not lost on the Rosenthal subcommittee, which demanded action.[73] The question of fairness was raised in a different forum. Because the commission's ban order applied only to Tris-treated finished goods, clothing manufacturers and retailers (many of them small firms) felt they bore the brunt of the agency's action. They aired these concerns before the House Small Business Committee.[74] John Moss's oversight subcommittee of Interstate and Foreign Commerce also joined the probes, emphasizing much the same criticisms as Rosenthal.[75] There, too, Chairman

71. Senate Committee on Commerce, Science, and Transportation, *Implementation of the Consumer Product Safety Act* (hearings before the subcommittee for consumers), 95th Cong., 1st sess., Apr. 19–21, 1977.

72. Peter Taylor, *Smoke Rings: The Politics of Tobacco* (London: Bodley Head, 1984), pp. 182–84.

73. *Consumer Product Safety Commission's Ban on Tris*, pp. 235–36.

74. House Committee on Small Business, *Banning Distribution of Tris* (hearings before the subcommittee on antitrust, consumers, and employment), 95th Cong., 1st sess., Apr. 28, May 19, 1977.

75. House Committee on Interstate and Foreign Commerce, *Consumer Product Safety Commission—Oversight* (hearings before the subcommittee on oversight and

Byington came under heavy fire; Moss made no secret of his personal dislike for the chairman, who mistakenly tried in one hearing to showcase his own children as evidence that Tris had shown no harmful effects—a moment that congressional staff present would cite years later as a textbook example of how *not* to behave in a congressional hearing.

By mid-1978, the CPSC, up for reauthorization, had become more politically vulnerable than at any time in its brief history—between December 1977 and June 1978 the GAO had released three studies criticizing agency performance.[76] The CPSC's image was so badly tarnished that the Carter administration briefly considered putting the agency out of its misery.[77]

The agency's congressional standing improved, however, once Byington announced his resignation, effective June 1978. He was replaced by Susan King, a political activist with scant background in consumer affairs. What she lacked in technical knowledge, however, she more than compensated for in political savvy. Unlike her predecessor, King succeeded in cultivating the subcommittees critical to the CPSC's congressional fortunes. A legislative staff aide who dealt with her routinely recalled that King "had political sensitivities that would rival any seismograph." Some consumer advocates in Congress also believed that, in an increasingly antiregulatory political environment, much more public flogging could fatally wound the agency. By autumn 1978, with commissioners and consumer activists mobilized on its behalf, the agency had been reauthorized for another three years.

Beyond encouraging leadership change, congressional scrutiny helped lead to concrete policy innovation. It focused the attention of commissioners and top staff on the need for more

---

investigations and the subcommittee on consumer protection and finance), 95th Cong., 1st sess., Sept. 26, 29, 30, Oct. 3, 1977.

76. The studies were General Accounting Office: *The Consumer Product Safety Commission Needs to Issue Safety Standards Faster* (HRD–78–3), Dec. 12, 1977; *The Consumer Product Safety Commission Has No Assurance that Product Defects Are Being Reported and Corrected* (HRD–78–48), Feb. 14, 1978; and *The Consumer Product Safety Commission Should Act More Promptly to Protect the Public from Hazardous Products* (HRD–78–122), June 1, 1978.

77. See note 67 above.

coherent treatment of "chronic hazards," a catchall term for substances (such as carcinogens) that may cause serious harm over long periods. In a 1978 report, the Moss subcommittee charged the agency with failure to act "in a timely fashion" to investigate a chemical and to move against it effectively once a hazard had been established. The report called for a "well-defined but limited CPSC chronic hazards evaluation program."[78]

The agency response largely placated congressional critics. By mid-1979, Chairman King could report to Senator Ford, in a remarkably friendly encounter designed to showcase both agency progress and Ford's role in promoting it, a process to scan the marketplace for such hazards. In marked contrast to the earlier halting responses and pleas of resource constraints, King laid out an orderly scheme by which the agency was proceeding.[79]

Of course, Congress was hardly alone in prompting change at the CPSC. Other forces included interest-group dissatisfaction, court decisions, White House appointments, and the collective judgment of the commission and its staff. Yet Congress served as a key forum for complaints. In public and private encounters with Congress, the agency was compelled to account for its procedures by persons whose goodwill it coveted. That multiple subcommittee chairmen were willing to give the matter attention made life unpleasant for the agency's leadership. As in cases recounted earlier, harsh assertions of an agency "out of control" were essential to the very exercise of that control. Here again we see at work the supreme irony of congressional oversight: the system works precisely by appearing to have failed.

The antagonism against Chairman Byington exemplifies the narrow and nakedly personal elements that can occasionally in-

78. House Committee on Interstate and Foreign Commerce, *Consumer Product Safety Commission's Regulation of Tris: The Need for an Effective Chronic Hazards Program*, Committee Print 95–58, 95th Cong., 2d sess., 1978, p. 3.

79. Senate Committee on Commerce, Science, and Transportation, *Chronic Hazard Programs* (hearing before the subcommittee for consumers), 96th Cong., 1st sess., June 14, 1979.

fect congressional supervision. Never popular with consumer groups—his selection by President Ford was thoroughly problematic from the first—Byington gained a reputation as a flamboyant, manipulative administrator that served him ill with Congress. The impression that he had deliberately surrounded himself with attractive female assistants merely compounded the perception of substantive failure. A fellow commissioner would later note that Byington's tenure had "brought unnecessary negative attention to the commission and its work. His resignation removed the target."[80]

By the end of the Carter administration, then, the CPSC's political fortunes had revived among congressional Democrats. The agency was anxious to point to benchmarks of dramatic improvement. For example, there were 545 product recalls in 1979 and 588 in 1980, as opposed to only 147 in 1977, the fewest in the agency's history.[81] Whether such numbers constituted an appropriate gauge of increased effectiveness was beside the point; such statistics helped blunt criticism among Democrats, who became, in general, protectors rather than assailants.

But by spring 1981, the Republican Reagan administration had made clear its desire to abolish the agency. "On balance," wrote OMB Director David Stockman, "we feel the public benefits to be secured by the agency in the future are not likely to exceed the costs, especially when one considers that many of the commission's responsibilities can be carried out more efficiently by other agencies."[82] One proposal called for the transfer of the agency to a cabinet department, perhaps Commerce. Severe budget cuts, amounting to some 30 percent of the agency's funding, were offered by OMB. Another proposal would have stripped the agency of its chronic hazard authority, suggesting EPA as a more appropriate place for it. The new chairman of the Senate subcommittee for consumers, the conservative Robert

80. Personal interview.
81. Molly Sinclair, "Safety Watchdog Stays Rocky Course," *Washington Post*, May 8, 1983, pp. L1, L5.
82. Merrill Brown, "Reagan Wants to Ax Products Safety Agency," *Washington Post*, May 10, 1981, p. A4.

Kasten (R-Wisconsin), signaled his interest in "a fundamental redefining of the commission's authority and structure."[83]

Democrats friendly to the CPSC mobilized for a counterattack, and ironically, public oversight devoted to Tris turned out to be part of the Democratic arsenal. In mid-April 1981, Albert Gore, Jr., then on the Dingell subcommittee, chaired a hearing designed to highlight the agency's usefulness. Said Gore:

Since 1978, the CPSC has improved its chronic hazard program significantly. The Commission has acted to reduce consumer exposure to many hazardous chemicals such as asbestos patching compounds, benzene paint strippers, and vinyl chloride in aerosol sprays. Most recently, CPSC has moved aggressively to seek civil penalties against companies allegedly involved in the illegal distribution of Tris-treated children's sleepwear after the ban was put into effect.

Yet just as the Commission has embarked upon a vigorous chronic hazard program, critics of the agency have proposed elimination of the Commission's chronic hazard jurisdiction or a sharp retrenchment in agency actions to regulate chemical hazards.[84]

The principal witness was Executive Director Richard Gross of the commission, who recounted the Tris saga and the agency's recent enforcement actions, noting that considerable amounts of treated fabric remained in warehouses throughout the country and "may represent about 100 potential cancers." He told also of several agency moves against firms accused of illegally disposing of such material, some of which appeared to have reached retail markets. A few weeks later, a hearing before the same subcommittee showcased a "major study" (actually a compilation of the existing evidence on Tris carcinogenicity) undertaken by the commission's staff. The committee again stressed the need for a continued CPSC presence.[85]

The agency has survived, albeit with diminished resources.

---

83. Merrill Brown, "Status Shift Suggested for CPSC," *Washington Post*, Apr. 8, 1981, pp. D7, D8.

84. House Committee on Energy and Commerce, *Regulation of Tris-Treated Sleepwear* (hearings before the subcommittee on oversight and investigations), 97th Cong., 1st sess., Apr. 15, June 4, 1981, p. 1.

85. Ibid., pp. 25–103.

The House Energy and Commerce subcommittee on health and the environment retained and enhanced the chronic hazard program. To counter the claim that the CPSC had inadequate capability, the agency was empowered to appoint ad hoc chronic hazard advisory panels consisting of outside professionals to provide technical expertise on selected substances.[86]

As the Tris affair exemplifies, Congress has demonstrated active interest in the CPSC mainly when a problem associated with a specific product arises, providing a tangible, comprehensible, and politically attractive focal point. Over the years this has occurred for aluminum wiring, urea formaldehyde foam insulation (UFFI), cellulose insulation, asbestos-insulated hair dryers, and all-terrain vehicles. These collectively represent only a vanishingly small fraction of the total agency agenda; as I suggested in the introduction, most of any agency's routine activities inspire little sustained congressional or constituency interest.

Members of Congress also occasionally write letters asking that the agency "look into" a report of death or injury associated with some product (usually in the member's home state) or expressing a position on a pending decision. The CPSC takes such communications seriously—the product-injury reports are pursued—but the overall impact is hard to assess. The CPSC's congressional liaison officer judged it peripheral at best.

For those issues that attract more than casual congressional attention, the struggle has been mainly to craft arrangements palatable both to Congress and various interest groups with a stake in the decision. For two products (cellulose insulation and lawn mowers), Congress preempted agency discretion by amending the Consumer Product Safety Act itself to specify the content of rules.[87]

As with the agencies discussed earlier, overseers generally prod most successfully when the change sought is concrete, noncontroversial, and clearly within the discretion of agency leadership. The hair dryer asbestos issue is a prime example. When

86. 15 U.S.C. 2077.
87. See 15 U.S.C. 2082 and Public Law 97–35, section 1212.

a Washington, D.C., television station reported in 1978 that certain models of hand-held hair dryers might discharge asbestos, public reaction was immediate and massive, triggering congressional attention.[88] Within a week after the original broadcast, the reporters who had broken the story and CPSC Chairman Susan King sat before Senator Ford's subcommittee.[89] Four days later, the same witnesses testified before James Scheuer, the chairman of the House Commerce subcommittee on consumer protection and finance.[90] Scheuer and his staff concluded that the agency should initiate a specific administrative change. The agency might well have moved more quickly on the hair dryer matter but for an inability to reassign funds otherwise committed. Could a contingency fund set aside for occasions when unanticipated product hazards required immediate investigation not enable the commission to respond faster in such cases? In discussion before the hearing, the House subcommittee and the commission agreed to the establishment of such a fund. The hearing was then staged so as to conclude with King's assurance to Scheuer that the commission would move immediately to set aside the money.

Things were dramatically different when Democrat Doug Barnard of Georgia, Rosenthal's successor as chairman of the House Government Operations subcommittee, looked into the alleged dangers of all-terrain vehicles (ATVs) in spring 1985.[91] A hearing featured the victims of ATV accidents, but the extent of the hazard was disputed. Barnard's conservative colleague Larry

88. The television station, WRC-TV, would later report on the continued availability of nutritionally deficient infant formula, triggering the events described earlier in this chapter.

89. Senate Committee on Commerce, Science, and Transportation, *Asbestos in Hand-Held Hair Dryers* (hearing before the subcommittee for consumers), 96th Cong., 1st sess., Apr. 2, 1979.

90. House Committee on Interstate and Foreign Commerce, *Hair Dryers Containing Asbestos* (hearing before the subcommittee on consumer protection and finance), 96th Cong., 1st sess., Apr. 6, 1979.

91. House Committee on Government Operations, *Consumer Product Safety Commission's Response to Hazards of All-Terrain Vehicles (ATV's)* (hearing before the subcommittee on commerce, consumer, and monetary affairs), 99th Cong., 1st sess., May 21, 1985.

Craig (R-Idaho) offered a long tirade challenging the need for regulation—after all, he noted, boating accidents killed far more persons—and accusing one unnamed commissioner (presumably Carter appointee Stuart Statler) of both unconcealed bias on ATVs and a consuming hunger for regulation. Thundered Craig: "Should we allow unelected bureaucrats to go around squashing businesses like bugs on a sidewalk?"[92] A further problem for Barnard was that there was no straightforward procedural hook for him to grasp. Even without Congressman Craig's opposition, Barnard was in the relatively weak position of prodding the commission, with its majority of conservative Reagan appointees, merely to exhibit greater urgency in gathering the data needed for possible regulatory action. There was neither a preexisting regulation to be defended nor a draft proposal that the subcommittee could "tip" toward final promulgation with the threat of bad publicity.

The Barnard hearing also marked the first formal sit-down oversight, unconnected to either the appropriations or reauthorization process, in several years. During that time, were overseers generally unaware of what was going on at the agency? Hardly, as they were kept regularly supplied with official and informal reports as well as leaks regarding commission activities and performance. The absence of formal discretionary oversight stemmed from several causes. First, scrutiny and direction through reauthorization and appropriations was considerable, as was debate in those forums. Because the agency had the misfortune to come up for reauthorization at the time that the Supreme Court raised anxiety about congressional oversight by striking down the legislative veto (see chapter 4), Congress shackled the agency with *two* veto provisions.[93] Other significant mat-

92. Ibid., p. 3.

93. One version specifies that both houses have ninety days after rule promulgation to adopt a concurrent resolution of disapproval. The other version provides that within sixty days one house may pass a disapproval resolution that becomes effective *unless*, within thirty additional days, the other house votes against the resolution. Both versions of the veto have been implanted in three

ters, such as the length of reauthorization and commission jurisdiction over fixed-site amusement rides, were hotly contested. Formal reauthorization thus absorbed some of the political energy that might otherwise have spilled out in nonstatutory inquiry. But, according to one commissioner, such effort was scarce for two other reasons. First, "a lot of the issues we deal with were not as sensational or sexy as things in FDA and EPA. Most of the issues don't grab you like Love Canal or exploding [Ford] Pintos or DES."[94] Moreover, such activity would not serve any useful purpose for those in a position to perform it, since "the forces that would be most likely to hold [such] hearings are largely satisfied." The commissioner quoted was, however, speaking some five months before the ATV issue erupted, further demonstrating how fragile political harmony can be in social regulation.

Advise and Consent

Congress and its committees also monitor and attempt to shape regulatory agencies through the appointments process. This effort is partly formal, since the Constitution grants to the Senate the power to confirm high administration appointees. Yet informal elements also exist: involvement by House members; bargaining between committees and the White House; efforts by members of Congress to elevate the political priority of certain issues or to extract promises of preferred behavior.

As an instrument of congressional supervision, the appointment process is necessarily both episodic and supplementary. The initiative lies with the president; the Senate confirms but does not appoint. Moreover, Congress ordinarily tends to see the president as entitled to the appointee he wants. And congres-

---

statutes enforced by the CPSC: the Consumer Product Safety Act, the Federal Hazardous Substances Act, and the Flammable Fabrics Act.

94. Diethylstilbestrol (DES) was for several years prescribed for women to prevent miscarriage. It was later found to cause vaginal and cervical cancer in the daughters of women who had taken the drug.

sional scrutiny of nominees by a committee in nomination hearings appears nearly useless for conventional performance oversight—review and assessment of recent agency activity. The reason is the simple implausibility of holding nominees accountable for, or expecting them to have detailed knowledge about, that activity. Indeed, presidents may appoint new blood precisely to obtain such innocence.

The prospects for scrutiny, challenge, and bargaining through appointments vary considerably but depend mainly on the agendas of and political ammunition available to committee overseers; they do *not* depend on how the public is faring under a given set of policies. Where an appointment does not touch on the electoral or policy concerns of overseers, creates no opportunity to prod the agency or its administration superiors to pursue or abandon some action, and offers no obvious handle for partisan enrichment, congressional interest will be minimal and confirmation probably routine. But where one or more of these obtains—and they sometimes have in regulatory politics—then all manner of bargaining, second-guessing, and delay are conceivable. In spite of inherent limitations as an instrument of supervision, the regulatory-appointments process consists of far more than the up-or-down floor vote on whether to confirm.[95] As with oversight appropriations committee hearings, however, the focus is nearly always on narrow, immediate, and concrete concerns. Protective impacts, by comparison, recede considerably as a focus of congressional interest.

Nomination and Confirmation

Congressional influence over nominations is often tacit; committee and subcommittee alignments may impose subtle parameters around the executive selection process. Though organized labor and its friends in Congress did not precisely dictate the selection of Eula Bingham to head OSHA, for example, any Carter administration choice offensive to labor would have been

95. G. Calvin Mackenzie, *The Politics of Presidential Appointments* (New York: Free Press, 1981).

difficult to conceive.[96] Sometimes, of course, subcommittee chairmen do push favored candidates, as when Sen. Robert Kasten (R-Wisconsin) unsuccessfully urged the White House to appoint a constituent and consumer-affairs consultant to the CPSC chairmanship.[97]

More typically, however, Senate overseers must content themselves with critical scrutiny of appointees and perhaps some bargaining over the makeup of the appointed group. The focus tends to be on personality, personal probity, broad regulatory philosophy, and the simple avoidance of political losses.

In this vein one can see a striking example of bargaining in the Senate Committee's treatment of Federal Trade Commission nominations in the 1970s. When President Nixon nominated self-described conservative Democrat Mayo Thompson of Texas to the FTC in 1973, liberals on Sen. Warren Magnuson's committee were predictably unenthusiastic.[98] Thompson seemed the farthest thing from the consumerist they wanted to head a recently reinvigorated commission. Magnuson therefore informally sought and received White House assurances that the next vacancy would be filled by someone with a demonstrated sympathy for the consumer perspective. The committee then favorably reported Thompson's nomination to the full Senate and confirmation ensued. The next commission vacancy, later that year, was given to Mary E. Hanford, a Republican consumer-affairs specialist.[99] After the voluntary withdrawal of another conservative nominee who could not get committee support for a full term, the Commerce Committee staff offered its own mem-

96. See James W. Singer, "A Farewell to OSHA," *National Journal*, Jan. 29, 1977, p. 179.

97. Sari Horwitz, "Naming of Chairman Awaited," *Washington Post*, Dec. 26, 1984, p. A19, and "Unfilled Seat on Panel to Tip the Scale," ibid., Jan. 31, 1985, p. A19.

98. The FTC examples are drawn from Robert A. Katzmann, *Regulatory Bureaucracy: The Federal Trade Commission and Antitrust Policy* (Cambridge, Mass.: MIT Press, 1980), pp. 143–45.

99. Commissioner Hanford would later be far better known as Elizabeth Dole, secretary of transportation under President Reagan and spouse of Sen. Robert Dole (R-Kansas).

ber, minority staff aide David Clanton, as a Republican on whom the committee would look with favor for both the unexpired and full terms. Clanton had served on the committee for several years, had the support of his boss, Minority Whip Robert Griffin (R-Michigan), and was judged ideologically compatible with the committee majority on FTC matters. Following a hearing that lasted barely ten minutes, Clanton easily won confirmation to both terms.

Most dramatically, the confirmation process can attempt to weed out persons about whom the GAO or some other source can unearth a smoking gun—conflict of interest, perhaps, or improper use of government resources. In June 1986 the Senate Labor and Human Resources Committee halted the controversial appointment of attorney Robert Rader to the Occupational Safety and Health Review Commission, the independent agency to which OSHA citations are appealed. Rader's record was judged sufficiently anti-OSHA—he had counseled employers on how to resist inspections—that it tipped a key moderate Republican, Lowell Weicker of Connecticut, into voting no. The resulting tie effectively ended Rader's chances for confirmation.[100] He had been found guilty of what one scholar has labeled a "predispositional" conflict of interest.[101]

Congressional Democrats assiduously highlighted the perceived foibles of Reagan administration nominees wherever possible. In 1982 the administration had to withdraw the nomination of F. Keith Adkinson to the FTC.[102] While a Senate committee staff aide, Adkinson had sought to cowrite a book with an organized crime figure, a collaboration terminated when it became evident that no publishable manuscript would result. Adkinson's superiors had not known of the arrangement. Public Citizen

100. Peter Perl, "Rader's Penalty: OSHA [*sic*] Nominee Fined over Legal Conduct," *Washington Post*, Apr. 17, 1986, p. A17, and "Panel Kills Nomination to Safety Review Board," ibid., June 19, 1986, p. A23.

101. Mackenzie, *Politics of Presidential Appointments*, chap. 5.

102. Caroline E. Mayer, "FTC Nominee Is Withdrawn by President," *Washington Post*, Mar. 30, 1982, p. D8. See also Senate Committee on Commerce, Science, and Transportation, *Nomination—Federal Trade Commission* (hearing before the full committee), 97th Cong., 1st sess., Nov. 19, 1981.

president Joan Claybrook charged that Chairman Terrence Scanlon of the CPSC had used government-paid staff for personal work (including antiabortion and church-related activities) and had improperly provided information to firms that were under commission investigation. Though Scanlon denied both charges, a GAO probe ensued.[103]

Assistant Secretary of Education Anne Graham's appointment to the CPSC was approved by the Senate Commerce Committee in November 1985. But Representatives Ted Weiss and Henry Waxman then received anonymous allegations that while at Education, Graham had used her government car on personal business and had thrown consulting work to her friends. Weiss and Waxman requested and got a GAO investigation.[104]

These cases exemplify the dynamics of creative congressional leverage over nominations. Congressional overseers are especially likely to seek such leverage when they differ sharply with the White House over basic regulatory philosophy and where (as at the multimember commissions) relatively frequent vacancies offer repeated targets. Chairman Magnuson, his staff, and political allies were well positioned in this regard during the mid-1970s. In the case of David Clanton, the committee achieved the ultimate in political judo; the selection parameters were successfully narrowed down to one person who could pass White House and congressional muster.

Far more likely, however, is the simple candidate veto. This is most readily achieved, even in the face of relative harmony

103. Scanlon became a CPSC commissioner in March 1983 and rose to the chairmanship in January 1985 through an appointment made (during a Senate recess) after the previous chairman, Nancy Steorts, resigned. Scanlon's "recess appointment" allowed him to serve as an unconfirmed chairman throughout 1985. (See Article 2, section 2, of the U.S. Constitution on this point.) Scanlon ultimately won confirmation in July 1986. On the controversy, see Bill McAllister, "Terrence M. Scanlon: Ending the 'Heavy-Handed' Approach to Product Safety," *Washington Post*, Mar. 30, 1987, p. A9. See also General Accounting Office, *Consumer Product Safety Commission: Allegations about the Chairman* (HRD–86–41BR), November 1985.

104. Keith B. Richburg, "Product Safety Nominee on Hold for GAO Probe," *Washington Post*, Nov. 29, 1985, p. A3, and "CPSC Member Criticized over Conduct: GAO Says Privileges Abused in Earlier Job," ibid., Apr. 29, 1986, p. A17.

between the White House and an agency's principal Senate overseers, whenever a nomination can successfully be cast in prosecutorial terms—that is, when questions can be raised about a nominee's probity. No matter how desirable politicians may find a nominee on policy or partisan grounds, none can afford to be seen embracing someone who appears to have violated fundamental norms of honesty or decency. Of course, assertions of such violation can easily become a surrogate for disagreements over policy. It was no accident that Representatives Weiss and Waxman happened to receive and follow up on damaging allegations about Anne Graham, since both headed key House subcommittees that they had long used as platforms for the vehement denunciation of Reagan deregulation initiatives. Obviously, this prosecutorial strategy has serious limits, because it relies on there being some character flaw or past abuse that can readily be brought to light. To the extent that an administration sends up "clean" nominees, opponents are robbed of the ammunition they need.

When basic ideological and partisan harmony exists between overseers and the White House and the candidate is clean, only a person whose views offend key members or the Senate as a whole is likely to have confirmation problems. This does not happen often. White House staffs do not like to lose or expend precious political capital defending nominees in trouble, so the administration considers candidate acceptability carefully, partly through informal consultation with Senate overseers.

Agenda Manipulation

The confirmation process also provides senators with a vehicle to comment on the mandates or procedural constraints under which nominees will be expected to work.[105] From the point of view of senators, the regulatory confirmation process ideally would allow them to extract promises of future toughness or leniency (better known in the language of politics as "flexibility"). When President Nixon created the EPA and appointed William Ruckelshaus its first administrator, for example, Sen. Edmund

105. Mackenzie, *Politics of Presidential Appointments*, chaps. 5, 6, 7.

Muskie (D-Maine), the leading Senate champion of environmental protection, raised the issue of tardy compliance with the National Environmental Policy Act, insisting that the Senate version of the pending Clean Air Act "makes you a self-starter, whenever you, unilaterally, see an environmental risk. You are given the responsibility to raise the red flag."[106]

Commerce Committee Chairman Magnuson and Chief Counsel Michael Pertschuk used written questions in advance of confirmation hearings to elicit nominee opinion—and, none too subtly, to reinforce nominee perception of the committee's preferences. Magnuson used this device repeatedly in the 1970s in pushing the FTC toward action on the ill-fated children's television issue. Nominees for the commission were routinely asked: "Can you comment on your views of advertising, particularly in the broadcast media and particularly that directed towards children? What do you see as the responsibility of the Federal Trade Commission to regulate such advertising practices?"[107]

Senators are also anxious to transmit signals that bear on the institution's prerogatives vis-à-vis the executive branch. Hence the following statement by Senator Muskie to Russell Train as the latter was about to become the second EPA administrator in 1973: "I would hope that the regulatory proposals that you develop under the statutes which are your mandate will not be subject to that [OMB] veto and that if there is an attempt to do so, you will resist it, and I hope successfully."[108] Rhetoric about congressional desires for political and policy "independence" are common but indicate, of course, precisely the opposite—that the nominee should depend on Congress rather than the White House for behavioral cues.

Naturally, pleas for special attention to one's electoral constituency are especially tempting. When Steven Jellinek came

106. Senate Committee on Public Works, *Nomination of William D. Ruckelshaus* (hearings before the full committee), 91st Cong., 2d sess., Dec. 1, 2, 1970, p. 45.

107. Senate Committee on Commerce, *Nominations: September–December* (hearings before the full committee), 93d Cong., 1st sess., Sept. 13, 25, Oct. 4, 5, 30, Nov. 19, Dec. 17, 1973, p. 34.

108. Senate Committee on Public Works, *Nomination of Russell E. Train* (hearing before the full committee), 93d Cong., 1st sess., Aug. 1, 1973, p. 8.

before Environment and Public Works in 1977 before taking over the EPA toxic chemicals program, Sen. Don Riegle (D-Michigan) made a point of bringing up the PCBs (polychlorinated biphenyls) that seriously threatened the health and economic well-being of his Michigan constituents:

> I hope that it is not just a matter of State selfishness that I raise this issue but, rather, the fact that we have unwittingly become sort of a test case with a very serious toxic chemical contamination of resources to be put to use to try to deal with this problem....
>
> I know from what you said to me it is your intention to see that is done.[109]

A major criticism of congressional oversight has been that it is rare and superficial, leading to self-directed, faceless bureaucrats. Yet the diverse and sometimes richly entertaining spectacle of congressional inquiry begins to suggest a more subtle set of difficulties at work. The agencies portrayed in this chapter are large and complex organizations, but they are hardly impenetrable or truly autonomous. Congressional inquiry has inhibited, sensitized, and changed these agencies, sometimes with a thoroughness bordering on the dramatic.

But note that good or effective congressional involvement must also be rather narrow and pointed. Congressional inquiry and comment is typically undertaken by specialized committees and by members with distinct agendas—reducing, increasing, or redirecting regulation, getting press coverage, or saving an agency from its enemies. Interest groups and firms desire and reward staunch allies, persons willing to carry their water in hearings, press releases, and in less public interactions with agencies and others. They do not want, or feel they can afford, circumspect referees.

Overseers focus on the policy positions of agency officials, their concrete behavior, and the implications of these things for dis-

---

109. Senate Committee on Environment and Public Works and Committee on Commerce, Science, and Transportation, *Nomination of Steven D. Jellinek* (joint hearing before the committees), 95th Cong., 1st sess., Sept. 28, 1977, p. 6.

tinct constituencies. Congress can apprehend, plausibly criticize, and most easily influence such things. Hence the apparent penchant for what might be called "prosecutorial" oversight. Such inquiry can be conducted without the need for a deep understanding of the more arcane technical aspects of regulatory issues and can be used to appear to evade the thorny question of politics. Overseers like to be seen as concerned merely with law enforcement, congressional intent, and the public interest—not with jockeying for partisan and political advantage. Technical questions and the achievement of regulatory policy goals seem less appealing targets for inquiry; the first is intimidating and intractable, the second merely ephemeral. Overseers can do little but add to the general clamor for effectiveness. One reason why the FTC engendered such free-swinging criticism in the late 1970s was simply the relatively nontechnical nature of its mandate. Members of Congress who might shy away from debating the safety of food additives or chemicals feel more confident in defending their notions of an unfair or deceptive trade practice.

Specific regulations not issued, killer products, embarrassing memoranda, or funds not delivered as promised, however, are all tangible things well within the grasp of, and easily highlighted by, congressional generalists. Targeting particular cases or behavioral bits gives an oversight effort cognitive and political focus, though it further undermines comprehensive evaluation. An extreme instance of this occurred in 1980 when Rep. Mickey Edwards (R-Oklahoma) and seven other House Republicans went to court to force Secretary of Labor Ray Marshall to comply with the letter of the law—specifically, section 4(b)(3) of the Occupational Safety and Health Act. That section had directed the secretary to report to Congress by early 1974 his recommendations "for legislation to avoid unnecessary duplication and to achieve coordination." But the report had never been submitted. In early 1980 Edwards began pestering the Labor Department for it, first during an oversight hearing and then in correspondence. Under court order, the Labor Department finally complied, reporting, innocuously enough, that no such legislation was then necessary.[110] Here was a case of narrowly effective (though minimally useful, except as embarrassment) congressional prodding.

Even more than most vehicles for oversight, legislative involvement in regulatory appointments is both episodic and analytically shallow. The occasional nominee may be alleged unfit to serve because of some past impropriety. More often, confirmation involves a somewhat more nebulous struggle over agency political environments, procedures, and regulatory agendas.

The appointments process also supports highly elastic definitions of the "good" appointee. Congress and president, business and labor naturally have different ideas about what defines such an appointee. So anxious are the respective players to gain compatible and reliable appointees, to maximize potential credit and avoid embarrassing losses, that getting the best or most knowledgeable candidate or obtaining the most profound protective effects can easily fade from consideration. It was no accident that the scientific and technical qualifications of CPSC appointees quickly eroded from the example set by the initial round of appointments (a group including a mechanical engineer, an electrical engineer, and a physical chemist). A different sort of person—the political activist, the ideologue, the reliable partisan loyalist—became just too tempting to resist.

Inquiry and comment by Congress seem most conspicuously and dramatically effective under one of the following three conditions: First, there may be a politically one-sided case. One or more committees may want change that generates little or no opposition elsewhere in the government. Second, if an agency action favored by overseers is near completion, with few or minor steps remaining, oversight can perhaps move the proposal the final few feet. Congressional attention and the prospect of hearings helped dislodge rules that the FDA had cleared but that remained blocked at higher policymaking levels. Inquiry hastened release of regulations implementing the Infant Formula

110. Bureau of National Affairs, *Occupational Safety and Health Reporter*, June 19, 1980, p. 75, and Jan. 8, 1981, p. 797.

Act and the adverse-experience reporting rule for medical devices. The same thing happened in 1985 with a proposal strengthening requirements that processed foods be labeled when they contain sulfites, a class of preservatives associated with potentially life-threatening allergic reactions in some persons.[111] Finally, inquiry is especially powerful when aimed toward blocking or rescinding concrete decisions rather than promoting them, particularly in the face of mass opposition or outrage.

Since much regulatory policymaking lacks these attributes, and since policy players outside Congress may be simultaneously active, however, the stamp of congressional overseers will often be far less visible. Disagreement or uncertainty within and beyond Congress clearly will blur or mute legislative impact on policy.

But this is not at all the same thing as saying that regulators are free to behave as they please, especially with regard to major issues. Two related and significant (if hard to measure) factors are at work: defensive anticipation by the agency and quiet (or tacit) cooperation between an agency and key overseers. Agencies must gauge the reaction within Congress to the policies they pursue. To do otherwise, especially for policies of interest to well-organized congressional constituencies, would be politically foolhardy. When making decisions, moreover, regulators often reflect at least some rough congruence with the perspectives of overseers *without* having to be bludgeoned into doing so through formal oversight. If this is so, then formal inquiry and comment by Congress may represent only the visible tip of a rather substantial iceberg.

111. Cristine Russell, "Rule to Label Foods for Allergenic Sulfites Wins Out," *Washington Post*, Mar. 29, 1985, p. A21.

Chapter 3
Dollars and Sense

Again, we are in a hearing room. This time we observe a subcommittee of House Appropriations. Much is as before: dais; witness table; prepared testimony; the chairman and his intense, anonymous staff aide. As before, members enter and leave throughout—if they show up at all. Yet these proceedings differ markedly from those described earlier. They occur regularly each spring but rarely last beyond a day, often running less than an hour or two. Fewer members of the working press attend, and cameras and photographers are rare, for there will be no victims and few fireworks. Lobbyists may be present but are less likely to testify.

Here high government officials dominate the witness list. A hearing to examine the Food and Drug Administration appropriation request, for example, may open with a brief statement by the Health and Human Services assistant secretary for health, followed by longer remarks from the commissioner of Food and Drugs, who heads the FDA. The deputy commissioner, chief counsel, and heads of various bureaus and divisions within the agency sit close by, armed with thick binders full of "justification material." The subcommittee chairman runs rapidly through a list of prepared questions and requests that cover a range of matters, some significant, others trivial. In 1985 Jamie Whitten, chairman of the House Appropriations subcommittee on agriculture and related agencies, asked FDA Commissioner Frank

Young about user fees, contracts, antibiotics in animal feeds, implementation costs, possible relocation of the agency's Minneapolis microbiologists, and work on nutritional problems.[1]

Once the chairman has run through his or her list, other members take their turns. When officials cannot offer a prompt and accurate response, they quickly agree to submit an answer later for the record. Under the circumstances, the questioning is bound to be perfunctory, sometimes ridiculously so. Agency leaders might appear to be undergoing a pale congressional imitation of a graduate oral exam.

These Appropriations subcommittee encounters—staged, superficial, and ritualized—are a small facet of what many deem Congress's most powerful process for monitoring and influencing regulators or anyone else—the power to appropriate money. Overseers and regulators take these sessions, as well as the larger process of which they are a part, very seriously.

Although the appropriations process tends to emphasize dry management issues (that is, dollar allocations among program categories), members of Congress may have a strong constituency incentive to question policy as well: they do not want those for whom they speak harmed. Like other oversight arenas, the appropriations process focuses on keeping regulatory implementation responsive to a panoply of administrative, political, and policy concerns manifested on Capitol Hill. The main themes, as before, are constituency sensitivity and procedural—especially fiscal—integrity.

The appropriations process contains some notable weaknesses. One, as economists never tire of observing, is a lack of focus on broad social costs. The major costs of regulation are not government expenditures but those of the firms and individuals who must comply; the most significant costs are said to be obscured.[2] And even regulators themselves note that the meager

1. House Committee on Appropriations, *Agriculture, Rural Development, and Related Agencies Appropriations for 1986*, pt. 3 (hearing before the subcommittee on agriculture, rural development, and related agencies), 99th Cong., 1st sess., Mar. 26, 1985.

2. Economists have offered explicit reforms to cope with this problem; see

proportion of the national budget consumed by most such agencies—the FTC and the CPSC combined get barely $100 million—makes them poor vehicles of fiscal restraint, weakening the incentive for detailed item-by-item scrutiny. Moreover, like the more generalized inquiry detailed in the previous chapter, appropriations oversight is remarkably detached from the question of protective impacts. For congressional overseers sitting on appropriations subcommittees, administrative means, especially budgets and personnel requirements, loom large. What the public gets for its money in an "ultimate" sense gets virtually no attention.

Yet neither Congress nor the public at large has protested these failures, primarily because the appropriations process works well at helping to ensure that agencies do not behave, and are not tinkered with by the White House or anyone else, in ways that offend congressional sensibilities. Appropriations supervision can be an effective bulwark against perceived agency overreaching. While it has sometimes been a vehicle for overcoming alleged regulatory timidity, the process is strongest in telling agencies what they should *not* undertake. Such prohibitions may apply either to the largest issues of regulatory enforcement or to staggeringly trivial questions of official deportment.

The Appropriations System

The executive branch takes the formal initiative in appropriations, partly because Congress must rely heavily on agency expertise to determine the resources necessary to implement programs and partly because Congress long ago ceded to the president formal responsibility for preparing a comprehensive budget for submission to Congress. Before budget reforms enacted in 1921, federal agencies "submitted uncoordinated financial requests directly to the Secretary of the Treasury, where they were packaged with little attention into a Book of Estimates

---

Robert E. Litan and William D. Nordhaus, *Reforming Federal Regulation* (New Haven and London: Yale University Press, 1983).

and forwarded to Congress."[3] As the government grew, Congress found this process overly burdensome and required co-ordinated submissions. Responsibility for coordination fell to a newly created Bureau of the Budget, originally part of the Treasury Department but later made a part of the Executive Office of the President. It is the recast Budget Bureau, the Office of Management and Budget (OMB), that today negotiates and oversees the preparation of the complete executive budget before congressional action.

The proposals that OMB gets have been developed first by budget officers in agencies and departments throughout the executive branch. At about the same time that an agency has its spring hearing before one of thirteen House Appropriations subcommittees, it completes its internal review for the next fiscal year. For example, while Congress considered, in early 1985, the budgets for the fiscal year starting in October 1985 (that is, FY 1986), agencies were completing their workups for FY 1987. If an agency is, like FDA and NHTSA, part of a larger executive department, one or more successive reviews occur at these higher levels before a final submission to OMB. Toward the end of each calendar year, OMB signs off and preparations are made to submit requests to Congress as part of the president's official budget. Early in the new year, about when the president gives his annual state of the union message, the complete budget and justification materials finally make it to Congress. Throughout this process the Appropriations Committee staff is in frequent touch with agency officials, informally monitoring the proposals as they traverse the executive branch. In fact, staff aides interact *continually* throughout the year with the agencies covered by their subcommittee's appropriations bill, collecting intelligence and communicating the subcommittee's (and especially the chairman's) perspective.

Once submitted, relevant budget items are parceled out to the House and Senate Appropriations subcommittees. The House traditionally takes the lead. Ideally, the agency hearings occur

3. Larry Berman, *The Office of Management and Budget and the Presidency, 1921–1979* (Princeton: Princeton University Press, 1979), p. 3.

promptly, and the relevant subcommittee concludes its deliberations in late spring with a markup—a session often closed to the public to facilitate a free exchange of views—in which it makes final adjustments in the language and dollar amounts of the appropriations bill. The bill and a draft committee report (a nonstatutory document that explains the bill and often indicates in considerable detail how funds are to be used) then go to the full committee. There, by tradition, a norm of reciprocity prevails, with each subcommittee's proposals receiving little or no scrutiny from members of other subcommittees.[4] Each of the thirteen appropriation bills goes to the House floor, where amendments or provisos limiting the discretionary use of funds (called riders) may be introduced. After consideration in the Senate, differences between the two versions are ironed out by a conference committee composed of members from the House and Senate Appropriations Committees.[5] Then, if all goes smoothly—and in recent years it generally does not—both houses pass thirteen identical bills, and a presidential signature ensues for each.

In recent years, the appropriations process has not often worked in such an ideal way. The reason is conflict. The Appropriations Committees' spending proposals are supposed to

4. In a recent study, two congressional scholars noted that among the most prestigious committees in the House, Appropriations had experienced the least change in the role of subcommittees in decision making. They reported: "The changes are least obvious on Appropriations, whose 13 subcommittees continue to do nearly all its work. The extremely large workload and size of Appropriations requires a division of labor and a heavy dependence by the full committee on subcommittee recommendations. A senior Appropriations aide explained: 'The full committee tends to rubberstamp the work of the subcommittees. Not too much has changed here.' If anything, another staffer added, the workload has increased, making it even less feasible for nonsubcommittee members to check the work of a subcommittee. Appropriations subcommittees continue to be the most autonomous in the House, and the members restrict their attention to their own subcommittees." (Steven S. Smith and Christopher J. Deering, *Committees in Congress* [Washington, D.C.: Congressional Quarterly Press, 1984], pp. 145–46).

5. For more on differences between the House and Senate Appropriations Committees, see ibid., p. 73.

fit within limits set by budget resolutions drawn up within the House and Senate Budget Committees and adopted by both houses. Disagreement and delay plague Congress as it seeks to reconcile appropriations with the budget resolution and with presidential priorities. In 1986, for example, Congress failed to pass *any* of its thirteen spending bills for fiscal year 1987. Fractious debate can erupt over controversial items in an appropriations bill. And since a regulatory agency's appropriation is considered on the same bill with other unrelated programs, a given agency's funding may be held hostage to a political fire storm erupting in a wholly different policy area. Although OSHA appropriations have been controversial in their own right, for example, they have also borne the burden of being lodged within one large funding bill for the Departments of Labor, Health and Human Services, and Education. When President Reagan signed the fiscal 1984 appropriations bill for these departments, it marked the first time in five years that these programs had been covered by such a bill. In prior years, controversies over federally funded abortions and school busing had derailed the process, forcing Congress to enact continuing resolutions to keep the wheels of government turning.[6]

The appropriations process nevertheless contains various means through which congressional sentiment can be communicated to an agency. Hearings constitute but a tiny fraction of this activity. Staff liaison, interest and entrepreneurship by the subcommittee chairman or other members, and the assorted provisions of yearly bills and reports all provide a powerful set of cues from the two congressional Appropriations Committees. And once a bill reaches the House or Senate floor, restrictive amendments expressing strongly held views are always possible.[7]

The Appropriations subcommittees generally are not bastions of "grandstanding" despite some striking exceptions. Relations between agency and subcommittee are routinized and muted at

6. See "Labor-HHS-Education Money Bill Cleared," *Congressional Quarterly Almanac–1983* (Washington, D.C.: Congressional Quarterly, 1984), p. 504.

7. In recent years the addition of riders to appropriations bills on the House floor has been made somewhat more difficult due to a change in House rules.

best, partly because of certain imperatives of the appropriations process. Everyone involved in appropriations knows that, whatever else happens, an annual bill must emerge that will pass the House and Senate. As one staff aide on the House committee put it succinctly: "An 'oversight' committee can stop with a press release. We have to get a bill out!" This has traditionally been a widely shared part of the ethos of appropriations.[8] Because appropriations hearings lack drama, moreover, public interest lobbies dependent on expanding the scope of political conflict through press coverage probably have little to gain through them.[9]

The Power to Persuade

In one critical respect the Appropriations subcommittees resemble others: the pivotal role of the chairman. A House or Senate Appropriations subcommittee chairman can wield enormous persuasive influence, and all regulatory agencies are constantly solicitous of their respective Appropriations chairman's concerns. This occurs mostly privately through informal staff-level contacts, letters, and "understandings," but when a chairman is dissatisfied with an agency, he may escalate the conflict, may even threaten to withhold support for resources. A chairman need develop only the will to commit sufficient time and energy to press his case to get an agency to listen to him.

Jake Garn and the CPSC

An instructive example involves the Consumer Product Safety Commission. Senator Jake Garn's (R-Utah) influence on the agency behavior in the following case was decisive even though it was, like most oversight, weak as a force for ensuring that beneficial protective impacts flowed from commission policy.

By the late 1970s, the agency's political troubles extended well

8. Richard F. Fenno, Jr., *Congressmen in Committees* (Boston: Little, Brown, 1973), p. 23.

9. Paul J. Quirk, *Industry Influence in Federal Regulatory Agencies* (Princeton: Princeton University Press, 1981), p. 141.

beyond the earlier rancor we saw regarding Tris; House and Senate reports that accompanied the CPSC funding bills during the late 1970s sharply criticized agency management. The House subcommittee wanted "more emphasis . . . on standards and surveillance rather than other activities such as information and education," believing that the agency had not adequately justified its performance in the former realm.[10] A Senate report portrayed the agency as wasteful and lacking in priorities.[11] In response the agency offered, during consideration of its fiscal year 1978 budget, just such a priority list, at least partially placating the committee, which noted that "a continuation of this trend will justify the dedication of additional budget support to the Commission's activities in fiscal year 1979."[12]

But in the early 1980s the issue of priorities arose once more, this time within the commission itself. In March 1982, some two weeks before he and his colleagues were scheduled to be examined by conservative subcommittee chairman Senator Garn on the FY 1983 budget, Stuart Statler, one of the CPSC's five commissioners, wrote Garn, accusing his own agency of failing to tie its budgeting to a sufficiently firm and justifiable set of regulatory priorities. Noting the "extreme fiscal restraints" under which the agency operated—its budget had been deeply slashed by the Reagan administration—Statler accused it of "striving to do a little bit of everything" instead of focusing its scarce resources productively. The existing priority lists represented, in his view, simple agglomeration and inertia rather than

10. House Committee on Appropriations, *Department of Housing and Urban Development—Independent Agencies Appropriation Bill, 1978*, House Report 95–380, 95th Cong., 1st sess., p. 24. The subcommittee also compared the CPSC with the Securities and Exchange Commission and found that the former was "devoting a disproportionate level of its resources to the administrative function."

11. Senate Committee on Appropriations, *Department of Housing and Urban Development—Independent Agencies Appropriation Bill, 1977*, Senate Report 94–974, 94th Cong., 2d sess., pp. 28–29.

12. Senate Committee on Appropriations, *Department of Housing and Urban Development—Independent Agencies Appropriation Bill, 1978*, Senate Report 95–280, 95th Cong., 2d sess., p. 24.

tough choices about objectives, and he believed the commission overly slow to address the problems. Complained Statler:

The Commission's inability or unwillingness to discipline itself to concentrate resources on priority projects stems in part from the way we approach the budget process. We tend to address the budget in a backwards manner. Commissioners review line items, rather than first determining where priorities lie, for a short-term and long-term agenda.... Decisions continue to be too often based on individual Commissioners' personal preferences, rather than adherence to agency-wide, clearly-defined, agreed-upon priorities.[13]

These complaints found a sympathetic ear in Garn, a management-oriented conservative. At the appropriations subcommittee hearing, he told commission chairman Nancy Harvey Steorts, a Reagan appointee, that "due to a lack of information on the commission's priorities, I would find it difficult to recommend a specific funding level for the commission." Garn wanted a "firm list" of the agency's top ten priorities and a breakdown on the percentage of the budget that would go to each. He also demanded that the commission develop a plan devoting "at least 60 percent of the Commission's resources" to the stipulated priorities.

Other commissioners were skeptical of Statler's position. One feared that if the commission devoted too much attention to the so-called priorities, staff units would be given a strong incentive to represent their work as priority items. Another worried that staff units whose work had not been given priority might suffer weakened morale. And if the priority list were too short, too much money would be unaccounted for, in effect working against the very intent of a priority-setting process.

Garn ultimately got what he and Statler wanted. Beginning with fiscal year 1983, a set of overall commission priorities was developed along with the annual budget. In exchange, Garn supported full funding for the priority items. Within two years, congressional and commission staff pronounced themselves rea-

13. Letter from Commissioner Stuart M. Statler to Sen. Jake Garn, Mar. 1, 1982, pp. 2, 3. Obtained from CPSC files.

sonably pleased with the way the system was working, and the agency got some political cover in the fight for dollars. Though Reagan's OMB strongly criticized regulation in general and the CPSC in particular, the agency-appropriations subcommittee arrangement apparently safeguarded those activities dearest to the commission. A former subcommittee staff aide later observed that "of all cuts that went through at OMB those priority list projects that were identified by CPSC were never touched at all."

The CPSC case illustrates the kind of opportunities for congressional signaling and negotiation that the budget process offers. Agency leaders must inevitably be attentive. They comply when not doing so might be politically costly, hard to justify, or both, but the process is not a one-way street. Even a powerful chairman cannot dictate behavior. Sometimes, by necessity, opportunistic extended bargaining and mutual adjustment take place. Had the commission leadership been unified and adamant in opposition, Garn might never have pursued his agenda. Or, having done so, he might well have been more effectively resisted.

In this instance, Senator Garn pursued broad procedural change without attempting to specify substantive content or outcomes. Though insisting on a list of specific program priorities, by all accounts he did not seek to intrude on the choice of priorities beyond asking that the list favor specific program objectives over a few generic issues—flammable upholstery versus children's health, for example. And although he did ask that the list set out specific timetables and goals, he did not insist in subsequent years that the agency devote any given percentage of funds to priority items.

Appropriations Reports

Appropriations reports are an important subcommittee tool for persuading agencies to follow a given course of action.[14] Osten-

14. Michael W. Kirst, *Government without Passing Laws: Congress' Nonstatutory Techniques for Appropriations Control* (Chapel Hill: University of North Carolina Press, 1969).

sibly, reports merely explain the budget allocation, but as congressional scholars have long noted, this does not begin to suggest their true influence. Through reports a committee, without cluttering up a statute, can hold officials accountable in a relatively detailed way regarding items considered important. One reason why the so-called runaway bureaucracy cannot, in truth, run very far is that attentive subcommittees can so easily make explicit exactly what they will and will not tolerate.

Reports give overseers the power of emphasis, a capacity to send special cues in a low-key way. A 1980 House Appropriations report urged OSHA "to develop and implement better methods of . . . targeting so as to prevent inspections of establishments with good worker safety and health records and concentrate in workplaces where the most serious problems exist." Soon OSHA reported that it was experimenting with new procedures that would draw inspections away from the safer establishments in high-hazard industries and toward the more dangerous ones.[15]

An agency ignores such nonbinding advice at its peril. In the words of an EPA budget analyst: "[Reports] become just as compelling [as the bill] because these are the guys that give us the money. We almost have to treat them like that because failure to do that is almost like taking your life into your hands. . . . You don't want to get your committees mad at you. They'll have you up there [testifying] every week."[16]

Yet this very usefulness can set the stage for dissatisfaction if a committee's leadership changes or if an issue considered by it is later elevated before the whole Congress in controversial terms. One of the more ironic examples of the persuasive force of appropriations reports involves the FTC's much-maligned effort during the late 1970s to develop regulations on the advertising of presweetened cereals to children. The goal was to enhance the dental hygiene of American children, and though the agency would ultimately be attacked as an overregulating national nanny, prodding by the Appropriations Committee had

15. Bureau of National Affairs, *Occupational Safety and Health Reporter*, Oct. 23, 1980, pp. 559–60.
16. Personal interview.

been instrumental in helping place the issue on the commission's agenda. As former FTC Chairman Michael Pertschuk pointed out, in the mid-1970s the House Appropriations Committee urged the FTC to "achieve . . . effective regulation of children's advertising," insisting that this was "a high-priority topic."[17]

Both Senate and House Appropriations Committees subscribed openly to this view. Only later, after a concrete proposal was in the offing, and after the *whole* Congress had been bombarded by the complaints of various business interests angry over alleged commission excesses, did the signals to the FTC change. In the context of the political seesaw that is social regulation, the commission paid for having done more or less as it had been told.

Appropriations reports routinely advance particular policies dear to the hearts of members, and these reports suggest an appropriations process that is brimming with concern about a variety of policy issues. Consider the reports filed by the House and Senate subcommittees on agriculture and related agencies for the FDA during the Carter and Reagan administrations. Both subcommittees assiduously followed the antibiotics-in-animal-feed issue discussed in the preceding chapter because both have long been home to members with substantial farming constituencies. The FDA move to restrict antibiotics in feed had direct and substantial implications for farmers throughout the nation, and so, in their respective reports, the subcommittees declared their support for more research in lieu of immediate regulatory action. To the subcommittees' members, the potential for drug-fed animals to foster drug-resistant bacteria was hypothetical, and they would not allow farmers to endure substantial hardship on what seemed slim justification. The House subcommittee, arguing that antibiotics had been administered "to billions of animals in the U.S. for more than twenty-five years without any indication that human health had been adversely affected," noted that its bill included $250,000 for additional research. The agency would be expected, said the subcommittee, "to hold in

17. Michael Pertschuk, *Revolt against Regulation: The Rise and Pause of the Consumer Movement* (Berkeley: University of California Press, 1982), p. 78.

abeyance any and all implementation of their proposal pending the final results."[18] The Senate subcommittee likewise wanted more research.[19]

The Senate subcommittee has also manifested an intense interest in the problem of adulterated orange juice. "The sale of this adulterated orange juice," it said, "has an adverse impact on the consumer who receives a poor quality product and works an economic hardship on growers and processors who produce a pure product."[20] The expression of concern and call for "a vigorous enforcement policy" stemmed from Sen. Lawton Chiles, whose Florida constituency depends heavily on the viability of that state's citrus industry.[21]

Reports, like the subcommittees that write them, display both broad public-spirited values and narrower constituency interests. In recent years, the subcommittees on agriculture have used reports to urge that the FDA:

- examine and pursue an "orphan-drug" program;
- take more effective action against pesticide residues on imported foods;
- delay action to ban the sugar substitute saccharin, "notwithstanding any other provision of law";
- study ways to expedite the approval of veterinary drugs for use in minor species;
- exercise caution in changing food labeling regulations;
- require the baby food industry "to monitor and report heavy

18. House Committee on Appropriations, *Agriculture, Rural Development, and Related Agencies Appropriation Bill, 1979*, House Report 95–1290, 95th Cong., 2d sess., p. 100.

19. Senate Committee on Appropriations, *Agriculture, Rural Development, and Related Agencies Appropriation Bill, 1979*, Senate Report 95–1058, 95th Cong., 2d sess., p. 84.

20. Senate Committee on Appropriations, *Agriculture, Rural Development, and Related Agencies Appropriation Bill, 1981*, Senate Report 96–1030, 96th Cong., 2d sess., p. 100.

21. For another example of congressional overseers exerting pressure on an agency (in this case the Overseas Private Investment Corporation) on behalf of the Florida citrus industry, see Clyde H. Farnsworth, "Mixing Politics and Oranges," *New York Times*, Apr. 19, 1986, p. 8.

metals content—with particular emphasis on lead—of the food as it is received and after it is packaged."

This was all in addition, of course, to the more general concern with management—personnel matters, funding levels, facilities, and the like. In fact, the farm-oriented subcommittees that oversee the FDA appropriations are, according to agency officials, often not interested in the budget per se. "The committees are interested in anything that might be of concern to their constituents, that might be in the news," says an official in the agency's division of financial management. "If the agency is going to put out a regulation on [the artificial sweetener] aspartame, they'd want to be sure they read it first." In his experience, the subcommittees almost never ask dollars-and-cents questions. Everything is an ad hoc response to agency policy and process. As a longtime congressional staff aide familiar with FDA put it: "The other house has its laundry list and we have ours."

Management can also be a convenient route to policy. Consider the merging of the two in the following excerpt from the House subcommittee's report for the FY 1985 budget:

The Committee is heartened to know that there appears to have been a breakthrough in the field of virology. Aside from the highly successful viral vaccines for polio, rubella, and smallpox, physicians have had no method to effectively treat the scores of viral diseases. Recently, new anti-viral drugs have been developed to attack viruses within the cell itself. Applications for approval of these drugs have been filed with the FDA, and the FDA is giving them prompt attention. The Committee believes, however, that the FDA should direct additional resources to this entirely new field, which holds such promise. Therefore, the Committee directs that at least two additional virologists be recruited and assigned to processing anti-viral drugs. The Committee appropriates $200,000 for this purpose.[22]

For the subcommittees, report instruction and informal negotiation have an important advantage over appropriations bill language: since they are not formal legislation, they are not

22. House Committee on Appropriations, *Agriculture, Rural Development, and Related Agencies Appropriation Bill, 1985,* House Report 98–809, 99th Cong., 2d sess., p. 107.

subject to the collective scrutiny of the whole House or Senate. Committees can pursue their respective agendas without having to forge consensus within the larger bodies or with one another. But from the point of view of the agency, and perhaps of overall policy coherence, the capacity of these different spheres to operate unconstrained creates problems. Agency officials must respond to both House and Senate committees and, they hope, keep both reasonably satisfied. This is not easy when committees take contradictory stances toward a regulatory practice or issue. In the late 1970s, for example, the two subcommittees on transportation were opposed on the question of public funding for citizen participation in National Highway Traffic Safety Administration rule making. The House subcommittee wanted to kill the funds, whereas the Senate restored them.[23] And each subcommittee can, even when not articulating a firm policy stand, ask for a report on the issue by a certain date. Like the kind of oversight inquiry discussed in the preceding chapter, such requests have the inevitable effect of forcing an agency to reassess, justify, and perhaps change its position.

The Power to Legislate

The strongest element of appropriations supervision lies in the constitutional power to enact spending requirements. Compared to the persuasive methods discussed above, lawmaking for appropriations and authorizations offers one great advantage while suffering a comparable disadvantage. To put it simply, agencies must obey the law. They cannot spend funds they do not have or employ them for purposes proscribed by statute. Agency heads who might, for some reason, try to sidestep the jawboning of a committee report are far more constrained when confronted with a statute. As noted in chapter 2, for example, OSHA's revocation of its nit-picking consensus standards came in response not only to general inquiry and prodding but to a specific mandate in the agency's appropriation bill for fiscal year 1977.

23. The Reagan administration moved early to eliminate such programs in the regulatory agencies.

If a committee, or the Congress as a whole, considers an agency to have overstepped its bounds or otherwise affronted institutional intent, the annual spending bill can be a powerful tool for reining in the offenders.

The disadvantage of lawmaking is that it is necessarily consensual and thus more difficult to achieve. But this potential difficulty is mitigated somewhat by the specialization and mutual deference that characterizes much congressional policymaking. Spending requests are examined and dollar amounts set almost entirely by the relevant subcommittees in each chamber, a specialization process that by constraining conflict partly facilitates the work of Congress. Even within the full Appropriations Committees, the norm of reciprocity makes each subcommittee extremely reluctant to comment on the work of others. Outsiders—members and staff not directly involved at the committee level—enter late in the game, especially when amendments are offered on the House or Senate floor. In the vast majority of cases, consensus between the two corresponding subcommittees is the major hurdle to enactment by the full House and Senate. And that consensus is further facilitated by the conveniently divisible measuring rod, dollars, with which the committees work. When the House and Senate disagree on how much money an agency ought to get, they can nearly always compromise on an acceptable figure.

Yet appropriations remains a sphere of continuing conflict. Social regulation, as I have discussed, stimulates strong constituency and ideological interests. These interests will differ over what to permit and what to reject, over where to cut or increase and by how much, and they will focus on anything from administrative trivia to grand issues of regulatory policy.

Given the symbolism, ideology, and economic stakes that often infuse public policy, it is not surprising to find that appropriations lawmaking sometimes operates more by passion than by reason. As we shall see, agencies can also be stuck with reputations that, valid or not, prompt potentially damaging resentment on Capitol Hill. And legislators can sometimes manipulate the appropriations process more because of the positions they hold or the respect they command than because their arguments are empirically defensible. Two agencies, EPA and OSHA, illustrate the profound power of appropriations lawmaking, as well as displaying a process often largely driven by concerns of constituency, turf, clout, and sheer symbolism. In the present context one is particularly struck by two things. First, appropriations oversight can be used effectively to keep any agency from taking actions that congressional opponents want to block. And second, the annual appropriations process is a ready stage for uncertainties, controversies, and hostilities that linger well beyond the enactment of the regulatory statutes generally thought to embody congressional intent.

Push and Shove at the EPA

Political scientist Richard Fenno has pointed out two competing imperatives characteristic of Appropriations Committees: they must support congressional programs while holding the line against excessive spending.[24] Failure to do either could land them in trouble with the rest of Congress. This helps explain the posture that the House and the Senate subcommittees on Housing and Urban Development–Independent Agencies have taken toward the EPA, whose $4 billion-plus budget, vast jurisdiction, and symbolic significance earn it a special place in both public consciousness and the congressional agenda. Both subcommittees have tried to give the agency, whose programs command substantial bipartisan support, sufficient funds to meet its burgeoning responsibilities while simultaneously manifesting strong concern that funding not increase faster than the agency's ability to absorb it.

In examining the Superfund program of toxic waste cleanup, the House subcommittee, chaired by Democrat Edward Boland of Massachusetts, has been inclined to ask the kinds of tough management-oriented questions that tend to get lost in the uproar over particular hazards and allegations of partisan manipulation. A 1984 staff study suggested that the EPA would find

24. Richard F. Fenno, Jr., *The Power of the Purse: Appropriations Politics in Congress* (Boston: Little, Brown, 1966).

it hard to spend for cleanup at vastly greater rates than it had been doing. Recalls a House staffer:

> The concern we are expressing . . . just in terms of fiscal 1985 was: can they effectively move from a $400 million program to a $600 million program? . . . It was not a very popular [effort], coming from a Democratic-controlled House. It was during an election year and Walter Mondale was visiting every toxic waste dump in the country promising to do it faster, sooner, better. Our attitude was just out of fiscal responsibility; we wanted to keep the brakes on. If you expand a program too soon you quickly overload the supply of contractors. You bid up the prices and you exhaust the supply of available experienced labor.[25]

Though EPA appropriators mainly reflect congressional concern for efficiency and effectiveness in key programs, more narrow issues also attract attention. At the other end of the spectrum, appropriations bills sometimes deal with administrative trivia, and officials may be disciplined for picayune abuses. At various times since the mid–1970s, EPA appropriations have dictated home-to-office transportation, prevented the allocation of agency funds for a personal cook or chauffeur, and prohibited officials from hiring private firms to water the office plants.

Most appropriations bill language, however, addresses a kind of middle ground between the broadest policy questions and headline-grabbing minutiae. It attempts either to put conditions on general administrative practice—for example, by setting limits on the discretionary transfer of funds among budget accounts or by mandating certain procurement protocols—or to dictate answers to specific policy questions that one or more congressional advocates prefer—for whatever reasons.

The history of EPA appropriations abounds with attempts, both successful and failed, to engage in such policy steering. During the late 1970s, for example, the House subcommittee added a provision that barred the EPA from using any funds to administer a program to limit or regulate parking.[26] This grew out of the EPA's proposal to mandate higher downtown parking

25. Personal interview with House staff aide.
26. "HUD, NASA, Veterans," *Congressional Quarterly Almanac—1977* (Washington, D.C.: Congressional Quarterly, 1978), p. 285.

fees for cities that failed to meet clean air standards. Though the 1970s Clean Air Act had provided explicitly for "land-use and transportation controls" as a regulatory option, the widespread political opposition to the EPA's package of proposals—from cities, state agencies, and Congress itself—turned out to be more than the agency could withstand. Notes one commentator: "No other controversy so damaged the EPA's public reputation as did its promulgation of transportation control plans."[27] The appropriations bill restriction was one palpable result.

In 1980 conservative Sen. Roger Jepsen (R-Iowa) won floor approval of an amendment barring the agency from issuing certain sewer-control regulations that would apply retroactively. Though generally sympathetic to environmental programs, Doug Walgren (D-Pennsylvania) won floor approval in 1982 for a rider that would have prohibited the use of EPA funds to implement mandatory state auto-emissions inspection programs. The cost, intrusiveness, and constituent displeasure resulting from such inspection and maintenance programs made them broadly unpopular, even among representatives otherwise supportive of environmental initiatives. At the same time, Ron Wyden, a Democrat from environmentally sensitive Oregon, moved to bar the use of EPA funds to reduce health standards regulating carbon monoxide. (Both the Walgren and Wyden provisions were later removed in conference committee.)

Conflict between Appropriations and other committees in the same house is always possible. When an authorizing committee wants something that Appropriations dislikes, the latter can always try to withhold necessary funds. For fiscal year 1982, for example, the House Appropriations subcommittee wrote language stating that none of the EPA's funds could be used to support the resource recovery and conservation panels established under section 2003 of the Resource Conservation and Recovery Act. The authorizing statute directed the EPA administrator to provide "teams of personnel, including Federal, State, and local employees or contractors" (that is, the panels) that

27. R. Shep Melnick, *Regulation and the Courts: The Case of the Clean Air Act* (Washington, D.C.: Brookings Institution, 1983), p. 299.

would, on request, "provide Federal agencies, States and local governments . . . with technical assistance" on waste matters. The House Science and Technology Committee (headed by Florida Democrat Don Fuqua), which has authorizing jurisdiction over EPA's research and development efforts, attempted to impose a floor on spending for these panels, apparently believing that the Appropriations Committees had not allocated sufficient money. That prompted the House subcommittee to withdraw the funds. Recalls a House subcommittee staff aide:

In FY '82, I'm sure the Fuqua Committee wasn't pleased because that language is in the bill. They would have to beat us on the floor, which isn't going to happen. Our position remains unchanged; we don't want that money spent for those panels. I don't even know what form those panels are supposed to take. I think that on thinking it over the authorizing committee's thinking was, "that's not such a great idea anyway. We might as well back off."[28]

That same year, Fuqua's committee had developed a list of favored projects, including Great Lakes research and aquatic weed control. But the Appropriations subcommittee resisted these as well. Chairman Fuqua may have been captivated by research on aquatic weeds, but Appropriations was not buying. As an EPA official later put it:

Fuqua . . . had been after us for some time on aquatic weed control. . . . But it's not seen as a major health threat, nobody's dying from it, and if general public health is our major motivating concern, you can see why it was not a priority. The Appropriations committee was not interested in pursuing these projects. I think there was a real intent to send a message from one committee to another. . . . I think there was a real effort to put Science and Technology in its place.[29]

One should not, therefore, be tempted to see the Boland subcommittee, or Appropriations generally, as a sanctuary of disinterested rationality. One reason, of course, is that members may use membership on Appropriations to serve the material

28. Personal interview with House staff aide.
29. Personal interview with EPA official.

interests of their constituencies.[30] The section on abatement and control of the 1983 bill directed, "Notwithstanding any other provision of law, that Inverness, Mississippi, shall be reimbursed for the costs incurred for construction of a hydrological control release lagoon." Why? An EPA official offers a lively explanation:

Once upon a time there was a community that built a sewage treatment plant that didn't work. They tried to give it back to the federal government: it was built with 75 percent federal money. They said, "We don't want it, you take it." Well, the problem is there's no provision to allow the federal government to take it back. They wanted not only for us to buy it back but they wanted the federal government to pay them to teach their alternate technology to others in the Delta.[31]

Enter Jamie Whitten, chairman of the House Appropriations Committee and natural advocate of Mississippi's interests. Explains a source within the House Appropriations Committee:

This is one of those instances where the boss knocked and we listened. . . . The way the world works is that full committee chairmen have a lot of power and members defer to them. It was sort of a little crumb, it was only about $60,000. It was just sort of understanding the realities of life. I think Mr. Boland probably just said, this is something that Mr. Whitten's interested in and everyone said yes. I don't think there was any discussion.[32]

Riding OSHA

During the 1970s, OSHA was perhaps the regulatory agency for which appropriations conflict proved most persistent. Far more than the EPA, OSHA generated congressional skepticism regarding the fundamental correctness of its routine practices.

---

30. If anything, the Appropriations Committees seem to have become more sensitive to constituency pressures than they were just a few years ago. During the 1970s, closed hearings became the exception for these committees. Also, "an Appropriations chair no longer can appoint subcommittees in such a way as to minimize constituency pressure and maximize willingness to reduce spending requests, as had been the practice in the 1960s" (Smith and Deering, *Committees in Congress*, p. 93).

31. Personal interview with EPA official.

32. Personal interview with House staff aide.

The examples that follow, however, suggest how far appropriations restrictions went to curtail the agency's enforcement discretion.

Appropriations lawmaking is strongest and most direct when telling an agency in explicit terms what it may *not* do. To be sure, offering money and encouraging positive action are hardly negligible forces. But the potential for such agency action, and its efficacy, depends on much—the amount of technical knowledge, the capacity for coordination within or among agencies or levels of government—that neither appropriations nor anyone else can control reliably. "Getting something done" in government can be a frustrating, even maddening, process. But if one wishes merely to *block* action, to keep an agency from doing something, success comes far more easily.

Between 1972 and 1980 OSHA was the target of repeated efforts to amend its appropriations bills so as to preclude certain activities nettlesome to various interests and their congressional spokesmen. The interests were largely small businesses and farmers; appropriations became the field of battle because the authorizing statute itself remained impervious to amendment, thanks mainly to the efforts of prolabor members of both houses. Even Appropriations subcommittees, however, were largely the bastion of labor sympathizers. Advocates of further restrictions tended to end run the committees on the floor, where they could avail themselves of the widespread resentment provoked by perceptions of the agency's field enforcement. This led to a series of restrictive riders aimed at halting "harassment" and unnecessary inspections. But because the agency's defenders within the Appropriations subcommittees controlled the politics of overall spending levels, even as OSHA found itself growing massively unpopular and faced with severe constraints on its enforcement discretion, its budget continued to grow. Between fiscal years 1973 and 1981 the agency's funding climbed from $89 million to $209 million.

From the first, the Appropriations Committees knew that OSHA enforcement made a lot of people mad. By spring 1972, barely a year after the legislation had taken effect, the House subcommittee on Labor-HEW, then considering the agency's FY

1973 funding, noted in its report that it had "received many complaints of overly zealous enforcement officers, and other complaints of great difficulty in getting assistance from the Department [of Labor] in interpretation of the standards and regulations." The committee added its expectation that "this be recognized by the Department in the training of new personnel and in the supervision of the program."[33]

The report language reflects the low-key appeals and negotiation that OSHA's patrons have always favored in dealing with the agency. But this did not appease others. When the bill reached the House floor, Paul Findley (R-Illinois) introduced an amendment to exempt firms employing twenty-five or fewer persons from complying with the Occupational Safety and Health Act. Findley's amendment passed by a vote of 213 to 154. At the same time, the House rejected an amendment that would have slashed $20 million from the $55 million sought by the House subcommittee by a vote of 160 to 205. Two weeks later, conservative Sen. Carl Curtis (R-Nebraska) failed to get floor approval for a twenty-five-person restriction but won by dropping the minimum size of a regulated firm to fifteen persons. In the conference committee, appropriators felt they had no choice but to include some restriction and agreed to the fifteen-person limit.

But then OSHA got help from a somewhat unlikely source: President Richard Nixon. During the summer, the president vetoed the entire Labor-HEW funding bill, deeming its provisions too costly. Eventually, Congress settled on a new provision that Senator Curtis had offered successfully on the Senate floor, barring funds "to pay the salaries of any employees . . . who inspect firms employing three persons or less" for compliance with the act. But another veto ensued, and the interim continuing resolutions that kept Labor-HEW programs alive contained no such restrictive language.

The following year passed without another major battle, but

33. House Committee on Appropriations, *Departments of Labor, Health Education and Welfare and Related Agencies Appropriation Bill, 1973*, House Report 92–1118, 92d Cong., 2d sess., pp. 10–11.

in the deliberations on the fiscal 1975 budget, small-business critics returned with renewed vigor. The agency, which still felt compelled to inspect and cite small firms (taking the position that to do otherwise would leave a large proportion of the nation's work force unprotected), saw its budget rise from $70 million to $102 million. But a virtual blizzard of floor amendments sought both to reduce the agency's overall budget and to attach the same sort of prohibitive language considered two years before. (One extreme proposal even sought to delete *all* funds for the agency.) In the end, a House-Senate conference agreed to language stipulating that "none of the funds appropriated by this Act shall be used to require recordkeeping and reporting ...from employers of ten or fewer employees." In addition, some $5 million was targeted for on-site consultation services, nonpunitive instruction to small firms trying to cope with OSHA rules.[34]

During discussion of the 1977 budget, efforts to curtail agency enforcement discretion took hold even more firmly. The debate was heated and hardly rational. Agency opponents seized on examples of allegedly foolish action that seemed to portray an agency of idiots. In doing so, they distorted the truth. As one student of OSHA policymaking recounts:

As part of a program to prepare booklets on job hazards for distribution to workers, OSHA had contracted to prepare a series of booklets for farm workers. Some brochures were designed for workers whose native language was not English; there was no intention to distribute them to, say, Kansas wheat farmers. The first booklet in the series was one of those so written. However, this was nowhere stated on the brochure itself, so as not to offend recipients. Instead, it ended up offending everyone else. To someone not aware of the background, the booklet appeared paternalistic and patronizing; one passage warned farm-workers to be careful lest they slip on cowdung. Outraged newspaper editorials followed.[35]

34. House Committee on Appropriations, *Making Appropriations for the Departments of Labor, Health Education and Welfare and Related Agencies*, House Report 93–1488, 93d Cong., 2d sess., p. 4. This is a conference committee report.

35. Steven Kelman, *Regulating America, Regulating Sweden* (Cambridge, Mass.: MIT Press, 1981), pp. 208–9.

OSHA withdrew the booklet, but not before passages had been derisively read on the House floor. Objections were also raised to the expense and intrusiveness of a proposed field sanitation standard for farmworkers. The agency sought to assure Congress that it was ridding itself of trivial rules. Agency enforcement personnel also would receive training in comportment.

But anti-OSHA sentiment proved too strong. "We did not create experts...," intoned Republican Joe Skubitz of Kansas on the House floor, "We created a monster, a monster which does not have the guts to question big business but centers upon small business that cannot afford to—or are afraid to—strike back."[36] Congress ultimately agreed, after much trading of polemical blows and parliamentary maneuvering, to two new restrictions on the agency. One prohibited OSHA inspectors from citing businesses for "first-instance" violations deemed nonserious unless at least ten such violations could also be found. The other prohibited OSHA regulation of farms employing ten or fewer persons.

Deliberation on the fiscal 1979 budget generated two additional restrictive provisos, one spawned inside the House Appropriations Committee itself. Representative Silvio Conte (R-Massachusetts) received information that workers at a Louisiana plant had complained of being shot at by recreational hunters on the property. OSHA had warned the company that the land should be posted, but Conte feared that the agency might cite the firm. This single incident apparently led to language stipulating that OSHA could not take any action "affecting any work activity by reason of recreational hunting, shooting, or fishing." In the Senate, Robert Dole (R-Kansas) won a provision stating that small businesses ("10 or fewer employees") could not be fined for nonserious violations if the employer had earlier taken advantage of the on-site consultation process and made a "reasonable good faith effort" to eliminate the hazard. Dole wanted, he said, to encourage the use of consultation programs.

The following year brought still more restrictions. Beverly Byron (D-Maryland) concluded that the OSHA policy of spot-

---

36. *Congressional Record* (House), June 24, 1976, p. 20366.

check monitoring of firms already inspected by the state was both wasteful and needlessly burdensome for small business. She successfully offered an amendment on the House floor to keep OSHA from conducting such follow-up inspections for six months after the state visit.[37] The Senate committee dropped the provision, but it was later restored, in slightly altered form. John Breaux (D-Louisiana) got a rider telling OSHA, in effect, to think carefully before taking any action on the Outer Continental Shelf. Breaux seemed to feel that OSHA had upstaged the Coast Guard, an agency overseen by the Merchant Marine and Fisheries Committee, on which he was a major player. Senators Frank Church (D-Idaho) and Richard Schweiker (R-Pennsylvania) made separate efforts to restrict OSHA's burden on small business still further. The result was a provision that, with certain exceptions, forbade OSHA from taking action against small firms with low rates of injury. OSHA, said Schweiker, should spend its time where the injuries are.[38]

With the coming of the Reagan administration, the era of "OSHA bashing" through appropriations riders ended. In large part, this reflected a sense that the agency had finally been defanged—and that an antiregulatory administration would take care of any further problems through administrative action. Since 1981 lawmakers have contented themselves mostly with nonstatutory efforts. Committee reports and the extensive informal contacts between subcommittee and agency career employees have remained a major source of political leverage for prolabor Democrats. Labor advocates have even turned the weapon of restrictive bill language to their own uses. When David Obey (D-Wisconsin), perhaps OSHA's staunchest advocate on the House Appropriations Committee, was angered by reports that a Virginia company had been given a compliance waiver while it studied the effects of a cotton dust standard on its workers, he resorted to such language. Such activity, he decided, was inappropriate "human experimentation," and so the fiscal 1985 appropriations bill forbade it.

37. Bureau of National Affairs, *Occupational Safety and Health Reporter*, July 26, 1979, p. 187, and Aug. 2, 1979, p. 211.
38. Ibid.

Administrations of either party generally dislike appropriations riders. The Reagan administration was no exception.
Thorne Auchter, head of OSHA for most of the first Reagan
term, lobbied to have the four oldest riders removed in 1984.
He found the Appropriations Committees in no mood to expend
the energy to refight old battles. A House Appropriations staff
aide sums up the problem well:

It's a matter of principle. Every administration, even the Reagan people,
they come in and they say, "This stuff doesn't belong in the appropriations bill." In the mark-up, the chairman always recommends leaving
it in and nobody ever says anything. Everybody's used to it; the agency
has done everything they have to do to comply.... Every year I always
mention to my staff director: "Hey, let's do something about this." And
he says, "Do you want to be the one to sit up and explain each one and
defend it?" And I say no. And that's that.[39]

The Appropriations Battleground

The system of regulatory appropriations is hardly a disinterested, rational search for perfect policies or the public interest.
It is instead decentralized, prolonged, and somewhat unpredictable political warfare. Members of Congress blend constituency interest, ideology, partisanship, personal preference, and
their own maintenance needs into a rich and sometimes con-
fusing stew of dollars, orders, and cajolery. Neither comprehensive nor entirely coherent, appropriations oversight
nonetheless constrains regulatory discretion on those matters
that well-placed or persuasive members, or coalitions, deem important. Such oversight is at once both formal and informal,
process and weapon. As such, its precise uses reflect the particular array of forces surrounding a program, especially the agendas and maintenance needs of committee members.

Appropriations oversight is well suited to combating what
overseers perceive as the most egregious cases of runaway bureaucracy. Although formal and informal appropriations tech-

---

39. Personal interview with House staff aide.

niques are superb for naysaying, it may happen—as in the case of the Federal Trade Commission—that Congress will give regulators one set of signals at one time and then reverse course later when constituency heat becomes unbearable. An agency may thus be left to appear unresponsive in the new climate. Because it works most directly and effectively to restrain rather than propel, appropriations supervision is less useful against perceived regulatory laxity than in opposing the agency that has gone too far. In the Reagan era, House Democrats could not use the appropriations whip as effectively as they would have wished to oppose administration policy, aware that such restraint would play into the hands of a deregulation-minded administration. Only when that administration wished to pursue positive but distasteful action such as OSHA's human experimentation or OMB review of proposed regulations might a funding cutoff be a plausible threat.

Appropriations supervision works wonders at assuring politically sensitive regulatory appropriation. Regulators must justify, at least in broad terms, what they are doing with the public's money. Congressional overseers, for their part, assure themselves that nothing is taking place that severely transgresses their basic interests and values, whatever those happen to be. Again, this is *not*, and cannot be anything like, comprehensive monitoring of or influence over agency behavior. Even with a vast increase in an already considerable staff, Congress could not hope to achieve this. But Appropriations Committee overseers seem little concerned with dramatically increasing their information from and about agencies. "There are many problems with Appropriations," one staff aide involved in the NHTSA budget said in an interview, "but information is not the problem." The reason for such a response is not only that overseers evidently have access to all the information they can use and more but that they do not in any case see their jobs in terms of "perfect" knowledge. Overseers are most anxious to enforce a profound sensitivity within an agency's leadership to the agendas of chairmen and committees. Appropriations overseers wish to know what obstacles agencies face in gratifying these sensitivities and how they might be overcome. In these respects Appropriations oversight is remarkably powerful. More difficult to cope with are the profound disagreements that infect social regulation and the enormous distance of appropriations oversight from the protective impacts it is often supposed to help produce.

Chapter 4
The Legislative Veto

Particular regulatory proposals by the agencies discussed here have on rare occasions compelled discrete decisions by the whole Congress to sustain or rescind them. Three kinds of conditions tend to generate such review. Perhaps the statute establishing the agency requires such scrutiny. Alternatively, a rigidity deliberately built into the law by Congress might ultimately drive an agency to take action that a significant number of legislators find unacceptable. Or perhaps an action approved, whether tacitly or overtly, by those with routine oversight jurisdiction sparks significant opposition throughout the country and thus within Congress as a whole.

The term *legislative veto* generally refers to various versions of a formal procedural requirement that Congress has imposed on the executive branch often since the early 1930s. In essence, an agency's proposed action—a Federal Trade Commission rule making, for example—is made subject to congressional assent. Veto provisions and proposals have differed somewhat regarding both the breadth of congressional participation required and the need for Congress to act affirmatively to allow the action. In various incarnations, legislative vetoes have stipulated that rejection by a committee, by a single house, or by the whole Congress would kill a proposal.

A passive version of the legislative veto allows proposed administrative action to take effect *unless* Congress rescinds it in a formal vote. In an active version sometimes suggested, an agency action would not become effective *until* Congress voted to allow it. For present purposes, I shall broaden the concept of a legislative veto slightly to include narrowly targeted prohibitions enacted through authorizing legislation and intended to halt or rescind an agency decision.

Champions of the veto argue that Congress is handicapped in constraining regulatory discretion unless it has available some mechanism by which it can formally intercede to block rules or other decisions it does not want. Opponents—who have included every president since Harry Truman—generally argue against such a vehicle on the grounds that it is unconstitutional, an encouragement to statutory vagueness, or a weapon for resourceful lobbies trying to thwart action that may be in the public interest.[1] Opponents won an important, and perhaps definitive, round in this continuing battle with a 1983 Supreme Court decision (*Immigration and Naturalization Service v. Chadha*) invalidating forms of the veto that had been repeatedly enacted into law over several decades.[2]

1. These latter two arguments are defended in Barbara Hinkson Craig, *The Legislative Veto: Congressional Control of Regulation* (Boulder: Westview Press, 1983). See also Mark V. Nadel, "Making Regulatory Policy," in *Making Economic Policy in Congress*, ed. Allen Schick (Washington, D.C.: American Enterprise Institute, 1983), pp. 252–54.

2. That the Supreme Court did not halt congressional passage of legislative veto provisions is evident from Louis Fisher, "Legislative Vetoes Enacted after Chadha," Congressional Research Service paper, Mar. 25, 1985. Fisher notes: "In the sixteen months between *Chadha* and the end of the Ninety-eighth Congress, fifty-three legislative vetoes (generally the committee-veto variety) have been enacted into law in eighteen statutes. Some of these legislative vetoes were about to be enacted at the time of the court's decision. Others have been introduced, reported, and enacted long after Congress became aware of the court's ruling.

"This total does not include legislative vetoes that might have been 'incorporated by reference' in continuing resolutions. It is the practice of Congress to fund programs not covered by the regular appropriations bills by referring to a bill at the most recent stage: as reported by committee, passed by one House, or adopted by the conference committee. The continuing resolution treats such bills as if they had been enacted into law. Some of these referenced bills contain

The court's decision to declare unconstitutional the most common forms of the veto as embedded in law has neither ended the debate over its appropriateness nor rendered Congress impotent in the face of the bureaucratic monolith. Where the underlying political impetus for rescission of agency action is strong, Congress can make its will felt whether regulatory legislation provides for a formal veto review or not. The formal legislative veto is neither as indispensable as its proponents claim nor as dangerous as its most vigorous opponents contend, and its formal use is infrequent in a Congress often divided over policy. Congressional influence will normally find other outlets.

The veto was first enacted long before the modern era of social regulation, originating in 1932 as a way for House Democrats, mistrustful of President Herbert Hoover but cognizant of institutional limitations and the need for presidential discretion, to provide for executive-branch reorganization authority while assuring themselves of the ability to block proposals of which they might disapprove.[3] By the end of the Carter administration, legislative vetoes of one sort or another had been implanted in some two hundred statutes. With the vast increase in the size and scope of the regulatory state that occurred in the late 1960s and 1970s, it was perhaps inevitable that a Congress unable to forge consensus on policy details or immerse itself deeply in the technical matters regulators must confront would turn to the legislative veto.[4]

---

legislative vetoes" (p. 1). Fisher also notes that some EPA funding has been made subject to such committee veto provisions.

3. The historical development of the legislative veto is traced in James L. Sundquist, *The Decline and Resurgence of Congress* (Washington, D.C.: Brookings Institution, 1981), chap. 12, and in Louis Fisher, *Constitutional Conflicts between Congress and the President* (Princeton: Princeton University Press, 1985), chap. 5.

4. The veto was attached to various measures, including: the Office of Education's program of grants for postsecondary education; rules issued under the General Education Provisions Act; exemptions from price and allocation controls on petroleum products; and rule making by the Federal Election Commission. The performance of these and other legislative veto provisions are found wanting in Harold H. Bruff and Ernest Gellhorn, "Congressional Control of Administrative Regulation: A Study of Legislative Vetoes," *Harvard Law Review* 90 (May 1977): 1369–1440.

Some advocates have suggested that *all* regulatory action be made subject to a legislative veto. Although denied this, proponents have won lesser victories, including some fought over three of the agencies examined here. Under the Consumer Product Safety Amendments of 1981, CPSC rule making became subject to a congressional veto. A two-house veto was attached to NHTSA rule making for passenger restraint standards in 1974. And in 1980 the FTC found itself saddled with a veto, due largely to the widespread conviction that the agency had overstepped its bounds with ill-advised regulatory initiatives such as the "kid-vid" rule. Enemies and skeptics of the FTC and the CPSC managed to extract veto provisions as concessions during reauthorization deliberations at which congressional support for these agencies seemed especially fragile.[5]

Vetoes and Regulation: Five Cases

I examine below five prominent instances where some sort of formal veto process was applied to regulatory proposals in the consumer protection area. The principal lesson emerging is that protracted political conflict and various kinds of uncertainty have proved far more significant forces in veto debates inside Congress than agency autonomy or bureaucratic imperialism. Not all of these cases involve laws containing veto provisions, nor was a veto achieved in each case. Indeed, the variation among them cautions against easy generalization. Yet these cases help us to see where the troubles with oversight lie—and where they do not. The cases recounted below include:

1. The 1973–74 attempt by NHTSA to mandate a seat belt ignition interlock for domestic automobiles. This device prevented a car from being started unless the front seat belts were fastened.

---

5. "FTC Funds Bill with Legislative Veto Clears," *Congressional Quarterly Almanac—1980* (Washington, D.C.: Congressional Quarterly, 1981), p. 233. See also "CPSC Authorization," *Congressional Quarterly Almanac—1981* (Washington, D.C.: Congressional Quarterly, 1982), pp. 572–73.

2. The 1977 NHTSA rule that would have required the installation of air bags as "passive-restraint" protection in new cars.
3. The FTC effort in the early 1980s to regulate more closely the transactions between used car dealers and their customers.
4. The FTC decision in the 1970s and early 1980s to attack abuses in the funeral industry.
5. The 1977 FDA attempt to ban, on the basis of cancer studies conducted in Canada, the widely used artificial sweetener saccharin.

The Seat Belt Ignition Interlock

In the first case we see constituent anger trigger a broad and negative congressional response to an agency decision. And although the agency was accused of stupidity and callousness, its troubles stemmed, ironically, from its attempted accommodation of regulated interests.

Since its creation in 1966, NHTSA has had to confront the question of protecting automobile passengers from potentially deadly contact with hard surfaces inside vehicles during accidents. Softer interior surfaces, a type of passive protection, help, but automotive safety advocates have long accepted that some mechanism for restraining occupants in the event of a crash is essential to reducing death and serious injury. The agency thus established a rule in 1967 requiring the installation of passenger-operated seat belts.[6] But largely because of low rates of seat belt use, the agency set out in 1969 to explore so-called passive restraints that would protect vehicle occupants without their active intervention. Over the next decade and a half, the odyssey of Motor Vehicle Safety Standard 208 on "occupant crash protection" would traverse some of the most technically difficult and politically treacherous terrain in safety regulation.

In 1971 the agency announced its intention to require passive restraints—these would almost certainly be inflatable air bags

6. Stephen Breyer, *Regulation and Its Reform* (Cambridge, Mass.: Harvard University Press, 1982), p. 97. See chap. 5 for a useful discussion of NHTSA standard setting.

that deployed in a crash—beginning in 1973. Auto manufacturers, however, argued that they would need more time to adjust, and NHTSA decided to accede, noting the industry's "extreme dislocations, and the attendant financial hardships that would be caused by requiring [the introduction of] major new systems."[7] As an interim measure, NHTSA decided to allow "the option of installing seat belt systems with ignition interlocks for the period up to August 15, 1975." Such devices would prevent an automobile from being started and driven unless the front seat belts were fastened. The agency believed that this option would permit automakers "to institute an orderly, phased introduction of passive systems."[8]

In 1971 Ford Motor Company officials had sought relief from the Department of Transportation (DOT) and (as the infamous Watergate tapes would later reveal) from President Nixon himself.[9] Former NHTSA Administrator Douglas Toms would later remark that, just before the 1972 presidential campaign, there had been talk of Henry Ford abandoning the Democrats to support Nixon. Said Toms: "If that meeting [at DOT] with White House officials had not taken place, DOT would never have raised the interlock as an alternative to the air bag." Later, however, the myth would flower that the interlock had been the brainchild of overreaching regulators.

Manufacturers responded in diverse ways, though the interlock seems not to have been their biggest concern.[10] Chrysler

7. 36 *Federal Register* 19254 (Oct. 1, 1971).

8. Ibid.

9. On the revelations in the Nixon tapes, see "Nixon Ordered Air-Bag Intervention," *Detroit Free Press*, Nov. 30, 1982, p. 1A. The quote from former NHTSA Administrator Toms and other pertinent material is contained in memoranda dated May 24 and June 4, 1974, from Special Counsel Michael R. Lemov to John E. Moss, chairman of the subcommittee on commerce and finance of the House Committee on Interstate and Foreign Commerce. Both are entitled "Ignition Interlock" and were obtained from the files of the Insurance Institute for Highway Safety, Washington, D.C. See also Joan Claybrook, "The Air Bag Issue: Whether and When," *Washington Post*, Sept. 1, 1976, p. A15.

10. Comments on proposed NHTSA rule making on the interlock are found in Docket no. 69–7, available on microfilm in Room 5109 at NHTSA headquarters, Washington, D.C.

suggested that the agency was pushing the device prematurely, before the full results of existing or less intrusive measures such as belt warning systems were known. General Motors also thought a warning system preferable and said that consumers might "become so annoyed by the inconvenience of the starter interlock feature that they would have the entire system disconnected." General Motors also asserted that the complex circuitry required could cause interlock failures, leaving drivers unable to start their cars in critical situations. Foreign automakers lodged the same sorts of objections. The Ford Motor Company, on the other hand, championed the device, apparently in the hope that it would forestall the introduction of inflatable air bags. American Motors endorsed the interlock for the "front outboard," but not the center, positions. In written comments to NHTSA, however, manufacturers generally seemed less concerned with the interlock than with other pending regulatory issues, such as the use of debated injury criteria to measure seat belt performance and the overall timetable on which NHTSA seemed to be operating for the development and introduction of passive systems.

The Ralph Nader-affiliated Center for Auto Safety objected strenuously to the agency's position on both procedural and substantive grounds. It complained that a delay for the automakers seemed to reflect ex parte (that is, off the record) contacts between the White House, the manufacturers, and the agency.[11] The center also argued that seat belts of any sort were far inferior to air bags as a means of protection, since the latter allow greater and more gradual dispersal of impact forces. Moreover, it argued, belts would not protect small children and "unusual-sized" adults as well as would air bags. And like the manufacturers, the center worried about technical problems and the potential for consumers to defeat the system.[12] In spite of these reservations, however, auto safety advocates generally favored the interlock over the status quo, in which belt use rates hovered well below 20 percent.

11. Letter from Ralph Nader and Lowell Dodge to John A. Volpe and Douglas Toms, Oct. 8, 1971.

12. Letter to NHTSA from Lowell Dodge, Jan. 31, 1972.

Detailed debate among the agency, manufacturers, and safety advocates over various aspects of the interlock provision raged on into 1972 and 1973, but congressional interest was slow to mount until the device's imminent appearance on 1974 model cars aroused public sentiment. It is important to note that the agency did not pull a fast one on overseers, who were quite aware of the issue. During spring 1973, for example, the subcommittee on commerce and finance of the House Interstate and Foreign Commerce Committee conducted extensive oversight of the agency while considering reauthorization of the National Traffic and Motor Vehicle Safety Act. The interlock proposal came up only in passing, as the subcommittee focused on a plethora of other matters deemed more pressing.[13]

But during that spring a trickle of angry constituent mail began to hit Congress. During the summer and autumn, as cars with interlocks arrived on the market, the trickle became a torrent. To many, this was a clear case of Washington bureaucrats having gone berserk:[14]

How can you possibly consider it any of your business whether I fasten my seat belt or not? To require ... me to fasten [the seat belt] before the car will start is the height of the ridiculous! [Letter to Rep. George Mahon of Texas dated April 20, 1973]

This is an invasion of privacy. To make seat belts available in cars and educate people as to the safety factors is fine. But to force a person to use a seat belt by tying it in to the ignition is wrong. [Letter to Sen. Richard Schweiker of Pennsylvania dated July 27, 1973]

I just don't believe that the government would take it upon itself to make even this small decision for me. ... I have a ruptured disc problem ... [and belts put] unbearable pressure on my back so I have never used them. ... Even without my back problem I think any citizen should be

13. See, e.g., House Committee on Interstate and Foreign Commerce, subcommittee on commerce and finance, *Amendments to the National Traffic and Motor Vehicle Safety Act of 1966—Part 1* (hearings before the subcommittee on commerce and finance), 93d Cong., 1st sess., Mar. 23, Apr. 13, 16, 17, 18, May 7–11, 29, 1973, p. 329.

14. These excerpts are taken from letters on file under Docket no. 69–7, copies of which are in possession of the author.

allowed to weigh the odds for himself. [Letter to Sen. Mike Mansfield of Montana dated September 4, 1973]

As an owner of a new 1974 automobile, I am appalled at the degree to which the U.S. Congress has invaded our personal lives. [Letter to Sen. Walter Mondale of Minnesota dated September 27, 1973]

The media, especially the automotive press, was quick to emphasize that the interlock was both defeatable and unnecessarily annoying.[15] And a single-minded Ford engineer named Emile Grenier quit his job to fight the interlock with newspaper ads and interviews, claiming that the device could prove hazardous under a variety of circumstances.[16] The agency worked hard to counter the adverse publicity, noting the interlock's relatively meager cost (about fifty dollars per car), the low rate of belt use, and other considerations.

What NHTSA found harder to fight, however, was the widespread sense of an intrusive government interfering with its citizens' rights, a view championed by a conservative New Hampshire Republican, Rep. Louis Wyman. He called the interlock "one of the most offensive invasions of the personal right of privacy to be dictated by the federal bureaucracy in recent years" and suggested, along with other critics, that the system posed "significant risk potential." His examples of the risk included: a woman trying to escape an attacker might be unable to because of the time it would take to buckle up; a motorist stuck at a railroad crossing might prove too flustered to start his car in time to avoid an onrushing train.[17]

By mid-1974, as the NHTSA reauthorization moved toward floor consideration in the House, public sentiment against the interlock was in full bloom; some consumers went so far as to pay mechanics to disconnect it. The bill reported out by the House Interstate and Foreign Commerce Committee reversed

15. See, e.g., Richard A. Wright, "Interlocks: Annoying, Defeatable," *Automotive News*, July 16, 1973, p. 71.

16. Paul Gainor, "Inventor Calls Interlock Lethal," *Detroit News*, Aug. 15, 1973, p. 20.

17. Louis Wyman, "The Case against Seat-Belt Interlocks," *Motor Trend*, May 1974, pp. 53, 108–9.

NHTSA policy by requiring the agency to give consumers a choice. Automakers would be able to satisfy the government by making some cars available with interlocks and some with a "sequential warning system," an integrated shoulder and lap belt connected to a buzzer or light.

But when the bill reached the House floor that summer, even this modification proved insufficient to stem the criticism. Wyman, then well into a Senate campaign and fighting allegations that connected him peripherally to the Watergate scandal, rose with what he called "a citizens' rights amendment" that would ban the interlock outright.[18] Chairman John Moss defended the committee's provision to allow a choice as "rational and reasonable," but the mood of the House proved irreversible: the Wyman amendment steamrolled to passage by a vote of 339 to 49. A House-Senate conference agreed to language providing, in the 1974 Motor Vehicle and Schoolbus Safety Amendments, that "no Federal motor vehicle safety standard may . . . [require] any continuous buzzer designed to indicate that safety belts are not in use or any safety belt interlock system."[19] Two weeks after bicameral acceptance of the conference report, NHTSA issued a notice that the interlock option was officially rescinded.

The Air Bag and the Legislative Veto

The end of the interlock did nothing to resolve a larger issue far more worrisome to the automobile industry, to safety advocates, and to NHTSA: the long-term future of passive restraints. Many inside and outside the agency believed that the demise of the much-maligned interim system had helped keep alive what had been their preferred regulatory option all along: air bags.[20]

18. The debate and vote is detailed in *Congressional Record* (House), Aug. 14, 1974, pp. 27805–27. For Wyman's tangential connection to Watergate, see Jonathan Kellogg, "Wyman Shifts on '72 Gift," *Washington Post*, Sept. 18, 1974, p. A4.

19. Public Law 93–492, section 109. See "Mandatory Seatbelt System Voided," *Congressional Quarterly Almanac, 1974* (Washington, D.C.: Congressional Quarterly, 1975), p. 688.

20. "Taking out Interlocks, Putting in Air Bags," *Business Week*, Oct. 12, 1974, pp. 30, 32.

The legislation that killed the interlock also imposed a legislative veto on all future passive-restraint rule making. The law said that if the agency promulgated an occupant restraint rule requiring a system other than seat belts, Congress would have sixty days to review the rule and pass a concurrent resolution disapproving it. Without such formal disapproval, the rule would take effect.

That provision was activated in the summer of 1977 by Carter administration Secretary of Transportation Brock Adams, who decided to phase in over three model years front-seat passive restraints—either air bags or a passive lap and shoulder belt that automatically encircled occupants. Full-size cars would have to comply by the 1982 model year, with smaller vehicles to follow in the two ensuing years.[21]

Adams's decision provoked strong opposition in both houses, and conservatives and members with significant automobile manufacturing constituencies quickly mobilized to rescind it.[22] In the House, a conservative Pennsylvania Republican, Bud Shuster, organized the opposition. By the beginning of the August recess, his veto resolution had some 160 cosponsors. In September testimony before the House Commerce subcommittee charged with evaluating the disapproval resolution, Shuster declared the pro–air bag arguments were based on "highly theoretical extrapolations" that were without foundation. He suggested, moreover, that "the air bag lobby has virtually captured NHTSA" and would stop at nothing, including distorting the facts and suppressing unfavorable data, to gain its objective. Shuster and his allies also portrayed the order as yet another example of imperialistic regulatory overreaching. Finally, in an attempt to portray air bags as positively dangerous, Shuster also cited scientific

21. 42 *Federal Register* 34299 (July 5, 1977). Adams's announcement reversed a decision by his Ford administration predecessor William T. Coleman calling for a large-scale "demonstration program" under which the automakers and the federal government would cooperate to test the practicability and effectiveness of passive restraints. See 42 *Federal Register* 5071 (Jan. 24, 1977).

22. See "Air Bags Mandated," *Congressional Quarterly Almanac—1977*, pp. 531–32. See also House Committee on Interstate and Foreign Commerce, *Installation of Passive Restraints in Automobiles* (hearings before the subcommittee on consumer protection and finance), 95th Cong., 1st sess., Sept. 9, 12, 1977.

opinion holding that the sodium azide used to inflate them was mutagenic and thus might well pose a health risk of its own.

The subcommittee, led by a pro–air bag chairman, ultimately voted against the resolution to rescind but passed it on to the full Interstate and Commerce Committee anyway on the grounds that it did not wish to obstruct a measure supported by so many members. After considerable parliamentary skirmishing in which air bag proponents sought to delay a floor vote, the full committee finally voted to table the resolution.

In the Senate, opposition to the Adams measure was out-gunned and outnumbered. The consumer subcommittee voted 5–0 to recommend that the full Commerce Committee kill the rescinding resolution. But when the committee met that October, Robert Griffin (R-Michigan) threatened to block action on any other legislation until the resolution was voted on. The committee complied but sent the resolution to the floor with a neg-ative recommendation. There it died when Commerce Chairman Warren Magnuson won a landslide 65–31 vote to table it.

One important consideration in the size of the resolution's defeat was doubtless the earlier loss in the House. Though the automobile lobby was formidable, consumer protection re-mained, as it does today, a popular issue. Even Representative Shuster was careful to position himself, to the extent possible, as proconsumer; air bags would be costly and might cause genetic mutations. With passage of the resolution impossible given the House action, a vote for it became a vote wasted—and one that a future opponent could use to paint an incumbent as anticonsumer.

The actions by both houses did absolutely nothing to settle the question of passive restraints; the legislative veto process was anything but definitive in this instance. Since the first cars af-fected by the Adams order were to be manufactured in the summer of 1981, opponents had plenty of time and many other avenues to block passive restraints. The order was challenged in court, where it survived scrutiny by a federal court of appeals in a 1979 decision.[23] Congressional opponents of air bags, denied

23. *Pacific Legal Foundation et al. v. Dept. of Transportation*, 593 F. 2d 1338 (D.C. Cir. 1979), cert denied, 444 U.S. 830 (1979).

a victory through the legislative veto, turned to the appropriations process. In 1978 Shuster got the full House, which had been kept from voting on the earlier resolution, to approve (237–143) an amendment to NHTSA's fiscal 1979 funding bill that would have killed money to implement the Adams order. This did not receive full congressional approval. The following year, Rep. John Dingell tried the same thing. These measures and similar activity in the Senate were largely symbolic, since technically the Department of Transportation did not need the money to enforce the standard until autumn 1981. Nevertheless, they were a convenient way of keeping the pressure on NHTSA and DOT to reconsider their position.

Anti-air bag forces received a temporary boost from the 1980 elections, which brought into power an administration committed to reduced regulation. But after the courts challenged a revocation of the DOT standard, the administration proposed to phase-in passive restraints unless a sufficient number of states began to mandate seat belt use. By the late 1980s, the major automobile manufacturers, facing continued government pressure and apparent consumer interest in air bags, had shown a gradual change of heart. Air bags began to find their way into an increasing proportion of manufacturers' models. How the air bag saga would ultimately play out remained anyone's guess.

But for present purposes certain things are clear. A legislative veto process will not settle an issue where contending sides are well organized and intensely committed. The contestants will use other available means in search of victory in the political process. And one might reasonably have taken *either* side in this air bag debate. Once again, the only conclusion possible is that the bureaucracy did not grossly overstep appropriate bounds.

The FTC's Used Car Rule

In the early and mid-1970s, such diverse forces as a Ralph Nader study group, an American Bar Association panel, the Nixon administration, and congressional consumerists moved to invigorate an FTC widely perceived to have neglected its twin jobs of antitrust enforcement and the protection of consumers against misrepresentation in the marketplace. An important legislative component in the commission's new, more active orientation was the Magnuson-Moss Warranty Act of 1974, which called for the FTC within a year to begin proceedings leading to the promulgation of a rule covering used car warranties and practices.[24]

In 1976 the FTC started things moving.[25] A lengthy and complex debate ensued, both within the agency and in the rule-making record, that principally resulted in honing down the scope of the rule. In 1979 the commission considered and rejected a proposal that would have mandated inspection of all used cars sold by dealers, with results to be disclosed on a window sticker, and in 1981 it voted to stop short of even optional inspections. Later that year the commission promulgated a rule that focused on maximum disclosure of warranty coverage, if any, and known defects.

The years that the used car rule lay in the regulatory pipeline had been politically unkind to the FTC. For various reasons, its supporters on key oversight committees dwindled, Congress as a whole became increasingly hostile to the commission's activities, and energetic commission chairman Michael Pertschuk came under especially intense fire as a coalition of business interests, representing both small and large firms, joined to fight an assortment of commission initiatives.[26] By the end of the decade, Congress was giving the agency distinctly different signals than it had five or ten years earlier. In its FTC Improvements Act of

24. Section 109(b) of the Magnuson-Moss Warranty–Federal Trade Commission Improvement Act (Public Law 93–637) stipulated that the FTC "shall initiate within one year after the date of enactment . . . a rulemaking proceeding dealing with warranties and warranty practices with the sale of used motor vehicles."

25. This account draws on interviews with participants. The history of the used car rule is covered in detail in 46 *Federal Register* 41328–30 (Aug. 14, 1981), and in testimony by FTC Commissioner Patricia Bailey in House Committee on Energy and Commerce, *Federal Trade Commission's Rule Regulating the Sale of Used Motor Vehicles* (hearings before the subcommittee on commerce, transportation, and tourism), 97th Cong., 2d sess., Dec. 2, 1981, Feb. 24, 1982, pp. 9–33.

26. See the personal account in Michael Pertschuk, *Revolt against Regulation: The Rise and Pause of the Consumer Movement* (Berkeley: University of California Press, 1982).

1980, Congress took what might be seen as the ultimate symbolic and substantive step: shackling the commission's rule-making authority with a legislative veto. The proposed used car rule was the first to come under the new requirement.

Both new and used car dealers and their lobbies, the National Automobile Dealers Association (NADA) and the National Independent Automobile Dealers Association, mobilized to fight the rule, complaining primarily about a provision forcing a dealer to disclose "known defects" to prospective buyers. Although the language of the rule did not require presale inspections by the dealers themselves—it did allow independent third-party inspections, however—they argued vehemently that its practical effect would be precisely to compel such inspections. This was their main line of attack in the House subcommittee on commerce, transportation, and tourism, then chaired by James Florio, who strongly supported the rule. Protested NADA President Wendell Miller: "Any conscientious dealer attempting to comply will be forced to inspect almost every used car if he is to run his business in a prudent manner and protect himself from multiple and random lawsuits that the rule will subject him to."[27] And in compelling inspections indirectly, said industry representatives, the FTC was violating congressional intent as stated in an earlier committee report expressly warning against administrative action to make inspections mandatory. All of this would hurt not only an ailing automobile industry but also consumers, to whom the price of inspections would be passed on.

These arguments were echoed by Rep. Gary A. Lee (R-New York), who introduced the resolution of disapproval in the House. Conceding that most of its provisions, such as the requirement that dealers disclose the existence of warranty coverage, were unobjectionable, Lee nonetheless wanted major surgery: "However, the proposed rule's secondary goal to mandate the businessman or businesswoman to attest to all known defects in their product in 14 major systems, with the stated language in the proposed feature that a thorough inspection is

27. *Federal Trade Commission's Rule Regulating the Sale of Used Motor Vehicles*, p. 75.

not required, is preposterous. For example, how can a business-person attest unequivocally to defects in the engine system without an extensive examination?"[28]

FTC Commissioner Patricia Bailey took the lead in defending the rule before Congress. She argued strenuously that it did not require inspections directly or indirectly, that the dealers themselves had earlier supported precisely the sort of disclosure provided for, and that reopening the rule making to strike out the offending section (as suggested by Congressman Lee) was unnecessary.

The fight continued throughout late 1981 and early 1982. The dealer lobby, with members in every state and congressional district, flexed its muscle as letters poured in to Congress protesting the FTC's decision. The NADA political action committee had given more than $1 million to various congressional campaigns in 1979 and 1980, and these contributions provided a critical source of industry leverage. Industry representatives were also careful to envelop their case with consumer-protection arguments of their own, reiterating their satisfaction with some of what the rule had to offer and emphasizing the potential costs to used car buyers.

The rule lacked a strong grass-roots constituency that could mobilize on its behalf anything to match auto industry opposition. With Congress already sensitive to the perceived excesses of the FTC, a vote to stop runaway regulators was politically attractive to many members, and agency officials and congressional supporters of the used car rule apparently came to the opinion early in the game that theirs was probably a lost cause, even after the special assistant to the president for consumer affairs announced her support for the FTC position.

They were right.[29] In May 1982, the full Senate voted 69–27 in favor of the veto resolution. A few days later the House followed suit. Late in 1984 the FTC put forth a revised used car

28. Ibid., pp. 2–3.
29. "FTC Rule Vetoed," *Congressional Quarterly Almanac—1982* (Washington, D.C.: Congressional Quarterly, 1983), pp. 346–47.

rule without the dreaded defects disclosure requirement. It took effect in 1985 with relatively little fanfare.[30]

Like the cases discussed earlier, the used car episode does not represent congressional reining in of an autonomously aggressive FTC. Many in Congress, including key overseers with jurisdiction over the agency, strongly urged that the rule be left alone. But once a well-organized and widely distributed business interest had expanded the scope of conflict in unfavorable terms before the whole Congress, the rule's prospects dimmed dramatically. This, of course, is precisely why many persons oppose the legislative veto in the first place.

A Veto Buried: The FTC Funeral Rule

As the FTC developed its used car proposal it also pursued a rule regulating the funeral industry's dealings with customers. Had the funeral rule run the congressional gauntlet *before* the used car proposal, the outcome of the veto debate could well have differed. As it was, a commission proposal to regulate funeral practices arrived on Capitol Hill in early 1983, after the election of a new Congress thought by Ralph Nader and others to be more sympathetic to consumerism than its predecessor and after bad publicity from the used car vote. (The press had played it as a tale of political action committee muscle at work.) For these and other reasons, the political climate for the funeral rule differed markedly from that surrounding the used car rule.

An internal commission study of possible regulatory action for the funeral industry began in the early 1970s. In 1979, after dozens of days of hearings and the receipt of thousands of exhibits and written comments, the commission first moved to establish a final rule. The commission proposal would have required that price information be given over the telephone, that consumers be able to purchase mortuary goods and services selectively rather than as part of an inseparable package, that prior permission be obtained for em-

30. Nell Henderson, "FTC's Used-Car Rule to Take Effect Today," *Washington Post*, May 9, 1985, p. B1.

balming, and that casket purchases not be required for cremation.[31] For several reasons that first proposal would be withdrawn for further study.

Congressional scrutiny of the FTC funeral rule is largely the story of one member's persistent opposition over several years. Chicago Democrat Marty Russo came to Congress as one of the "Watergate babies" elected in 1974. In the late 1970s, Russo, a gun-control advocate who would support the used car proposal, decided that, in the FTC's attempt to constrain the funeral industry, he had found a federal bureaucracy overreaching without sufficient cause. In 1979, when the House debated the FTC reauthorization, Russo offered a floor amendment that would have effectively stopped the funeral proposal by denying the commission authority to spend funds on it. He wanted, he said, to "prohibit the Federal Trade Commission from issuing [the rule] or a revised version of it."[32] He was doing this, he said, "because the American people want less intervention in their daily lives, not more."

But, as his own later commentary makes clear, there was more to it than that. As part of a House Small Business subcommittee that looked at FTC handling of the funeral rule during his first term in Congress, Russo became convinced both that the proposal was an unnecessary invasion of state and local government turf and that the rule making had been characterized by procedural irregularities that biased the result against industry. Russo concluded that the commission was operating without justification. As he later told Susan and Martin Tolchin:

I showed up one morning at a hearing and we had this guy named Arthur Angel [from the FTC]. I asked him how many complaints do you have. A couple of thousand? He said not that many. It got down to six. They had read Jessica Mitford's book [*The High Cost of Dying*] and that was the impetus, and based on that they made up their mind that they were going to move from there to some kind of rule. I said,

---

31. Described in 47 *Federal Register* 42262 (Sept. 24, 1982).
32. *Congressional Record* (House), Nov. 14, 1979, p. 32472.

based on six complaints you are going to continue an investigation of small business? I don't understand this.[33]

On the House floor Russo quoted Chairman Pertschuk as saying that, in its early days of commission consideration, "there was a sense of vendetta against the funeral industry."[34] Whether or not this was true, Russo's amendment undoubtedly benefited from the "vendetta" atmosphere that generally colored congressional thinking about the FTC at the time. Russo's amendment passed easily, 233–147, although a House-Senate conference later deleted it while Russo was hospitalized. But partly as a result of agency uncertainty in light of the reauthorization debate, and partly because of a court decision on an unrelated rule, the funeral rule proceedings went into hiatus, after which the rule underwent yet more revision.

Meanwhile, Congress remained active. The 1980 FTC reauthorization statute explicitly narrowed the scope of any permissible commission rule making for the funeral industry. But the FTC was still free to: (1) move against misrepresentation; (2) stop funeral providers from threatening competitors; (3) keep funeral providers from conditioning the sale of some goods and services on the purchase of others; and (4) restrain providers from furnishing goods and services for a fee without prior approval.

When a revised rule was proposed to Congress in late 1982, subject to the legislative veto process adopted with the 1980 reauthorization, Russo, along with industry lobbyists, was still poised for a fight. But the funeral directors were not as fast off the mark as the used car dealers had been, nor as unified in their opposition. The National Funeral Directors Association (NFDA) did argue that federal regulation would "take away a fiduciary trust between the bereaved and a funeral director" and that certain requirements would prove impractical. Said an association spokesman: "A widow, who may have just kissed her

33. Susan J. Tolchin and Martin Tolchin, *Dismantling America: The Rush to Deregulate* (Boston: Houghton Mifflin, 1983), p. 175.

34. *Congressional Record* (House), Nov. 14, 1979, p. 32472.

husband goodbye for the last time, is not in any mood to have
all these prices thrown at her." But the executive director of the
New York State Funeral Director's Association said that the FTC
proposal "really isn't a problem" and that in some places funeral
directors had long ago accommodated to state and local disclosure laws.[35] An FTC staff person who worked on the rule in its
latter stages told an interviewer that the NFDA was far more
resistant to regulation than the National Select Morticians, which
represented a more "upscale" clientele and tended to work better
with the commission. The latter group, for example, "wasn't
opposed to itemization or to giving price information over the
phone." Moreover, the funeral directors could not make the
powerful claim, available to the auto dealers, that they would be
forced willy-nilly into a costly activity (inspections) that ran
squarely against congressional intent.

And unlike the used car rule, the funeral proposal had grass-
roots support. The American Association of Retired Persons
had, for several years, made the funeral rule one of its lobbying
concerns. Senior citizens are obviously high consumers of mortuary services, and the costs associated with a death are considerable, especially for persons on fixed incomes. Their huge
numbers, wide distribution, and high rates of participation make
the elderly a formidable political voice. They comprised a natural
and effective constituency *for* the rule.

Given all of this, the segments of the funeral industry most
firmly opposed to the rule were hard pressed by spring 1983 to
find many allies besides Representative Russo. Not one senator
was willing even to introduce a disapproval resolution. The antiregulatory fever that had swamped Congress a few years earlier
was clearly receding, including its antipathy toward the FTC.
"We were worried about the Senate," says a commission staff
person then involved in congressional liaison. "The industry lobbying groups were over there but nothing happened."[36] Even
Sen. Robert Kasten, who had torn into the used car proposal,

35. Michael deCourcy Hinds, "A New Try for Truth-in-Funerals," *New York
Times*, Feb. 27, 1983, p. E7.
36. Personal interview with FTC staff attorney.

supported the funeral rule. And as had happened in the 1977 passive restraint vote, the lack of support in one house helped take the starch out of the other. House members did not want an anticonsumer vote that would not count for anything wrapped around their necks.

The end of congressional consideration was almost anticlimactic. One congressional staff aide involved in both the used car and funeral rule debates recalls that "there was a different feel in the air" the day of the House subcommittee's vote on the latter.[37] The subcommittee unfavorably reported Russo's resolution to the full Committee on Energy and Commerce. There the resolution lay when the *Chadha* decision emerged from the Supreme Court. But even without *Chadha*, the resolution was dead.

Whether the funeral rule made for sound policy or not, the case certainly shows a Congress aware of the proposal and endorsing it. Of course, this may have had more to do with political expediency than policy effectiveness. But Representative Russo's entrepreneurship was certainly effective in enhancing congressional attention to the rule. Even before FTC rules had been made subject to a legislative veto, Russo had found a way to make himself heard via an authorization bill. He lost, ultimately, because he was outgunned politically, not because the FTC was out of control.

Saccharin the Sacrosanct

The most intensely debated provision in the food and drug law is the so-called Delaney clause, which stipulates that "no

37. As one source puts it: "After sustaining an overwhelming veto favoring the [used car] dealers, consumer groups immediately appealed to the judiciary and to the public. They won at law and Congress lost decisively in the communications media. Newspapers and television stations headlined a Congress that had 'knuckled under' to powerful dealership interests.... Shortly thereafter, when the FTC submitted its regulations on funeral homes and children's television advertising, Congress evinced little interest in a repeat performance" (Robert S. Gilmour and Barbara Hinkson Craig, "After the Congressional Veto: Assessing the Alternatives," *Journal of Policy Analysis and Management* 3 [Spring 1984]: 388).

additive shall be deemed to be safe if it is found to induce cancer when it is ingested by man or animal, or if it is found, after tests which are appropriate for the evaluation of the safety of food additives, to induce cancer in man or animal." In passing the law, Congress reflected a widespread fear of cancer, a major touchstone in debate on health and safety issues. Everyone hopes that this dreaded killer will be eliminated, and the Delaney clause embedded this hope in law. But it also set the stage for unpleasant choices when old friends turned out to be potential enemies.

Nowhere have these choices been tougher than for artificial sweeteners. Originally approved by the FDA in 1951, the sweetener cyclamate grew in popularity during the 1950s and 1960s to become the most popular sugar substitute. By 1969 the American public consumed some 17 million pounds of cyclamates annually. But by the following year, tests had implicated cyclamate as a suspected carcinogen, and the FDA moved to ban it, a decision reaffirmed in 1980. Although the ban was a hardship for producers, the impact on the average consumer was mitigated by the availability of an alternative: saccharin.

But by March 1977 the FDA had proposed a ban on saccharin, citing Canadian tests results indicating its carcinogenic potential. With cyclamates already off the market, the ban would leave no approved sugar substitute available to millions of consumers, and so the proposal sparked a fire storm of controversy unlike anything the agency had ever experienced. Created to safeguard the public, the FDA now found that same citizenry outraged that a favored product would be snatched away.

Congress quickly reflected the public outcry. The House Interstate and Foreign Commerce Committee's subcommittee on health and the environment, chaired by Florida Democrat Paul Rogers, was at the center of the storm. Rogers, who had managed to carve out a substantial reputation for himself as Mr. Health, could ordinarily be counted a strong FDA supporter, but as he opened a hastily called oversight hearing on the FDA's proposed ban on March 21 it was clear that he and other committee members would be listening to the mailbag as much as to the experts testifying before them. Along with other nonscientists, congressmen questioned whether a study in which rats seemed to have been deliberately overdosed could reasonably trigger a ban: "We will want to know why FDA has decided to ban saccharin based on the results of a study in which rats were fed the equivalent of 800 bottles of diet soda a day, an amount hundreds of times higher than the average American could be expected to consume."[38]

Other members noted the potential impact on the nation's ten million diabetics. New York Democrat James Scheuer observed that saccharin had "never produced a single case of cancer in a human being," and Florida Democrat Claude Pepper warned sardonically that "some of our esteemed leaders in the field of medicine tell us that there is a substance called aflatoxins that is found in peanuts. This is an ominous development. Before long, we might have to ban peanuts."[39]

Agency officials explained that the law gave them no choice and that the tests had been conducted in accord with accepted scientific practice. The quantities of saccharin fed to the rats and the subsequent extrapolation of the resulting data to humans represented sound science, not agency stupidity. Moreover, said agency defenders, it could be plausibly argued that the FDA had been *slow* to act rather than precipitous. Sidney Wolfe of the Health Research Group applauded the proposed ban, citing ten additional "cancer-positive studies" and arguing that "the proper design of animal research studies for cancer is a matter of consensus among research scientists."[40]

But Congress as a whole was inclined to stop somewhere short of a ban. Opposition from the Pharmaceutical Manufacturers Association and other industry groups was strong. An agency

38. House Committee on Interstate and Foreign Commerce, *Proposed Saccharin Ban Oversight* (hearing before the subcommittee on health and the environment), 95th Cong., 1st sess., Mar. 21, 22, 1977, p. 1.

39. Ibid., p. 15.

40. Ibid., p. 241. See also Linda E. Demkovich, "Saccharin's Dead, Dieters Are Blue, What Is Congress Going to Do," *National Journal*, June 6, 1977, p. 857.

suggestion that saccharin be designated an over-the-counter drug rather than a food additive (an attempt to allow diabetics and others with health needs continued access while curtailing it for others) fell flat, particularly with the soft drink and food industries, which accounted for 90 percent of saccharin use. A business lobby, the Calorie Control Council, launched an advertising campaign ridiculing both the FDA and the studies on which it had based its decision.[41]

Ultimately, the key political force was the mass resistance, even panic, that overwhelmed constituents in every state and district. As Baltimore Democrat Barbara Mikulski testified: "The way my mail and phone calls are running, the proposed saccharin ban is a larger issue and has more opposition than any other matter I have dealt with since I have been in public office." Mikulski conjured forth the specter of Prohibition and the possibility of a black market in saccharin. She recommended more study, and that turned out to be a nearly irresistible position for most members of Congress. Divided scientific opinion over just how carcinogenic saccharin was made it easy for members in both houses to cite the need for more information. The House adopted appropriations language delaying any ban to the end of the 1978 fiscal year and calling for more scientific scrutiny in the meantime. A similar move came in the Senate. These were ultimately withdrawn when the authorizing committees indicated they would move quickly on a bill.

This they did. By the end of October, both houses had passed legislation postponing a ban. The Saccharin Study and Labeling Act signed into law by President Carter on November 23 imposed an eighteen-month moratorium on any possible ban, required that the FDA undertake further study and report the results to Congress, and mandated a two-sentence warning on all food products containing saccharin: "USE OF THIS PRODUCT MAY BE HAZARDOUS TO YOUR HEALTH. THIS PRODUCT CONTAINS SACCHARIN WHICH HAS BEEN DETERMINED TO CAUSE CANCER IN

41. An excellent discussion of this effort is Key Lehman Schlozman and John T. Tierney, *Organized Interests and American Democracy* (New York: Harper and Row, 1986), pp. 188–90.

LABORATORY ANIMALS." In spite of the FDA's earlier opposition to a special exemption for saccharin, the agency was mollified enough by the labeling requirement to counsel the president to sign the bill.

Following the new law, the FDA then contracted with the National Academy of Sciences (NAS) for studies of saccharin and food additives. In 1979 two NAS panels reported that an immediate ban was probably unnecessary despite a finding that saccharin seemed to be a low-potency carcinogen. Deeming the Delaney clause unworkable, they recommended instead that agency officials be given greater flexibility to factor in risks versus benefits in making their decisions on additives, a procedure they routinely followed in the drug approval process. But a vote to weaken the Delaney clause remained too close to a vote for cancer in the minds of many. Congress could resolve only to extend the moratorium every couple of years thereafter.[42]

Overwrought political rhetoric to the contrary notwithstanding, the saccharin episode hardly shows a foolish or untamed FDA. Instead, regulators responded to what seemed an ironclad congressional mandate only to be told they should make an exception. The end product was a balancing of risks and benefits that satisfied Congress while leaving the agency cast, unfairly, as a villain. In this respect, the saccharin case is not at all unique.

A fundamental point to remember in all the legislative veto cases considered is that such cases are rare. Congress has had only a handful of instances in which to consider seriously a collective after-the-fact veto for the agencies discussed. This suggests either a Congress massively inattentive to the workings of important regulatory bureaucracies or one that is capable of affecting the practices and policies of those agencies primarily

42. By the early 1980s, the FDA had tested and approved yet another sugar substitute, aspartame, after years of scientific and political debate. Aspartame too remained under a cloud despite manufacturer claims that it was "the most tested food additive in history." A comprehensive and critical overview of the controversy over sugar substitutes is Linda C. Cummings, "The Political Reality of Artificial Sweeteners," in *Consuming Fears: The Politics of Product Risks*, ed. Harvey M. Sapolsky (New York: Basic Books, 1986), pp. 116–40.

through alternative means. Of these two possibilities, only the latter is plausible. No fair reading of the record of formal regulatory oversight by Congress—and this would leave out a vast amount of informal or tacit oversight—could support the conclusion that legislators ignored or were unaware of what regulators were up to. Congress as a whole may be only mildly or sporadically attentive to the performance of the agencies discussed here, but the subcommittees and staff with ongoing oversight responsibility are kept thoroughly informed of what and how the agencies are doing. The principal reason that oversight of the sort described in this chapter is so infrequent is that it is so rarely necessary. Other tools (committee-generated provisions in authorizing or appropriations legislation, committee reports, letters, informal contacts, and gentleman's agreements) typically suffice to head off or modify agency actions that might antagonize members and the assorted constituencies for which they speak.

The paucity of cases can also be attributed to the relative uselessness of the veto as applied to the problems that plague regulation. Consider regulatory delay: The capacity to send things back to the drawing board does not mean much if the problem is that things never get moving in the first place. As noted in chapter 3, congressional Democrats searching for a weapon to oppose a Reagan administration perceived hostile to regulation and slow to take necessary action often found the ability to *block* things relatively unhelpful.

Asked if the legislative veto implanted in the agency's authorizing statute had been a significant impediment to FTC rule making, a high-ranking career staff official in the consumer protection unit said that it had not, citing both the Reagan administration's general reluctance to work through rule making and the procedural morass of the Magnuson-Moss Act as far greater impediments. The findings of a General Accounting Office study of the impact of congressional review on the FTC are generally consistent with this view.[43] The legislative veto provisions in the

---

43. General Accounting Office, *Impact of Congressional Review on Federal Trade*

CPSC authorization statute have never been tested, despite that agency's vast jurisdiction, mainly because of a preference for working through negotiated agreements instead of rule making. Indeed, given the principal charge leveled against the CPSC earlier—that it failed to put out *enough* rules—it is unclear why the legislative veto was ever thought appropriate. But political reforms may reflect impulses other than instrumental rationality.

What these cases do accomplish is to shatter the popular image of a Congress riding to the rescue with its formal veto power when the regulatory bureaucracy has gotten out of hand. *None* of these occasions may fairly be said to have arisen due to the failure of other mechanisms (such as the appropriations process) to catch a problem created by imperialistic regulators.

If congressional capability to review and perhaps rescind regulatory actions collectively is hardly a panacea for what ails regulation, neither is it the horror of horrors it is sometimes made out to be by opponents. Again, the paucity of cases here suggests that Congress will usually find it unnecessary to exercise or even approach a veto. Veto provisions arguably give well-organized and/or widely distributed interests an advantage, but such interests are bound to be effectively represented in Congress whether the legislative veto as such exists or not. The *Chadha* decision did not fundamentally alter the nature of the American political process. Some versions of the legislative veto may be unconstitutional, but the veto is hardly, by itself, the policy-wrecking back door into the administrative process that liberals have sometimes alleged, even though one may expect agencies to think hard about how a proposal will play before the whole Congress.

The political dynamics of congressional vetoes will necessarily include, and probably be driven by, forces other than scientific and technical rationality. And as the air bag and funeral rule examples suggest, the appetite for a veto will almost certainly diminish in one house if it seems to lag in the other. The funeral rule experience also indicates that the reaction to previous action

---

Commission Decisionmaking and Rulemaking Processes (GAO/HRD–82–89), Aug. 17, 1982.

can spill over into the decision at hand. Members of Congress naturally consider how a vote will look as well as what a vote will do. None of this is avoidable or especially alarming. Where representatives are directly and individually accountable to voters the result could hardly be otherwise. But it is difficult to argue that such factors, at work through congressional vetoes, have horribly corrupted the democratic process as it pertains to the programs discussed here.

Arguably, the most significant single effect of legislative vetoes has been to help generate congressional consensus behind the statutes into which they have been placed.[44] When activated for consumer protection programs, collective review has not so much kept errant regulators "in line"—that has not been necessary—as it has generated constituency-centered second-guessing of a few discrete regulatory decisions.

44. See William West and Joseph Cooper," The Congressional Veto and Administrative Rulemaking," *Political Science Quarterly* 98 (Summer 1983): 288–97.

Chapter 5
Distant Goals

To what degree, if at all, are we likely to be made *substantively better off* as a result of the sort of congressional oversight activity recounted thus far? Put differently, will all this aggressiveness in prodding and constraining regulatory bureaucracies make us a better-protected people?

No full and final answer can be given here; probably none is possible. But there are good reasons to question the protective significance of any political oversight. Even as oversight significantly constrains, guides, and legitimates the behavior of regulatory bureaucracies, it is likely to make us better off in a purely protective sense only on a rather random or accidental basis. Even when regulators operate exactly as their political overseers would like—doing more, or less, or doing it differently—the resulting performance will be only dimly related to the enhancement of protective impacts.

I do not pretend to offer here any comprehensive catalog of ultimate policy effects. As the authors of an insightful volume on "urban outcomes" suggest, such an endeavor is doomed from the start:

Who knows what the final consequences of schooling are for individuals? We don't...and neither does anyone else. The ramifications of freeways, for instance, are so diverse—employment, social interaction, racial conflict, agricultural and industrial production—no one can project them in the distant future, let alone separate these consequences from others with different causes. One blanches at the very thought.[1]

And yet something more modest is both feasible and appropriate here: reasoned judgment on the means-ends connection in light of both the behavior discussed and the requirements oversight would have to satisfy to advance true protective impact. In this chapter, therefore, I suggest more comprehensively why policy impacts are not easily manipulated or enhanced through congressional intervention of any plausible kind.

The three primary themes we must now examine are: *political indifference, political and technical uncertainty*, and *implementation complexity*. Such forces, singly and in combination, go far toward explaining why oversight is, at bottom, a shortsighted, *means-focused* political enterprise, little concerned with or able directly to promote distant protective ends.[2] We will see that overseers: (1) cannot conceptualize or focus on ultimate goals; (2) have little or no incentive to do so; and (3) would face enormous, probably insuperable, challenges were they to attempt it.

Political Indifference

Politicians do not think much about policy goals. So bald a claim may raise the eyebrows—and perhaps the ire—of many persons regularly attentive to or involved in politics. After all, politicians, especially as elections draw near, seem to speak endlessly of goals, of their desire for using more or less or different government to create a better life. Since the hard business of making trade-offs, of sacrificing some particular thing in order to have more of another, is so terribly unpleasant and so politically risky, candidates seem to talk of *nothing but* goals. But they rarely, if ever, concentrate on goals in the sense of ultimate policy impacts. Such

1. Frank Levy, Arnold J. Meltsner, and Aaron Wildavsky, *Urban Outcomes* (Berkeley: University of California Press, 1974), pp. 3–4.
2. Readers familiar with social science literature on organizations and bureaucratic behavior will doubtless recognize that I derive the line of analysis taken here from themes developed by such scholars as Herbert Simon, Charles E. Lindblom, Aaron Wildavsky, Edward C. Banfield, and others.

impacts are too hard to envision, and there is typically little incentive to do the work required to project them. Most of what passes for consideration of goals in the hurly-burly of Washington politics is actually a discussion of means. When members of Congress speak of increasing or decreasing the quantity of almost anything, including regulation, they are engaging in just this sort of behavior.

On the regulatory front, it is striking how frequently discussion centers on the sheer quantity of regulations, inspections, citations, seizures, or prosecutions as indicators of success or failure. An increase or decline in the amount of such things is generally taken as evidence of a job done well or poorly. This may not be wholly out of line if one views program purposes broadly, as repositories of symbolism and public aspiration rather than as purely "instrumental" mechanisms. That the CPSC and OSHA had managed to put forth only a handful of regulations in their first few years of existence caused severe and sustained anxiety on Capitol Hill, as if doubling or tripling the number of substances for which rules had been issued would necessarily have provided enhanced protection of the public health. Such benefits *could*, of course, have resulted from an increase in rules or from the promulgation of any given rule. But whether this were true would depend, among other things, on what substitute behaviors, risk shifts, or new incentives the rule created. Politicians often miss this aspect of policymaking.

Let us return briefly to two episodes of FDA oversight pursued by House Democrats. In the case of medical device regulation, Chairman John Dingell and his staff on the House Energy and Commerce oversight subcommittee criticized the lack of class II standards or retroactive class III approvals.[3] Their principal focus was not ultimate safety but a more severe interpretation of the agency's obligations under the 1976 legislation. The overseers felt they could make a solid case that the FDA was not sufficiently enforcing the law. The subcommittee seemed to spend little effort asking whether a focus on preamendment class III devices or performance standards for those in class II actually

3. See chapter 2 material on medical device regulation.

constituted the best use of the agency's time as a way to maximize the public's benefit or whether the absence of regulation had caused real and widespread injury. The text of the law suggested that there ought to be greater effort at comprehensive enforcement, and that was enough to get Chairman Dingell, a man with a reputation for being easily roused by anything smacking of an affront to legislative intent or prerogatives, up and charging.

Similarly, whether additional real protection might be afforded infants by more stringent controls on infant formulas was not the focus in that case. Nor was the question of whether alternative strategies, directed at other infant products, might have achieved the same results. Congress and the press had found a conspicuous hole in the web of protection, which created the opportunity for oversight entrepreneurship, leading to a demand that something be done. Congress thus insisted on writing strict and detailed interim standards into the law.

As some academic students of Congress have suggested, members are powerfully driven by their political maintenance needs.[4] Policymaking by members of Congress, especially where they play a highly visible role, tends to be at least constrained by (some would say dictated by) the desire to retain both public office and favorable recognition within some larger elite—perhaps a network of supportive clienteles or the legislature itself.

Yet it is easy to overstate the role of reelection in determining members' policy stances. The claim here is not that politicians will do *anything* to get and hold office or that they do not care about the significance for the general public of policies they

---

4. David R. Mayhew, *Congress: The Electoral Connection* (New Haven and London: Yale University Press, 1974), and Morris P. Fiorina, *Congress: Keystone of the Washington Establishment* (New Haven and London: Yale University Press, 1977). Although some members of Congress may indeed be rather single-minded seekers of reelection, I prefer to think that for many, reelection is more nearly a constraint on the pursuit of other goals such as good public policy. On this point see Richard F. Fenno, Jr., *Congressmen in Committees* (Boston: Little, Brown, 1973), chap. 1. See also Martha Derthick and Paul J. Quirk, *The Politics of Deregulation* (Washington, D.C.: Brookings Institution, 1985), pp. 141–44, and Steven Kelman, *Making Public Policy: A Hopeful View of American Government* (New York: Basic Books, 1987), chap. 10.

promote. But members of Congress, especially those identified with particular policy networks, find themselves pressed to define a consistent posture and place in the network. A subcommittee chairman prominent for a "prohealth" or "prosafety" position on FDA or OSHA matters maintains and enhances his or her career by being allied with like-minded interest groups that will supply information, publicity, contributions, and other forms of assistance.

These groups, in turn, have their own maintenance needs.[5] Liberal public interest lobbies often depend on generating a perception of corporate or bureaucratic indifference to vital public values and needs. This mobilizes contributors and helps stir the public to support policies favored by the groups. Leading the charge may also legitimize group leaders in the eyes of their members.

Members of Congress, moreover, have limited amounts of time to devote to any one thing; everyone must vote on bills, attend to constituents, deliver speeches, and perform a multitude of other tasks that compete for their attention and sap their energy. Put all this together, and even the advocates of regulatory toughness will be more interested in how their behavior is perceived by economic, electoral, or ideological constituencies on which they depend, and how the activities of their pet or target agencies are regarded, than with distant impacts. When overseers complain that OSHA's citations or inspections have fallen off, they are naturally doing so with an eye on how organized labor regards these developments as well as because workers may be harmed. OSHA may well undermine worker health by failing to cite or inspect; I do not imply here, even in a roundabout way, support for a program of wholesale regulatory relief. The point is that an OSHA supporter in Congress is highly unlikely to inquire into regulation with anything like genuine analytical disinterest, seeking to maximize economic or other quantitatively stated values without regard to politics. He or she will not behave like the prize student in a public policy

5. James Q. Wilson, *Political Organizations* (New York: Basic Books, 1973).

seminar. The same is true of pro- or antiregulation members attentive to any agency.

A good example of this is congressional treatment of the Delaney clause embedded in the food and drug law. Many critics have argued that these provisions place an impossible burden on the FDA, since the degree of risk abatement implied is simply not feasible. Members of Congress familiar with the provision are all too aware of the problems it poses. But it is fear of political consequences, rather than an obsession with the public health, that has inhibited statutory revision. A staff aide put the matter bluntly:

> If you took everybody on the Hill who matters on FDA issues, people like Teddy Kennedy and Ted Weiss, and put them into a room and asked them, "Do you think the Delaney clause is any way to regulate?" they will tell you it isn't. I know because I've heard the conversations. But none of them will vote to weaken or remove it because none of them wants to see the third paragraph of the *New York Times* story where Sidney Wolfe [of the Health Research Group] tells everybody that their representatives have just voted to increase their risk of getting cancer.[6]

As another aide, also close to debate on the issue, put it: "Politics is the art of avoiding blame and claiming credit. With Delaney, there's just too much potential blame to go around and not enough credit." In the face of refusal to change the law, the Reagan administration reinterpreted the clause in a way that some feared might provoke congressional wrath without either resolving the issue *or* enhancing public protection.[7]

As noted earlier, what attracts widespread congressional and public attention most readily is the horror story. In social regulation, this may stem from allegations of insufficiency or malfeasance within either the agency or the business community it oversees. Dramatic instances of death and injury attract attention to overseers and help drum up support for the cause they have embraced. But there is no reason, a priori, to believe that these events, or the political reaction to them, will drive an agency in

6. Personal interview with House subcommittee staff aide.

7. Richard M. Cooper, "Stretching Delaney Till It Breaks," *Regulation* (November-December 1985): 11–17, 41.

directions that ultimately enhance the public health or welfare. Criticism of perceived holes in the FDA's approval process has become, over the years, a virtual industry in some quarters of Congress. But long-term benefit to the public health has not been the focus of these endeavors. The congressional perspective is confined almost entirely to *process* and the political benefits that may be reaped by prodding or criticizing it.

Agencies do respond, sometimes even change, as a result of all this proregulation scrutiny. With a bit of digging one can easily uncover instances where congressional oversight has worked, both broadly and narrowly, in this sense:

- The Fountain subcommittee's impending inquiry into the drug Oraflex induced FDA management to alter drug-review procedures marginally to assure that reviewers had to check agency files more thoroughly for evidence of adverse reactions in premarket tests.
- After a scare regarding asbestos in hair dryers, overseers succeeded in getting the CPSC to set up a special contingency fund to handle emergency assessments.
- Congressional complaints about the inadequacy of OSHA's health standards program helped raise and sustain that issue as a priority for the agency's leadership, setting the stage for the Carter administration's push in that area.
- Prodding by the Dingell subcommittee on medical devices triggered a reassessment and some shifting of priorities at the FDA's Center for Devices and Radiological Health.
- The complaints of the Dingell subcommittee were also critical to EPA's rescission of its 1985 decision to abandon its responsibility for asbestos. Ultimately the agency moved, in 1986, to phase out asbestos use completely.
- The pummeling that EPA took at the hands of several committees in 1982–83 resulted in massive turnover among the agency's leadership ranks.

Such concrete payoffs may also come in areas where public hearings have not been held. Most congressional inquiry does not occur in hearing rooms, and an absence of hearings should never be construed as inattention to what is happening, or not happening, inside agencies. During the first Reagan term, the Dingell subcommittee investigated numerous regulatory matters through simple requests for documents and private interviews with agency personnel. That is how overseers do nearly all their real learning; hearings are staged more to dramatize issues for the public or for other legislators than to instruct members and staff. Recommendations or referrals are sometimes made by letter.[8]

It is not just the public character of much oversight that diverts its focus away from ultimate protective ends. Even the nonpublic staff-level efforts are driven by the kinds of activities or events— appointments, pending proposals, stalled regulations, funding, allegations of impropriety or waste, tangible holes in the regulatory safety net—that overseers can readily grasp or exert efforts to influence. And, of course, staff are constrained by the larger political attachments of the members for whom they work.

In short, Congress—or more accurately, committee-level overseers—sometimes wins in the public and private battles to push a regulatory agency to do more. But whether such political triumphs mean victory for the public health and welfare is an open question, one from which members of Congress and their staffs are remarkably detached. When asked several years later if the CPSC emergency fund had ever been used, a staff aide who had helped engineer its acceptance had no idea; it had not occurred to him to wonder. Thus, he could hardly have reached the issue of the fund's contribution to beneficial public impacts, a symptom of the proregulation overseer's focus on proximate

8. During the Ninety-seventh Congress, for example, the staff of the House Energy and Commerce subcommittee on oversight and investigations learned of studies at the University of Kansas showing that under some circumstances the consumption of soy protein could cause problems in iron absorbency. Without much fanfare, the subcommittee referred the matter to the FDA, which took specific steps toward focusing greater attention on the questions involved. A committee report would later brag that the FDA had "[s]hifted the order of their priorities from some of their continuing research in other areas in order to place more immediate emphasis on the soy issue" (House Committee on Energy and Commerce, *Report on the Activity of the Committee on Energy and Commerce for the Ninety-seventh Congress*, House Report 97–1002, 97th Cong., 2d sess., p. 357).

process and on the political rewards for manipulating or attacking it.

The problem is not all in Congress. The bureaucracies themselves also often seem less motivated by the achievement of genuine protection than might be expected. Regulatory agencies, like all organizations, seek to maintain themselves. Doing so requires among other things friendly, or at least stable, political environments. Confronted by external threats, agencies will either fight or adjust, which may undermine the attainment of formal protective goals.

A striking case of such behavior was OSHA in the 1970s. The agency's wholesale adoption of the existing and ultimately troublesome industry consensus standards for safety reflected a short-run concern with political maintenance. The agency wanted to show that it meant business and forestall criticism from the political left. Later on it became clear to a wide spectrum of policy analysts that many of these standards were absurdly irrelevant to real safety concerns.

Perhaps an even more glaring example arose in the aftermath of the criticism the agency received for its slowness in reacting to complaints from workers at a chemical plant in Hopewell, Virginia. Unfortunately, it turned out that a serious (and highly publicized) health crisis was in the making. Once the crisis was revealed, the agency responded by giving employee complaints top priority in its inspections scheduling, with the proportion of inspections based on complaints reaching 38 percent of the total by fiscal year 1978.[9] But although this policy change may have mollified some workers and unions, it severely hampered any effort to direct scarce agency resources toward high-hazard firms or industries, as the General Accounting Office revealed in a 1979 report to Congress that noted complaints tended to come "from the types of businesses that OSHA would not visit on its own initiative and do not appear to address serious hazards or,

9. This explanation of events draws on interviews with former agency officials that confirm the account in Albert L. Nichols and Richard Zeckhauser, "Government Comes to the Workplace: An Assessment of OSHA," *Public Interest* 49 (Fall 1977): 54.

in some cases, any hazards."[10] A high GAO official reiterated
this finding at a 1980 Senate hearing: "Complaint inspections
often did not detect any violations of standards, seldom detected
serious violations, and rarely detected serious violations that related to the subject of the complaints. For 80 percent of the
complaints we reviewed, no violations were found that related
to the items complained about. Less than 4 percent of the complaint items were cited as serious violations."[11]

The attachment to politically attractive means over ends is also
evident in efforts to promote or protect agencies. The members
of Congress and staff engaged in shoring up the agency's image
and political support. Again, when this is the real purpose of
oversight it is quite beside the point to speak of impact in any
protective sense because the perspective at work is far more
limited. The same is obviously true of oversight that aims to limit
an agency.

Indifference to the larger protective ends of regulation also
afflicts another element of congressional oversight: analysis and
assessment. Virtually everyone who has ever looked at congressional use of its capacity to predict policy results or evaluate past
practices has concluded that Congress is inherently disinclined
to perform and use disinterested analysis. Instead, Congress uses
analysis as a weapon of political combat.[12] In the words of then

10. See Bureau of National Affairs, "GAO Says Complaint Inspections Delay
Inspections of Serious Hazards," *Occupational Safety and Health Reporter*, Apr. 19,
1979, pp. 1674–75. See also General Accounting Office, *How Effective Are OSHA's
Complaint Procedures?* (GAO/HRD–79–48), Apr. 9, 1979.

11. Senate Committee on Labor and Human Resources, *Oversight on Administration of the Occupational Safety and Health Act, 1980—Part 1*, 96th Cong., 2d
sess., Mar. 18, 21, 28, 1980, p. 415.

12. In this regard see: Charles O. Jones, "Why Congress Can't Do Policy
Analysis (or Words to that Effect)," *Policy Analysis* 1 (Spring 1976): 251–64;
Robert H. Haveman, "Policy Analysis and the Congress: An Economist's View,"
in *Public Expenditure and Policy Analysis*, ed. Robert H. Haveman and Julius Mar-
golis, 2d ed. (Chicago: Rand McNally, 1977), pp. 577–91; Michael J. Malbin,
*Unelected Representatives: Congressional Staffs and the Future of Representative Gov-
ernment* (New York: Basic Books, 1980), chap. 9; Erasmus H. Kloman, ed., *Cases
in Accountability: The Work of the GAO* (Boulder: Westview Press, 1979), p. 5; and

congressman and later OMB Director David Stockman, analysis tends to be a "fig leaf," employed to cover policy positions that comport with a member's existing interests or values.[13]

Analysis is only as good as the premises on which it is based. And these premises derive naturally and heavily from members' views of how alternative policies affect proximate and narrow interests rather than distant or broad ones. In fact, Congress is not even the right place to look for a truly technical grasp of most of the issues with which it must deal. As John Kingdon has written:

> With some notable exceptions, Congress is not the place to find the detailed, technical type of expertise found in the bureaucracy, in the community of academics and consultants, or among the interest groups that are occupied with the detailed impacts of programs and new proposals on the operations of their members. Certainly among senators and representatives themselves, again with some exceptions, "expertise" in the congressional context is really a system in which generalists learn enough about a given subject matter to help other generalists, their colleagues. Even many of their aides exhibit similar characteristics.[14]

Uncertainty: Political and Technical

For all of this relative indifference, discrete instances of congressional intervention probably do advance ultimate protective goals under some *very* limited conditions. Where the threat to the public health or safety is reasonably clear and immediate, and something can promptly be done that removes the danger without the surreptitious or inadvertent introduction of a new threat, oversight activity has a fairly high probability of actually helping to save or lengthen lives. Consider automobile seat belts. Also, though it is impossible to know for sure, Congressman Mike

---

David Seidman, "The Politics of Policy Analysis," *Regulation* (July-August 1977): 22–37.

13. Quoted in Malbin, *Unelected Representatives*, p. 234.

14. John W. Kingdon, *Agendas, Alternatives, and Public Policies* (Boston: Little, Brown, 1984), p. 40.

Synar's intervention in the Tar Creek case may eventually be seen to have satisfied these conditions. But it is hard to know just *how many* cancers or other problems could be avoided by getting the EPA to channel resources to a particular area or whether some alternative use of funds might prevent more. Rarely can overseers perform the regulatory equivalent of snatching innocents from before a firing squad, especially in the health area.

Assume, for the moment, something manifestly nonsensical— that the impediment of relative political indifference described in the preceding section did not exist. Assume that all overseers were consumed by an absolute passion for searching out and enhancing the ultimate protective ends of a regulatory program. Two kinds of uncertainty would still present serious, perhaps insuperable, difficulties preventing oversight from coming to grips with ends in a straightforward way.

One kind is political. In complex policy areas, it is impossible to really be sure what ends are. This is true on two levels relevant to the present discussion. On one hand, authorizing statutes for regulatory and other programs are notoriously vague about goals. This is largely unavoidable, since Congress has neither sufficient knowledge nor (usually) the consensus to be more specific. The result is the kind of statutory language that critics condemn as hopelessly fuzzy—laws that speak of preventing "unreasonable risks of injury" or of activities that "endanger the public health or welfare" or of "contaminant(s) which may have an adverse effect on the health of persons."[15]

But even if such language could be made more precise, the real ends of policy would still be prone to shift, because policy preferences evolve constantly. New information, the elevation of new values, the diminution of old concerns, and the revelation of previously unforeseen trade-offs imply that what we want by way of protection will shift, depending on our perceptions of what we have to give up to obtain that protection. To put the

15. This language is drawn from the Consumer Product Safety Act, the section on mobile source emissions of the Clean Air Act, and the Safe Drinking Water Act, respectively.

matter a bit differently, instead of means being driven by ends, our ends adjust to our perception of the available means.[16] It is partly for this reason that a major regulatory statute conspicuous for relative semantic precision on objectives—the Clean Air Act—has been subject to repeated implementation delays and exceptions.

How important is it to safeguard ourselves from cancer? Very important indeed, if political rhetoric, legislation, media attention, and surveys are even roughly indicative. Yet when the Delaney clause forced the FDA and the country into a particularly unpleasant choice over saccharin, Congress backed off. The same thing has happened in air pollution policy—deadlines have been repeatedly extended in particular cases even as the rhetoric of full protection continues.

As a staging area for competing ideas and constituency interests, Congress is well suited as a forum for changing protective ends. But even in a regulatory bureaucracy uninhibited by overt legislative signaling or influence, policymaking would still have to consider this factor, though perhaps in somewhat less dramatic form. The process by which policy decisions are reached would still have to confront an ever-flexible array of trade-offs, uncertainties, and surprises. As David Braybrooke and Charles Lindblom have observed: "For many subjects of policy, there is apparently no possibility of arriving at a precise conception of one's objectives independent of specific policy choices."[17] The thorniest questions of social regulation easily qualify as such subjects.

The more familiar brand of uncertainty is purely technical. Along with political disagreement and sheer cost, this remains one of the most pervasive and enduring policy challenges, especially to programs created explicitly for handling health and safety matters. Unfortunately, overseers can do little, whether singly or together, to make much of a short-run dent in this information problem. At best, Congress might prod agencies

16. David Braybrooke and Charles E. Lindblom, *A Strategy of Decision: Policy Evaluation as a Social Process* (New York: Free Press, 1970), chap. 5.

17. Ibid., p. 96.

and private institutions to gather more data and to think harder about the plethora of risks and uncertainties associated with regulatory questions. This it does with funds, grants of authority, personnel increases, and less concrete forms of encouragement. Sometimes, as with the saccharin case, Congress may spotlight a particular issue for a special infusion of resources. But this is about as far as Congress can go directly toward reducing technical uncertainty.

Even with the firmest political support researchers, agency officials, and others would have their work cut out for them.[18] Risk assessment is a fiendishly tricky business, often characterized by "missing or ambiguous information on a particular substance and gaps in current scientific theory."[19] Causation between substances and their possible effects is often not scientifically well established; evidence of a concrete threat that can be universally deemed conclusive is hard to come by. Even a relatively well studied substance like asbestos is brimming with uncertainty. Moreover, hazard may lurk anywhere, and individuals face exposure of unknown or unpredictable size and frequency to many thousands of substances and products.

The risk assessment process has four steps:[20] hazard identification, dose-response assessment, exposure assessment, and risk characterization. Each is fraught with uncertainty.

Hazard identification relies on such techniques as epidemiology and animal bioassays, each of which has severe potential shortcomings. The former looks at measured association between exposure and effect that may be hard to find, especially if "the risk is low, the number of persons exposed is small, the latent period between exposure and disease is long, and expo-

---

18. This discussion draws heavily on three sources: Senate Committee on Governmental Affairs, *Benefits of Environmental, Health, and Safety Regulation* (prepared by the Center for Policy Alternatives at the Massachusetts Institute of Technology), 96th Cong., 2d sess., 1980; Baruch Fischhoff et al., *Acceptable Risk* (New York: Cambridge University Press, 1981); and National Research Council, *Risk Assessment in the Federal Government: Managing the Process* (Washington, D.C.: National Academy Press, 1983).

19. *Risk Assessment in the Federal Government*, p. 28.

20. Ibid., chap. 1.

sures are mixed and multiple."[21] Animal bioassays, by contrast, depend on the validity of inferences from animals to humans. Though the scientific community relies routinely on such inferences, they are not precise. And since ethical considerations prohibit much of the human testing that would resolve such doubts fully, a grand leap to greater precision seems doubtful.

Dose-response assessment often relies on extrapolations among dose levels and from animals to humans, both of which are open to disagreement. This was the cause of much of the furor in the saccharin debate as well as the basis for EPA's 1983 estimate that up to three additional cases of cancer could occur among a thousand persons given typical lifetime dietary exposure to the grain fumigant ethylene dibromide, or EDB, for which the agency later announced an emergency ban.[22] Especially at low dosages, unknown factors may throw off the results of such assessments.[23] Moreover, exposure to multiple substances makes assessment that much more difficult. A British study reported excess cancer mortality at an EDB manufacturing plant, a finding of rather feeble usefulness, since exposure to benzene and arsenic had also occurred there.[24]

Exposure assessment also relies on extrapolation from small groups to whole populations. Meteorologic or geologic factors must be accounted for, as must the dietary, recreational, or other habits of those who might be exposed. How should one treat special risk groups such as the elderly, asthmatics, children, or pregnant women? Consider the comments of Dr. Robert Harris of the Environmental Defense Fund during the voluminous congressional deliberations on the CPSC's handling of Tris: "The dilemma which the public faces is this: Tris in children's sleepwear is not present in consistent amounts. It varies by a

21. Ibid., p. 22.

22. For a scathing critique of the regulatory response to EDB, see William R. Havender, "EDB and the Marigold Option," *Regulation* (January-February 1984): 13–17.

23. *Benefits of Environmental, Health, and Safety Regulation*, p. 13.

24. House Committee on Government Operations, *Government Regulation of the Pesticide Ethylene Dibromide [EDB]* (joint hearings before certain subcommittees), 98th Cong., 2d sess., Mar. 5, 6, 1984, p. 24.

factor of 100. In other words, you have some garments which have very high concentrations of Tris.... How is the consumer to know whether that garment has a high amount of Tris or a low amount?"[25] How are regulators to know either?

Finally, in risk characterization, one is at the mercy of the uncertainties accumulated through prior stages. In addition, this stage requires fine judgments to be made about the relative degrees of risk to various subgroups; the characterization must be presented in a way to provoke helpful responses both within the public and among policymakers who will have to make key decisions concerning appropriate strategies of risk *management*. Much is necessarily subjective at this stage.

None of this is to say that the system cannot work, that smart, well-trained, and resourceful specialists cannot generate reasonable assessments. But each step, even in ideal circumstances, is difficult and unsure, regardless of what distant, busy politicians may do to ease matters. On a good day, all that congressional overseers usually can do is offer money, point in some direction or other, and say, "Look into it."

The direction they point to and the tools they offer will likely reflect not only technical needs as perceived by the agencies but the political ones that confront overseers. One can only hope that the two may be reconciled productively. The 1981 congressional decision that allowed the CPSC to appoint chronic hazard advisory panels (CHAPS) for substances of particular concern marginally enhanced the agency's access to outside expertise but also reflected a desire among the agency's political supporters to forestall any effort to shift chronic hazard authority from the agency.[26] The political content of this decision does not appear to have compromised its technical merits, though it is easy to imagine this happening. For example, there might well have been a legislative attempt to specify panel appointment criteria on political grounds.

25. House Committee on Government Operations, *Consumer Product Safety Commission's Ban on Tris* (hearings before the subcommittee on commerce, consumer, and monetary affairs), 95th Cong., 1st sess., Apr. 4, May 17, 1977, p. 141.
26. See section 28 of the Consumer Product Safety Act.

Two aspects of the policy problem to which politicians pay remarkably little attention are the problems of risk redistribution and substitution.[27] By redistribution, I mean that new products or processes or regulation itself may shift risk from one group of persons to another. By substitution, I mean that the same forces may reduce one sort of risk while increasing another. Overseers are prone to perceive (and thus attack) one risk at a time, as interest groups and the press rivet their attention to one problem after another.

The saccharin and Tris issues were both largely risk substitution problems. For diabetics and obese persons, the cancer risk from saccharin consumption had to be set against the danger to them from these other problems. In the Tris case, use of the substance arose only because of 1971 Commerce Department regulations (later embraced by the newly created CPSC) stipulating flammability standards for children's sleepwear. Tris was introduced to meet these requirements. The Tris case is especially horrifying not only because many children—how many, no one can say exactly—were exposed to some additional cancer risk but also because, as congressional inquiry ultimately revealed, the original flammability standard that triggered Tris use apparently lacked foundation in data.[28]

27. A good starting point for thinking about this issue is a series of articles published in *Regulation* in the mid-1980s: Peter Huber, "Exorcists vs. Gatekeepers in Risk Regulation," *Regulation* (November-December 1983): 23–32; Peter Huber, "The Market for Risk," *Regulation* (March-April 1984): 33–39; Chris Whipple, "Redistributing Risk," *Regulation* (May-June 1985): 37–44; and Havender, "EDB and the Marigold Option." More generally, see Yair Aharoni, *The No-Risk Society* (Chatham, N.J.: Chatham House, 1981).

28. In an addendum to the Moss subcommittee's report assessing the CPSC's performance in the Tris affair, Republican James M. Collins of Texas wrote: "Pursuant to its authority under the Flammable Fabrics Act, the Department of Commerce promulgated the first children's sleepwear standard on July 29, 1971, for sizes 0–6X. The first significant thing that I uncovered about the development of this first standard is that the Department of Commerce had in its possession no reliable data of deaths or injuries from sleepwear fires.... "Former CPSC Commissioner [Lawrence] Kushner, who was at the National Bureau of Standards at the time of the adoption of the standard confirmed... that no such data existed.... Even more disconcerting is that former Chairman

Although Congress may occasionally identify, in retrospect, similar instances of weak assessment, it remains generally insensitive to the larger and more common problems of risk shifts. Instead, overseers tend to highlight whatever risks are either new or newly recognized, ignoring the trade-offs among new and old. At least one knowledgeable critic has claimed that both the EPA and Congress overlooked the considerable risks of the substances likely to replace the banned EDB for the spot treatment of grain-milling machinery.[29] Certainly, in their joint hearings on EDB in March 1984, subcommittee chairmen Mike Synar and Ted Weiss of the House Government Operations Committee dramatized only the dangers of the one substance, leaving to a future day the problem of substitutes.[30] This happens not just because, as some cynics might suggest, congressmen are interested only in headlines. Short-run political payoffs are a powerful incentive, of course, but more is at work. Congressional and bureaucratic structure and process are characterized by considerable fragmentation and subunit autonomy. And both must cope with emotional issues that erupt suddenly. Under such circumstances, a helter-skelter serial approach is arguably a rational, perhaps inevitable, response by busy and cautious members to the regulatory oversight challenge.

Even where social regulation is not focused on technically arcane health and safety issues, knowledge can be limited. The regulation of sales practices by the FTC must, to be both reasonable and effective, rely on data that can be spotty or hard to interpret. Getting a valid portrait of routine business practices, especially those that might be thought abusive, and linking it to a concrete pattern of consumer injury that agency action can remedy is harder than it may sound. This is particularly prob-

---

John Byington admitted at the same October 3, 1977, hearing that the Commission still had no such data." (House Committee on Interstate and Foreign Commerce, subcommittee on oversight and investigations, *Consumer Product Safety Commission's Regulation of Tris: The Need for an Effective Chronic Hazards Program*, House Committee Print 95–58, 95th Cong., 2d sess., August 1978, p. 54.)

29. See note 22 above.

30. *Government Regulation of the Pesticide Ethylene Dibromide [EDB]*, pp. 1–6.

lematic when the firms in question are widely dispersed small businesses, which is precisely why FTC Chairman James Miller strenuously opposed his own agency's funeral rule. Miller argued that "the Commission does not have a reliable description of the industry, much less a working knowledge of how it operates. The facts presented are often contradictory, are heavily anecdotal and may not be representative of industry practices."[31] One need not take a position for or against the funeral rule itself to concede that Miller's concerns are broadly appropriate given the agency's tricky regulatory domain. Congressional oversight may result in funding that allows the agency to collect more data and thus be more certain of its ground. It also might, through the prospect of legislative veto, encourage regulators to be more certain before committing themselves on a given rule. But that is the outer range of what congressional involvement can do to resolve uncertainty about the technical facts surrounding most regulatory questions.

Implementation Complexity

Since the early 1970s, public policy scholars have been examining the process of implementation with mounting intensity.[32] The resulting analyses, taken together, emphasize that government programs often fall short of the goals envisioned for them due to some combination of limited resources, political opposition, incompatible organizational agendas and processes, unforeseen imperatives, and institutional ponderousness. Signaling and prodding by overseers are subject to the same kinds of forces: whether a policy initiative originates in a formal statute, a presidential executive order, or a series of oversight efforts in Congress, it remains vulnerable to implementation complexity. The implementation problem surely includes the indifference and uncertainty described in the preceding two sections of this

31. 47 *Federal Register* 42303 (Sept. 24, 1982).

32. An excellent starting point for someone unfamiliar with this literature is Jeffrey L. Pressman and Aaron Wildavsky, *Implementation*, 3d ed. (Berkeley: University of California Press, 1984). See esp. the bibliography at pp. 261–71.

chapter, but it is much broader, because it embraces the full panoply of political and administrative impediments—namely, political opposition and institutional complexity.

Political Opposition

What overseers want may be controversial, especially if what they want goes to the fundamental protective tasks of the agency in question. If they want some agency regulation or process sped up, another set of overseers in Congress or the White House will likely either oppose the acceleration or, at the very least, advocate different priorities. As Harvey Lieber notes, this has been an enduring feature of the federal politics of hazardous waste management:

[A key pattern] is that of congressional initiative and agenda setting as well as vigilant, often critical oversight of the implementation process. As in other ecological areas, Congress's role was that of "environmental protector" with the ideas and initiative emanating from Congress, especially its Democrat members. [But] the Executive Branch, whether Democrat or Republican, has consistently given the solid and hazardous waste programs a low priority, resulting in a confused and delayed regulatory issuance and implementation process.[33]

As we saw in chapter 2, the efforts in some quarters of Congress to get the FDA to move against antibiotics in animal feeds foundered on farm-interest opposition located elsewhere in the legislature. Democrat challenges to new OSHA enforcement policies incurred resistance in the Reagan administration's continuing determination to pursue a less intrusive and adversarial course. Under the provisions of two executive orders, the Reagan OMB intruded aggressively, and to a degree that may never be fully known, into the regulatory rule-making process, frustrating the proregulation designs of congressional Democrats.[34]

33. Harvey Lieber, "Federalism and Hazardous Waste Policy," in *The Politics of Hazardous Waste Management*, ed. James P. Lester and Ann O'M. Bowman (Durham: Duke University Press, 1983), p. 62.

34. Two critical assessments of the executive orders are: Morton Rosenberg, "Beyond the Limits of Executive Power: Presidential Control of Agency Rule-

Institutional Complexity

The sheer combination of processes and wills that must be concerted to implement policies successfully is remarkable. Often
multiple political jurisdictions, or bureaucracies, or bureaucratic
subunits must be consulted and cooperation secured. Rarely will
all these elements share immediate priorities or compatible procedures. Resource limitations, including lack of vital knowledge,
may hinder the process at one or more critical points. The decisions and actions of various participants may be hard to co-
ordinate due to different schedules, procedures, and priorities.
Political scientists Jeffrey Pressman and Aaron Wildavsky have
referred to this mixed basket of problems as "the complexity of
joint action."[35]

Overseers find narrow, concrete changes easier to induce than
broad or nebulous ones. This is perhaps most easily seen in
agency responses to committee and GAO criticism of slowness
in fulfilling basic regulatory tasks. Typically these tasks are gargantuan and fiendishly complex, such as the faster implementation of health-oriented regulations and product approvals.
General Accounting Office studies, many done at the behest of
subcommittee and committee chairmen with a continuing interest in the programs examined, have often found regulatory
agencies deficient in this respect. For example, the CPSC originally failed to develop standards faster largely because it lacked
an effective way to decide what it should regulate and because
the law saddled it with a novel but ultimately infeasible process
that facilitated political participation by interested parties more
than the actual production of final standards.[36] The GAO noted
that the FDA drug-approval process has been subject to a variety
of obstacles, including:

---

making under Executive Order 12,291," *Michigan Law Review* (1981): 193–247,
and Ann Rosenfeld, "Presidential Policy Management of Agency Rules under
Reagan Order 12,498," *Administrative Law Review* 38 (Winter 1986): 63–101.

35. Pressman and Wildavsky, *Implementation*, chap. 5.

36. General Accounting Office, *The Consumer Product Safety Commission Needs
to Issue Safety Standards Faster* (HRD–78–3), Dec. 12, 1977.

- Imprecise FDA guidelines, subject to varying interpretations.
- Scientific and professional disagreements between FDA and industry.
- Slow or inadequate FDA feedback to industry and lack of promptness in notifying drug firms of deficiencies in applications.
- Lengthy chemistry and manufacturing control reviews.
- Incomplete new drug applications and industry's slow rate of resolving deficiencies.[37]

FDA's approach to reviewing and specifying regulations for over-the-counter drugs (OTC) was assessed as "reasonable" but "slow" in 1982. But a combination of scientific uncertainty, a court challenge, and an evolving legislative and procedural environment meant that the completion of the OTC project, begun in 1972, would take far longer than had been anticipated.[38]

In mid-1984, the GAO noted that the EPA's implementation of the Toxic Substances Control Act (TSCA), passed in 1976, had been somewhat uneven. As a result of "organizational and staffing problems," the agency initially seemed to have no long-range focus to guide its implementation of the law. One part of the law, section 8(c), required that the agency issue a regulation telling chemical firms how to handle reports of significant adverse reactions. As a result of "higher TSCA priorities, complexities of rulemaking, and internal organizational changes," the final regulation was not issued until August 1983—some six and a half years after the law became effective. The agency's overall section 8 information-gathering powers remained, as of 1984, an area of continuing difficulty.[39]

None of these problems is amenable to immediate and un-

37. General Accounting Office, *FDA Drug Approval—A Lengthy Process that Delays the Availability of Important New Drugs* (HRD–80–64), May 28, 1980.

38. General Accounting Office, *FDA's Approach to Reviewing Over-the-Counter Drugs Is Reasonable, But Progress Is Slow* (HRD–82–41), Apr. 26, 1982; see esp. appendix 2.

39. General Accounting Office, *EPA's Efforts to Identify and Control Harmful Chemicals in Use* (GAO/RCED–84–100), June 13, 1984; see esp. pp. 8, 49–55.

ambiguous redress as a result of the embarrassment wrought by oversight. Congressional inquiry may help induce or set the stage for change by raising the priority of some set of issues within an agency's leadership, but when overseers seek complex, long-range change instead of small and discrete adjustment, the prospects for success fade dramatically.

Political opposition and institutional complexity are also jointly at work when questions of firm compliance with rules arise. Firms may resist stringent regulatory requirements if they find compliance excessively costly, resulting in delayed implementation and diminished benefits. Thus, if overseers insist on stringency they may, ironically, lessen the prospects for achieving protective impacts by prompting resistance from individual firms. One must remember that the promulgation of a final rule does not necessarily end debate between firms and government officials. Rule implementation may be subject to painstaking negotiation.[40]

Let us make two additional observations. First, broad societal changes (for example, heightened living standards, increased education, urbanization) almost certainly lead to far greater and more significant gains in health and safety than even the most diligently and resourcefully run regulatory programs.[41] Just as the modern capitalist economy creates the negative spillovers that regulation is supposed to mitigate, so does it presumably spawn positive ones as well. Second, much risk is beyond the reach of *any* conceivable regulatory scheme, however well intentioned its architects. Individual product users may simply be ignorant or careless, no matter how vigorously exhorted to informed and careful behavior. In short, good things happen that regulators do not produce, and bad things happen that regulators cannot prevent. The same can be said, by extension, of attentive political overseers.

---

40. Laura Langbein and Cornelius M. Kerwin, "Implementation, Negotiation, and Compliance in Environmental and Safety Regulation," *Journal of Politics* 47 (August 1985): 854–80.

41. Aaron Wildavsky, "Richer Is Safer," *Public Interest* 60 (Summer 1980): 23–39.

Moreover, if increased injury and death rates stem from greater rates of product use, all one can often do is fight harder to make each unit safer and each consumer more careful; use restriction may be politically implausible. Consider the findings on automotive fatalities of the House Appropriations subcommittee on transportation:

> According to information provided for the record of NHTSA's fiscal year 1986 budget hearing, the relationship between increases in fatalities and increases in vehicle miles of travel seems to have been re-established in 1984. Vehicle miles of travel (VMT) increased by about 4.6 percent while fatalities rose by about 3.1 percent. The Committee had been encouraged by statistics in 1982 and 1983 showing a decline in fatalities even though VMT had been increasing. The apparent re-establishment of the fatalities-VMT linkage lends added support to the belief that highway safety is influenced to a far greater degree by economic factors than by NHTSA policies or programs.
>
> The Committee is hopeful, however, that the recent trend started by state governments to enact mandatory safety belt laws combined with the passive restraint requirements of Federal Motor Vehicle Safety Standard 208 will counteract this trend and produce significant reductions in highway fatalities and injuries. . . . It is hoped that the introduction of passive restraints into the United States auto fleet beginning in September 1986 will also have significant impact on highway fatalities and injuries.[42]

In the present context, the preceding passage is exemplary in three respects. First, note what it does *not* include—any mention of driving restrictions as a way to lower fatalities; such a proposal would be politically unthinkable. Second, note the highly speculative, downright flimsy analysis of the connection between VMT and fatalities, a relationship that could easily prove spurious for the single year mentioned. This evidently feeds a clear policy predisposition: economic factors matter more than NHTSA, a plausible bias but a bias all the same. And third, the hopeful tone of the report accurately reflects the fundamental

42. House Committee on Appropriations, *Department of Transportation and Related Agencies Appropriation Bill, 1986*, House Report 99–256, 99th Cong., 1st sess., pp. 64–65.

impotence of politicians bent on securing protective policy impacts. Under the circumstances, hope is about all they have.

Implications

Even if they wanted to, overseers could not readily create positive policy impacts. But they do not generally focus on doing so anyway. Neither regulators nor their policy choices nor political oversight reflects a single-minded drive for public protection. Regulatory structures and programs appeal to politicians in the first place largely for their symbolic value. Once created, programs must inevitably be shaved, expanded, or otherwise modified so as to make them tolerable to various policy players, which absorbs considerable (and, in my observation, most) of the energy of overseers. Far from being alarming, this bespeaks a certain systemic flexibility, a recognition of the real complexities of policy that simplistic rhetoric and sweeping statutory mandates often paper over. Political, and not only congressional, oversight facilitates such adjustments. Values besides pure protection should always be brought to bear on public programs.

For this reason, the basic questions of regulatory and oversight reform are: Which values ought to be elevated, by what means, and at what sacrifice to other considerations? Is there a more sensible, effective, and politically acceptable way to treat regulatory programs? Over the years the list of proposals has grown large indeed, but this very variety is symptomatic of why so little headway toward regulatory and oversight reform has been made.

Chapter 6
Lessons

The tension between congressional perceptions of regulatory action as either excessive or insufficient constitutes a fundamental and unavoidable challenge to both setting and achieving goals. Numerous additional uncertainties and complexities, abundant in social regulation and only minimally rooted in congressional dynamics, further impede the realization of protective goals.

What role, then, can congressional supervision reasonably be expected to play in social regulation? What, if anything, can be done to improve such supervision? To answer these questions, it is important to set forth first some summary observations about the nature of congressional regulatory oversight. It is also necessary to evaluate the prospects for significant and useful change in the status quo, which will be done in the final chapter.

The Role of Regulatory Oversight

Oversight's primary significance lies in helping incrementally to define and enforce, despite all the uncertainty described earlier, some working conception of the "appropriate" in policymaking and administration. Political supervision does not and never will guarantee the fulfillment of protective goals. "Politics," by its very nature, must perceive regulatory policy as *more* than purely protective. In a large and complex democracy, administrative behavior and public policies must always be formulated and implemented in a context of competing values. Behavior and policy must strike a balance among various considerations: protection, the size and distribution of costs, accountability, administrative and economic efficiency, equity, ethical constraints, fiscal integrity, and political legitimacy.[1] Oversight, for all its inherent self-interest and the undeniable sloppiness that has been noted in previous chapters, nonetheless (1) helps attach the flesh of such considerations onto the bare bones of broad and often vague legislation; (2) polices the policy choices of bureaucrats to whom considerable discretion has necessarily been given; and (3) challenges—sometimes it is the Washington equivalent of guerrilla war—the administration in debates over policy implementation. Oversight is at heart, then, a process of fitful policy adjustment that raises problems and disagreements for congressional and agency policymakers.[2]

That policymaking must reconcile multiple considerations and still be effective in a purely instrumental sense accounts for dilemmas confronting society on any number of policy fronts. Low crime rates are universally appealing, but not every means of achieving them (routine mass arrest, incarceration without trial, abolition of the right to counsel) is compatible with the kind of democracy we collectively embrace. Other means—the death penalty is the most obvious example—may be more compatible but hotly debated. Social regulation generates similar tensions. Regulators not only set protective goals, but they must do so while remaining sensitive to a plethora of contextual issues. Congressional and White House oversight provides an ongoing, opportunistic debate about which of these many concerns ought to be elevated at any given time. Each smaller battle occurs within the

1. The best short statement of this balancing act is James Q. Wilson, "The Bureaucracy Problem," *Public Interest* 6 (Winter 1967): 3–9. On the tension between bureaucratic rationality and responsiveness, see William F. West, *Administrative Rulemaking: Politics and Process* (Westport, Conn.: Greenwood Press, 1985). West uses FTC rule making for his case material.

2. As noted earlier, this process inherently involves the "socialization of conflict." See E. E. Schattschneider, *The Semisovereign People* (New York: Holt, Rinehart and Winston, 1960).

framework of a larger context involving whether regulation should increase or decrease, the distribution of perceived burdens and benefits, and the balance of institutional power.

Five Key Themes

The prospects for major change of any kind are obviously constrained by what overseers *themselves* generally want from or for regulatory agencies. Any proposal that threatens to sidetrack the pursuit of such ends will meet congressional resistance or indifference. Alternatively, any change promising enhanced capability in such tasks might be presumed to enjoy a built-in, if perhaps latent, congressional constituency.

Recent history is reasonably clear regarding what regulatory overseers typically want. One may divide the congressional agenda into at least five analytically separable categories: regulatory expansion and agency protection, regulatory restraint, prosecution, distribution, and efficiency. Of course, in the rough-and-tumble of real oversight, these orientations often overlap or conflict; such is the messiness of the political contest.

Regulatory Expansion and Agency Protection

Much oversight argues that aggressive regulation must be encouraged and may not have gone far enough. Two opposite postures regarding agency culpability are possible.

One is exemplified by the various subcommittee chairmen who have repeatedly raked the FDA's executives and managers over the coals for not minding the public health and congressional intent. The FDA is especially vulnerable in this respect because it has a vast and complex regulatory domain, because harm is often subject to dramatic revelation, and because the agency has the delicate chore of *approving* products before marketing. The agency is easily portrayed as standing directly alongside manufacturers in creating public harm.

More broadly, perceived holes in the regulatory safety net will provide useful ammunition to congressional overseers challenging any administration's effort to ease the burden on business. Conflict will center on such matters as statutory provisions, appointments, funding bills, OMB review, and the pace or direction of program implementation.

In a different vein, overseers may wish to coddle an agency. Hearings are either to be avoided altogether (since they may do little more than provide a forum for enemies) or may be held mainly to offer a threatened agency and its allies a means to promote a message of benign usefulness. This is what supportive subcommittee overseers clearly had in mind for OSHA and the CPSC; the former had been attacked as intrusive, the latter as merely ineffective.

Regulatory Restraint

Of course, much intervention runs in the opposite direction; it aims to prevent or check perceived overreaching by the agency. It is here that the direct manifestations of congressional interest become most dramatic. As several persons interviewed noted, if trying to push a reluctant agency into taking aggressive action can be difficult, blocking or rescinding controversial action proves remarkably more straightforward. The demands of OSHA on small enterprises, the proposed saccharin ban, the seat belt ignition interlock, the FDA moves to restrict the use of antibiotics in animal feed and to change the standard of identity for ice cream, the effort to require air bags in automobiles—all of these brought action to impede regulatory zeal.

Prosecution

Overseers may also attempt to expose legal, ethical, and procedural violations. This can be an attractive procedure; it allows members and their staffs to pursue and expose behavior that virtually no one is prepared to defend. When an oversight effort can be cast in terms of unethical or blatantly unlawful conduct, there is no natural constituency anxious to rally to the defense of the alleged activity. Firms and interest groups that would generate a veritable mountain of paper and a blizzard of phone calls on other matters fall silent when the issue is framed in terms of alleged misbehavior by a bad apple. Rather than getting overseers bogged down in debates over the merits of fiendishly technical and complex policy choices, prosecutorial oversight offers the luxury of relative clarity regarding both what behavior is appropriate and how one determines whether that behavioral standard was met.

Prosecutorial oversight can often provide a convenient path to larger policy aims. When CPSC Commissioners Terrence Scanlon and Anne Graham were accused of having made improper use of government resources, the political impetus for using the prosecutorial tactic originated in congressional distaste for the substantive regulatory policies that the Reagan administration was pursuing. So blatant was the motivation of the source leaking the results of a GAO investigation that a *Washington Post* reporter felt obliged to note that the leaker was "an interested party who has been a frequent critic of Graham."[3]

Distribution

One good way to attract the attention of a member of Congress is by putting something into his or her district that provides jobs, prestige for the member or district, or some valued service. But an even *better* way to attract it is by threatening to take that something out.[4] That is why, to take a classic example, proposals

3. Keith B. Richburg, "CPSC Member Criticized over Conduct," *Washington Post*, Apr. 29, 1986, p. A17. In some cases, however, regulatory policy recedes to become even more a backdrop to other partisan and institutional tensions. Environmentalist forces interested in acid rain surely welcomed the 1986 inquiry into the activities of former presidential aide Michael Deaver, who had been accused of functioning improperly as a conduit of influence for the Canadian government. But, just as certainly, other core issues were the continued access of former White House insiders and the elucidation of limits beyond which they ought not to go. From the standpoint of the primary policy dilemmas faced by regulators, however, such activity is of minimal importance.

4. James Q. Wilson notes that "individuals and groups are politically more sensitive to sudden or significant *decreases* in their net benefits than they are to increases in net benefits. That is, they are more sensitive to, and thus more easily mobilized for political action about, circumstances that make costs seem likely to go up or benefits to go down than they are when they foresee a chance to reduce costs or enhance benefits. They are, in short, more *threat*-oriented than opportunity-oriented." See "The Politics of Regulation," in *Social Responsibility and the Business Predicament*, ed. James W. McKie (Washington, D.C.: Brookings Institution, 1974), p. 139. See also the discussion in R. Kent Weaver, "The Politics

to enhance systemwide efficiency by closing light-volume rural post offices have always met intense resistance.[5] Regulatory agencies, like other government programs, create winners and losers through both their larger substantive policy choices and the deployment of tangible agency resources. Agency leaders, if politically astute, expect congressional interest in proposals to close offices, shift personnel, or reduce funding. Money traditionally spent in one place often cannot be diverted to some other use without a fight, regardless of how valid the reasons may seem.

This distribution rationale may combine with others. If office closings are deemed part of a concerted political attack on an agency's capacity to govern, the themes of agency protection and distribution blend. The proposed transfer of the National Institute for Occupational Safety and Health (the agency on which OSHA relies for technical studies) stirred the concerted opposition of Maryland's representatives, who attempted to paint the move as a policy shift rather than a pure management initiative.[6]

Compared to, say, the Pentagon, regulatory agencies generally dole out a mere pittance in local funds. The EPA water pollution program, however, contains a conspicuous exception. By 1981 some $22 billion had been spent on thousands of wastewater-treatment facilities in cities and towns throughout the United States, with billions more obligated.[7] The size, scope, and com-

of Blame Avoidance," *Journal of Public Policy* 6 (October–December 1986): 371–98.

5. See, e.g., Michael Brostek, "Rural Post Offices," in *Cases in Accountability: The Work of the GAO*, ed. Erasmus H. Kloman (Boulder: Westview Press, 1979), pp. 93–99.

6. House Committee on Education and Labor, *Oversight on the Proposed Transfer of the NIOSH Facilities from Rockville, Md., to Atlanta, Georgia, and Cincinnati, Ohio* (hearings before the subcommittee on health and safety), 97th Cong., 1st sess., July 28, Sept. 15, 1981. A similar case occurred when overseers blocked the proposed closing of four (of ten) FTC regional offices early in President Reagan's first term. Under a compromise, staff cuts were more evenly distributed, and all the regional offices remained open.

7. House Committee on Public Works and Transportation, subcommittee on investigations and oversight, *Implementation of the Clean Water Act concerning Ocean Discharge Waivers (A Case Study of Lawmaking by Rulemakers)*, 97th Cong., 2d sess., 1982. Hereafter cited as the *Levitas subcommittee report*.

plexity of the program have made for a troubled implementation history. It is hugely difficult to design, construct, operate, and maintain so many facilities in accord with a multitude of administrative and technical requirements. These problems, along with the obvious pork barrel incentives, have made the construction grants program a natural target of continued congressional interest.[8] The one thing most certain to arouse Congress, however, is any hint that funds thought to be deserved may be denied. As a former EPA regional administrator recalled:

Upon realizing how many step 1 and step 2 applications were lying dormant in my region 6 office (grant dollars were tied to these steps), so that no one was getting the benefit of the dollars, I began to take a very hard look at what could be done to stop unnecessary grants where a finished product would never see the light of day. My staff began an intensive review of the State of Arkansas and I realized that 13 small communities on the priority list should be using some form of innovative/alternative technology. When I announced I would no longer fund mechanical plants for communities unable to cope with them, it set off a great furor in the State of Arkansas. I was bombarded by congressional pressures to release those dollars. I sent EPA teams in to Arkansas to look at each community and decide what would be the best solution.[9]

Efficiency Enhancement

Efficiency—maximizing valued output per unit of valued input, or vice versa—is often the last thing on the minds of members of Congress looking at regulatory programs. Efficiency is always in tension with other values, including protective stringency. For example, in May 1986 Chairman Ted Weiss of the House Government Operations subcommittee on intergovernmental relations and human resources questioned FDA representatives about the antidepressant Merital, which was associated with al-

8. See, e.g., House Committee on Public Works and Transportation, *Implementation of the Federal Water Pollution Control Act (Concerning the Performance of the Municipal Wastewater Treatment Construction Grants Program)* (hearing before the subcommittee on investigations and oversight), 97th Cong., 1st sess., July 14–16, 21, 23, 1981.

9. Ibid., p. 4.

lergic reactions. Weiss's real agenda, however, was to challenge, in the name of safety, newly adopted procedures designed to speed drug approvals. Argued Weiss:

No one quarrels with the need to make Government efficient in regulating the investigation and marketing of new drugs. But the law does not permit FDA to subordinate its responsibility for assuring drug safety and efficacy to any other objective....

Recently, however, FDA's new attitude appears to emphasize approving more drugs, often at a faster rate, notwithstanding diminishing resources and large increases in new drug applications. If the subject of today's hearing is any indication, the result of FDA's new policy has been reduced protection for the American public.[10]

Overseers also embrace various conceptions of efficiency when examining or reacting to regulatory agency behavior. They may endorse greater coordination among agencies and thus less wasted effort and funds. Or they may, like Senator Garn homing in on the CPSC, insist on tuning means to ends more efficiently *within* the agency.

Much of this involves quieter, more routine supervision. The appropriations committees of both houses, along with the GAO, are the primary instruments of detailed inquiry into the match between tangible resources and the proliferation of subtasks through which agencies pursue their larger missions.

Inevitably, overseers do not monitor efficiency with anything like objectivity or perfect coverage. And efficiency, too, overlaps with the other four themes. It is sufficiently elastic to provide a convenient shield for both pro- and antiregulation claims. If regulators are not working hard enough, they are being inefficient. But if they are thought to intrude where their scrutiny is not needed (or wanted), that too is inefficient.

For Congress, administrative and fiscal efficiency are relatively easy targets while *policy* efficiency is not. The first two look inward, obsessed with the details of resource allocation within or among bureaucracies. The last concerns the impact of the agency's policies on the larger world. Overseers routinely challenge

10. Opening statement by Ted Weiss at "Hearing on FDA's Regulation of New Drugs: The Merital Experience," May 22, 1986, p. 1.

agency requests for more personnel or the ponderousness of decision processes and pay little attention to the kinds of inefficiencies that regulatory policies create or promote *outside* the agency. This is why economists have often attacked aspects of air pollution policy, arguing that the country spends far more than necessary to achieve pollution abatement because various interests discourage less costly alternatives.[11]

The multiple, overlapping themes pursued by overseers are symptomatic of a pervasive difficulty, long familiar to commentators on Congress: the lack of policy integration.[12] Since each bundle of regulatory policies and practices is considered by so diverse and fragmented a body, there can be no overall sense of institutional priorities or collective endorsement of agency activity. Rather, various members and groups in Congress hunt and pick on activities of interest to them. This situation arises from a lack of institutional discipline and the overwhelming tendency to break off chunks of activity for scrutiny and manipulation.

Regulatory Mythmaking and the Irony of Oversight

Much confusion about what oversight is and does is sown both by imprecision in describing the oversight challenge and by a certain amount of deliberate political mythmaking. Overseers face three central, and progressively more difficult, problems: (1) learning what agencies have done, are doing, or plan to do; (2) influencing administrative behavior and policy decisions

11. See Robert W. Crandall, "Air Pollution, Environmentalists, and the Coal Lobby," in *The Political Economy of Deregulation: Interest Groups in the Regulatory Process*, Roger G. Noll and Bruce M. Owen (Washington, D.C.: American Enterprise Institute, 1983), pp. 84–96. See also Lawrence J. White, *Reforming Regulation: Processes and Problems* (Englewood Cliffs, N.J.: Prentice-Hall, 1981).

12. Theodore J. Lowi, *The End of Liberalism: Ideology, Policy, and the Crisis of Public Authority* (New York: Norton, 1969); James L. Sundquist, *The Decline and Resurgence of Congress* (Washington, D.C.: Brookings Institution, 1981), chap. 14; and Don K. Price, *America's Unwritten Constitution: Science, Religion, and Political Responsibility* (Cambridge, Mass.: Harvard University Press, 1983), chap. 4.

along preferred lines; and (3) promoting goal attainment. Only the third remains thoroughly problematic.

If nothing else, decades of habit and institution building have given Congress truly formidable resources for simple monitoring—uncovering and inspecting agency activities. Generally speaking, Congress lacks knowledge of this sort mainly to the extent that it deliberately prefers ignorance, as with Central Intelligence Agency activities in the 1950s, or simply does not bother to learn, as with the NASA space shuttle program before the explosion of *Challenger* in 1986.[13] With thousands of staff assistants, myriad progress reports, and informal sources within the bureaucracy, the modern Congress is well equipped to perform such monitoring. If anything, the hail of paper coming from agencies, not lack of information about agency behavior, is the far more serious problem. Even when the executive resists, whether through the rare claim of executive privilege or through unsanctioned criminal cover-up, a tenacious Congress is anything but helpless. And, to the extent that monitoring is found weak, structural cures are apparent: greater reporting requirements, larger congressional staffs, and more designated oversight committees to keep an eye on programs. Of course, these cures may promote hazards of their own: further policy disin-

---

13. In 1956 Sen. Leverett Saltonstall of Massachusetts stated: "It is not a question of the reluctance on the part of CIA officials to speak to us. Instead, it is a question of our reluctance, if you will, to seek information and knowledge on subjects which I personally, as a member of Congress and as a citizen, would rather not have, unless I believed it to be my responsibility to have it because it might involve the lives of American citizens" (quoted in Stansfield Turner, *Secrecy and Democracy: The CIA in Transition* [New York: Harper and Row, 1985], p. 145). On the lack of inclination to scrutinize the shuttle program, see Kathy Sawyer, "Oversight Was Blurred: On the Hill It Was 'NASA Knows Best,'" *Washington Post*, Apr. 6, 1986, pp. A1, A6.

Yet national security and foreign policy do provide somewhat more formidable challenges to Congress's monitoring and influence-wielding capabilities than does social regulation. The reasons are that a high degree of enforced bureaucratic secrecy is essential and that the president may deploy military force with great speed and suddenness (and little, if any, consultation with Congress) in response to an imminent crisis.

tegration and an even more intense blizzard of bureaucratic paper.

The question of influence over administrative behavior and policy choice involves two central considerations: the extent of consensus among overseers and the complexity of their demands. Many issues that arise within Congress are politically one-sided. Either a lone subcommittee chairman and his staff may be solitary voices or multiple voices may all sing the same tune. If so, and if the demand can be accommodated promptly by an agency, then it almost certainly will be. If the GAO recommends, for example, that a department secretary transmit a certain set of instructions to subordinates or to other parts of the government, compliance is a straightforward matter; the secretary either sends the letter or does not. But whether the subsequent priority setting, decision making, and coordination necessary to fulfill the ultimate intent of those instructions actually occur is another matter altogether.

A subcommittee may be lucky or shrewd enough to have leverage at a critical stage in the decision-making process, especially when it is necessary mainly to prompt or rescind the decision of one or a few key players. A dramatic example of such leverage was the EPA decision in January 1986 to propose both an immediate ban on some asbestos products and a decade-long phaseout of all remaining asbestos uses.[14] Strikingly, the proposal came barely a year after an announcement by Acting Deputy Administrator James Barnes that would have surrendered authority over asbestos to OSHA and the CPSC. Relying on section 9 of the Toxic Substances Control Act, which allowed the agency to refer a substance elsewhere for regulatory disposition, Barnes's announcement had sparked a political fire storm.[15] Chairman John Dingell's oversight subcommittee staff launched a prolonged investigation, concluding that Barnes had

14. Statement by Lee M. Thomas, administrator, EPA, Jan. 23, 1986.
15. House Committee on Energy and Commerce, subcommittee on oversight and investigations, *EPA's Asbestos Regulations: Report on a Case Study on OMB Interference in Agency Rulemaking*, 99th Cong., 1st sess., October 1985.

knuckled under to unlawful OMB pressure. Congressional and environmentalist critics objected that Barnes's interpretation of section 9 of TSCA was a smoke screen for Reagan administration insensitivity to environmental and public health concerns. Within the EPA, a kind of palace revolt erupted as scores of agency employees signed a letter that branded Barnes's justification "an insult to our intelligence and to the public's."[16] Five weeks after the Barnes announcement, the agency announced it was putting the decision "on hold" pending further study. Nine months later, the EPA went ahead with the ban and phaseout.

Congressional attention could be so dramatically influential only in combination with other circumstances peculiar to the case. The EPA had been moving fitfully toward tough regulatory action on asbestos since 1979, and as recently as April 1984 then-EPA Administrator William Ruckelshaus had made clear the agency's intention to "substantially eliminate" asbestos both because of its pervasive and severe health risks even when controlled and because suitable substitutes were available.[17] But by later that year, progress had been stymied by the OMB, which objected to the proposed ban and phaseout largely on the grounds of policy efficiency: OMB questioned whether the rules' benefits would exceed their costs. The OMB also doubted the EPA's scientific conclusions and interpreted section 9 so as to justify a transfer of authority over asbestos.[18]

Congressional investigation and criticism were important to the decision to forge ahead with asbestos elimination. But so was the larger context in which the issue developed. Congressional pressure was not comparable in the other direction. Moreover, the agency had been moving all along toward an outcome that overseers favored. The challenge, in a nutshell, was that ongoing plans to ban and phase down had been derailed by the deputy administrator and the OMB's involvement; the essential role of oversight was to help push the agency "back on track." So it

16. Quoted in ibid., p. 2.
17. Quoted in ibid., pp. 15–16.
18. Ibid., pp. 23–29.

seems hardly a miracle that congressional criticism so quickly helped to provoke an about-face. It was not as if the Dingell subcommittee had to undertake the more forbidding task of getting the agency to consider, out of nowhere, the threat posed by asbestos and to decide whether to regulate it. But without congressional outcry at a critical juncture, it is hard to imagine how things would have turned out as they did.

The asbestos story points once again toward the central political challenge confronting Congress and the nation in regulatory oversight: the elusiveness of consensus regarding what is appropriate and reasonable. Unfortunately our attention is often diverted from this reality as the main facets of the oversight task have given rise to mutually reinforcing myths about the nature of the regulatory oversight problem. Although Congress has an effective means to learn what the bureaucracy is doing, we tend to persist in seeing bureaucracy's doings as "impenetrable." In spite of multiple avenues of formal and informal political influence in regulatory policy, we are persistently reminded by some policy and reform advocates, many within Congress itself, of regulators' dangerous independence. Given the attentiveness of agency executives to congressional cues, we can join Herbert Kaufman in wondering about the "puzzling" tendency of Congress to contain some of "the most vehement complainers about the autonomy of the bureaus."[19]

Kaufman conjectures (correctly, in the case of social regulation) that the image of runaway bureaucracy may originate in simple political disagreement reflected in conflict within Congress, between Congress and the White House (or OMB), and ultimately, of course, within society at large.[20] Serious and prolonged disagreement also arises between overseers and the agencies within their jurisdiction, but there exists ample room for negotiation and various strategies through which such disputes can be handled. The very existence of such disagreement, however, is no reason to see regulators as free agents.

19. Herbert Kaufman, *The Administrative Behavior of Federal Bureau Chiefs* (Washington, D.C.: Brookings Institution, 1981), p. 169.
20. Ibid., p. 170.

An important reason for perception to the contrary lies, I believe, in the inherently ironic nature of oversight, especially when undertaken in a context of political turbulence to restrain an agency. The irony, as I argued earlier, is this: the system works precisely by creating the impression of its failure. To galvanize congressional and public sympathy against some perceived abuse or excess, politicians and lobbyists tend to use extreme language, sounding the alarm against an unresponsive bureaucracy. Congressional policy entrepreneurs face a continued struggle to elevate their concerns and enlist the aid of others toward some preferred course of action. Rhetoric that plays on the perceived autonomy of renegade regulators is simply too useful to forgo. Thus aroused, Congress reins in the offending agency with an appropriations rider, amended authorization, or embarrassing publicity. Or, perhaps, the mere threat of such action is enough to persuade the agency to reconsider its position. In either case, the system has done its job; the desired message has been effectively delivered. A lingering by-product, however, is the impression of rogue bureaucracy.

This was largely what befell the FTC during the Carter administration. Business lobbies and their congressional sympathizers put out the word that the FTC was out of control. The large majority of members, generally indifferent to the commission's activities, were besieged by complaints from local Chambers of Commerce and other groups. Hence Congress came to believe that things were terribly out of whack. While the FTC may have made errors of judgment—and many of its defenders will today acknowledge that it did—it was hardly making major policy decisions for which congressional monitoring and encouragement had been absent. Nevertheless, the business community and its allies helped create the image of an agency run amok.

Interest groups hold no monopoly on the drive to capitalize on perception of institutional failure. Candidates for Congress, incumbent or not, get considerable mileage out of "running for Congress by running against it."[21]

21. Richard F. Fenno, Jr., *Home Style: House Members in Their Districts* (Boston: Little, Brown, 1978).

Another possible contributor to an exaggerated perception of autonomy may lie in confusion over the term itself. There is a tendency, especially among nonacademic generalists, to use "autonomy" and "discretion" loosely, without specifying the level at which they operate. But it is always important to distinguish between the *field enforcement* discretion of inspectors and other relatively low-level officials who often go about their tasks in relative isolation from the scrutiny of a central office and the *policy-setting* discretion of managers and executives.

It is not hard to see why the former type of discretion resists fine tuning by executives and elected officials. The behavior can be hard to observe routinely and may spawn small-group or subcultural dynamics that resist manipulation. Lower-level officials must also make "spot" judgments about what is appropriate, perhaps in the face of nebulous cues from above.[22] And at least one sensitive student of administration has suggested that leaders may often deliberately (for various reasons) screen out information from below.[23]

The exercise of policy-setting discretion, however, is far more visible, necessarily embracing a much wider circle of participants, any one of whom may blow the whistle on behavior or decisions that conjure dissenting views. By various means, overseers may both determine what is being done at this level and communicate their sense of how, if at all, it should be done differently. Even when middle- and upper-level managers engage in tactics designed to frustrate what they deem the premature release of information or policy options, overseers are anything but helpless.

Yet no one any longer supposes that politicians can make decisions that administrators merely execute. Agencies, regulatory or otherwise, are not empty vessels into which political au-

22. See Michael Lipsky, *Street-Level Bureaucracy: Dilemmas of the Individual in Public Services* (New York: Russell Sage, 1980); James Q. Wilson, *Varieties of Police Behavior: The Management of Law and Order in Eight Communities* (Cambridge, Mass.: Harvard University Press, 1968); and Peter M. Blau, *The Dynamics of Bureaucracy: A Study of Interpersonal Relationships in Two Government Agencies* (Chicago: University of Chicago Press, 1955).

23. Herbert Kaufman, *Administrative Feedback: Monitoring Subordinates' Behavior* (Washington, D.C.: Brookings Institution, 1973), chap. 4.

thorities or interest groups simply deposit their preferences. The power of regulatory bureaucracy is less the ability to get away with things while Congress has its back turned than the ability to shape the legislature's sense of what policies are appropriate and, perhaps, to play off contending forces against one another. Bureaucracies can powerfully shape their institutional environments, providing ideas and perceptions to which other actors respond. Regulators will also (as did the FDA in the case of the drug Zomax) stand their ground if they can make a defensible case.[24]

The claim here is that the perception of regulatory discretion is frequently *inflated*—so often, in fact, as to distort both the true nature of the regulatory oversight problem and, as a result, debate about necessary change. It can take Congress time and effort to curb an errant agency, but the main thing required to achieve this is simple political will, not some ephemeral anti-bureaucratic magic. When informal prodding does not work or appears insufficient, Congress can always fall back on more finely tuned drafting of the statutory authorization in question. Promoting regulatory accountability is surely an arduous task, but those who labor at it are inclined to overstate the difficulty either as a way to build a case for some favored reform or to expand the scope of conflict in a particular realm of policy activity. One simply cannot expect overseers to offer balanced interpretations of either the system in which they operate or the results they get.

A particularly blatant example took place in the early 1980s. The EPA came under fire for that part of its water pollution program dealing with ocean discharges of partially treated municipal waste. In 1977 amendments, Congress had given the EPA discretionary authority to waive the requirement for full "secondary treatment" in some cases. But by 1981 not one such waiver had been granted. The subcommittee on investigations and oversight of the House Committee on Public Works and Transportation traced this outcome to a determined resistance

24. See "FDA Response to the Thirty-first Report by the Committee on Government Operations: 'FDA's Regulation of Zomax' " (typescript, no date). Available from the Food and Drug Administration.

on the part of Assistant Administrator Thomas Jorling and others at the agency who apparently held to a stricter interpretation of who could qualify for a waiver than some observers believed Congress had intended. The subcommittee chairman was Georgia Democrat Elliott Levitas, who had made something of a name for himself bemoaning the autonomy of regulators and trumpeting the benefits to be reaped through broader use of the legislative veto. Levitas viewed this as a glaring "Case Study of Lawmaking by Rulemakers," the subtitle of the 1982 committee report that reviewed the history of the EPA's handling of the waivers.[25]

But even in this instance, Levitas ultimately had to concede three points. First, "problems in resolving some of the more complex technical and scientific issues" posed by the statutory language contributed to the delay. Second, the proposed regulations implementing the waiver provision were challenged in court by parties "complaining that the rules were either too broad or too restrictive." Third, and most significant for present purposes, congressional attentiveness eventually *paid off*. Late in 1981 amendments to the Federal Water Pollution Control Act tightened the authorizing language and clarified congressional intent.[26] The Levitas subcommittee's report, clearly meant to be read as an appalling regulatory horror story, actually is nothing of the sort.

The Regulatory Precipice

In influencing the behavior of regulatory agencies, Congress is most dramatically effective when the situation has placed both the legislature and the agency at a kind of high-profile decision precipice. Under one general scenario, a policy decision has reached the point of final promulgation after perhaps years of percolation through the bureaucracy. But just as the agency is about to take its final leap into the *Federal Register*, or even shortly

25. *Levitas subcommittee report.*
26. Ibid., pp. 14, 38, 45.

after it has, Congress reaches out and negates the action. The rest of us, the audience, cheer or boo, a response that may leave an imprint on subsequent congressional behavior (as it did in the case of the FTC funeral rule). This blocking activity is no mean trick for a Congress persuaded of agency overkill; it mainly requires loud screams of protest.

The alternative tipping scenario occurs when a decision has reached a political bottleneck high in the bureaucracy. As noted earlier, the idea is that the OMB or the department secretary may have held up the proposal. Once again, some focused rhetoric may be just the thing to shove the decision the last few feet and over the edge, as in the asbestos case and others.

But congressional influence is generally *not* so dramatic and clear. Agencies and their overseers often will have worked out a rough accord on what decision should reach the cliff long before it does. By contrast, a given decision may remain well away from the precipice, snared in thickets of controversy and uncertainty.

Chapter 7
Prospects

The intense conflict, uncertainty, and programmatic diversity of the oversight system suggest the need for caution in approaching large-scale change. The situation demands incrementalism, modest experimentation, protracted negotiation, and the puncturing of destructive stereotypes. Rather than a greatly increased or diminished quantity of oversight, or a major shift in the balance of institutional power between Congress and the president, what is most needed is a more pragmatic and thoughtful adjustment of the current oversight regime. In particular, we should try to inject more foresight into oversight.

Congress wants coolheaded priority-setting and implementation in regulatory programs. But as regulators know only too well, Congress also treasures its right to intervene to raise the priority of any given item or even to reverse a position previously taken. It might, therefore, seem tempting to dismiss Congress as a crowd of ignorant, self-promoting meddlers. Clearly, there is a political impetus for a member of Congress to use the bureaucracy as both launching pad and whipping boy. It is also clear that members of Congress face huge demands on their time, that the legislature enjoys quite limited technical expertise, and that its legislative product often fudges key issues.[1] Members

1. On the time pressures that afflict members of Congress, see Steven Kelman,

of Congress also refuse to think like economists; congressional concern for overall policy efficiency ranges from dim to nonexistent.

If it made sense to think of Congress purely in such terms, then the central imperative of regulatory (or any other) oversight reform would seem obvious: to get legislative meddlers, to the extent possible, *out* of the supervision business, perhaps increasing the president's role correspondingly or even trusting in the self-restraint of the civil service. Yet no one seriously offers such a solution, for short of a political and cultural revolution, it is both implausible and undesirable. An independently elected and densely specialized Congress will inevitably (if unpredictably) seize the opportunity and incentive to guide and challenge agencies. Without a national government reconstituted along authoritarian or parliamentary lines, and unless a less adversarial political culture suddenly emerged, this path to "reform" is a dead end. The abandonment, or dramatic lessening, of congressional scrutiny would surely imply a concentration of power in the executive incompatible with accepted notions of inhibited government.[2]

Congress must remain a player in the regulatory arena. Its presence is vital to any prospect for regulatory reform on two levels. First, reforms aimed explicitly at oversight would need direct congressional participation to make them work, because they require an infusion of time, attention, staff assistance, and other scarce resources. Second, even innovation not aimed di-

---

Making Public Policy: A Hopeful View of American Government (New York: Basic Books, 1987), pp. 53–58.

2. In an otherwise perceptive recent statement regarding where the politics of social regulation ought to head, Gary C. Bryner errs, in my opinion, by suggesting that "[a]d hoc, sporadic hearings and informal interventions of congressional committee members and their staffs interferes with the ability of agencies to accomplish the tasks given them, and should be prohibited." This is entirely unrealistic. On the other hand, Bryner's judgment that "Congress ought to direct more of its attention to the beginning of the rule-making process—as it writes statutes, and as agencies set priorities and establish their regulatory agendas" is, I believe, beyond argument. See his *Bureaucratic Discretion: Law and Policy in Federal Regulatory Agencies* (New York: Pergamon Press, 1987), p. 216.

rectly at Congress's role (for example, altered agency mandates or novel policy approaches that can be implemented without new law) must still gain a measure of legislative acquiescence. They must be deemed legitimate to survive over the long run.

Political activity everywhere inevitably bears the hallmarks of personal political self-interest, but this is not precisely the same as the classic tension between the public interest and smaller clienteles. Narrow political and economic interests contend with broader ones every day, and there is no denying the often-noted advantages the former enjoys in contests with the latter, a serious difficulty for pluralist democratic systems.[3] But this "interest-group liberalism" cannot be fought by wishing away the essence of politics. All political life is fueled in part by individual ambition. Discussion, discovery, and reform are impossible in public life without the catalyst of such impulses, and it benefits us little to talk as if politics can or should be bled dry of them. The unavoidable task is to channel and discipline such forces toward some higher and broader purpose. The inclination to political self-promotion evident in congressional oversight is not by itself sufficient grounds for cynicism, radical change, or panic.

Inevitably, the debate over how better to supervise regulation has not been entirely calm and judicious. Discussion has been colored by deep intellectual and partisan disagreement derived largely from differences over the problems oversight reform ought to deal with. Advocates of reform, often talking completely past one another, have tended to concentrate on one of two goals: (1) increased institutional—especially congressional—power over agencies, or (2) driving policymaking toward greater concern for broad social costs.[4]

3. Theodore J. Lowi, *The End of Liberalism: Ideology, Policy, and the Crisis of Public Authority* (New York: Norton, 1969).

4. In their article defending a constitutional amendment to override the Supreme Court's *Chadha* decision on the legislative veto, for example, Sen. Dennis DeConcini (D-Arizona) and Robert Faucher glide over a major reform proposal, the legislated regulatory calendar, as an "indirect approach to legislative control of agencies." In fact, the calendar is aimed at least as much at creating cost-sensitive decision making as at enhanced congressional "control." DeConcini and Faucher, as is typical of those adopting a "congressional power" perspective on

In the late 1970s and early 1980s, attention to broad-scale oversight reform gained considerable congressional attention. Liberals and conservatives alike cited the need to get control over a bureaucratic state seen as distant and propelled largely by political inertia. On everything else, reform advocates quickly disagreed. Many favored broader application of the legislative veto, others regulatory (that is, cost-benefit) analysis. Still others supported sunset legislation, requiring termination of programs not explicitly reauthorized.[5] The natural advantage that narrow, well-organized economic interests enjoy over broader ones lay behind various suggestions for more open government.[6]

Anxious to enhance *both* political accountability *and* cost-sensitive policymaking, some analysts have offered a "regulatory budget."[7] Such a budget would, in a manner akin to the annual governmental expenditure budget, take account of the *private-sector* costs of regulation and would limit the costs agencies could impose. At its root would lie "the approval by the full Congress of both a total ceiling on all mandated private expenditures and individual ceilings broken down by agency or even by rule."

Considering such a budget impractical on various grounds but keeping its objectives firmly in mind, some critics of regulation have endorsed a legislated regulatory calendar. Under the calendar process, the executive would submit a few costly major

---

regulatory reform, simply elect not to engage in a cost-focused debate. See their "Legislative Veto: A Constitutional Amendment," *Harvard Journal on Legislation* 21 (1984): 57.

5. Lewis Anthony Davis, "Review Procedures and Public Accountability in Sunset Legislation: An Analysis and Proposal for Reform," *Administrative Law Review* 33 (Fall 1981): 393–413.

6. Various measures have been proposed to ensure that agencies formally record their contacts with outside parties as a check on the power of narrow economic interests. Suggestions have also been made that public participation in agency rule making be subsidized by the agencies in question, as was done at the FTC. See *Government Regulation: Proposals for Procedural Reform—Ninety-sixth Congress, First Session* (Washington, D.C.: American Enterprise Institute, 1979), pp. 50, 52.

7. On this paragraph and the following one, see Robert E. Litan and William D. Nordhaus, *Reforming Federal Regulation* (New Haven and London: Yale University Press, 1983), chaps. 6, 7, and pp. 139, 177, emphasis in original.

proposed regulations for consideration by special standing committees in each house and then by the whole House and Senate, with few or no amendments allowed. The agencies would proceed with rule making, but only after Congress had addressed the broad areas of choice. Proponents argue that Congress could even use the calendar process to trade off among the regulatory costs generated by different agencies. "Congress could thus recommend relaxation of a particular worker safety proposal while, *at the same time*, recommending the strengthening of another environmental or antidiscrimination proposal." Others argue that this places congressional generalists in the position of voting on matters they do not sufficiently understand.[8]

For all this, what is most conspicuous about the debate to date is how little real change it has yielded. In 1982 the Senate passed, without dissent, S. 1080, an omnibus package of reforms including legislative veto and regulatory analysis requirements, only to see it die in the House Rules Committee at the end of the Ninety-seventh Congress. Thereafter, congressional interest waned.

The Reagan administration was at least partly responsible for the failure to pass reforms. Its regulatory relief program was undertaken more or less unilaterally. Perhaps this was unavoidable, but little energy or political capital was expended on hammering together even the outlines of a governmentwide consensus. Unwise appointments at the EPA blew up in the administration's face, as scandal engulfed that most visible of regulatory agencies in 1982–83. The OMB review process, seen as an unapproved, mysterious, and possibly unlawful back door for business, came to be widely resented on Capitol Hill, where even the Republican Senate sought guarantees of greater open-

---

8. John Mendeloff, "Regulatory Reform and OSHA Policy," *Journal of Policy Analysis and Management* 5 (Spring 1986): 440–68. Mendeloff observes astutely that Congress could easily limit "the authority of agencies to issue rules, requiring a return to Congress" or employ any number of alternative control strategies that would involve it more deeply in each rule making. It does not, however, simply because "the political costs of responsibility are often viewed as outweighing the benefits" (pp. 449–50).

ness and the House ultimately threatened to defund the OMB's Office of Information and Regulatory Affairs.

The last major change enacted before the Reagan presidency was the Paperwork Reduction Act of 1980. The law satisfied the congressional quest for symbolic reform—getting excess government off the back of the American businessman—while leaving essentially undisturbed the powerful alliances and constituencies that underlay particular regulatory programs. It was, like campaign finance disclosure and ethics reform in the wake of Watergate, politically low-cost change for many lawmakers.[9] The 1982 Senate bill shared this advantage. And by offering multifaceted reform—legislative veto, regulatory analysis, and a larger role for the courts—the bill attempted to unify the separate regulatory reform constituencies.

The inclination to exert control over agencies by stressing—indeed sometimes pretending—how much they have evaded control presents a significant puzzle to modern American government. Even as the system works, it threatens to undermine confidence in the efficacy of political practice. Evaluation suffers because of an inaccurate picture of policy implementation. This tendency also pushes us farther toward symbolic instead of substantive action. To the extent that politics becomes an exercise in raising issues and creating conflicts rather than resolving them, we are more likely to grow frustrated and thus be drawn to mainly symbolic remedies. Expanding the scope of conflict on one issue, moreover, makes it more likely that the same will happen with related issues, a daunting prospect at best.

Uncertainty contributed to the deadlock over what kind of change makes sense both in regulatory programs and in the oversight efforts targeted at them. Ideas like the regulatory budget and the legislated regulatory calendar have yet to generate anything like the sort of intellectual consensus within the academic community that might help pave the way for successful congressional policy entrepreneurship. Such consensus consid-

9. On the political attractiveness of campaign finance and ethics reform see Thomas Byrne Edsall, *The New Politics of Inequality* (New York: Norton, 1984), pp. 42–46.

erably facilitated economic deregulation in transportation; economic analysts were virtually unanimous that continued regulation was unjustified at best and terribly harmful at worst.[10] In social regulation, by comparison, analysts exhibit little agreement on how much deregulation or other change there ought to be (if any), how it ought to be accomplished, or what adjustment in Congress's overall role might be most useful.[11] About the only position that corrals most persons is a general support for exploring alternatives to the rigidity of command-and-control standard setting. Ironically, its very intellectual fecundity impedes the analytic community from making as strong a reformist mark as it otherwise might. Once agreement is reached, however, and congressional leaders are persuaded that it is in their interest to embrace it, this could change dramatically.

Any set of reform proposals must confront the indifference or resistance of individual members and of the various regulatory policy networks. Members satisfied that they can successfully pursue the oversight theme of their choice for programs that immediately interest them will be hard to convince that they should support change that may cause institutional turbulence for little or no concrete payoff. A major difficulty for reformers of an economic bent, beyond their inability to agree on any straightforward plan of attack, is the lack of any palpable constituency for overall economic efficiency outside the analytic community. As one observer has put it: "The chief problem facing those worried about the inefficiency of risk regulation is that most people are not."[12] This state of affairs will be hard to change. It will not change just because smart people produce good ideas. Those ideas must be sold. Momentum must be generated within Congress and among attentive publics.

Even business will shy away from changes that promise dim and distant benefits or that might even backfire. (Certainly the

10. Martha Derthick and Paul J. Quirk, *The Politics of Deregulation* (Washington, D.C.: Brookings Institution, 1985).

11. See, e.g., the debate on reforming OSHA in the *Journal of Policy Analysis and Management* 5 (Spring 1986).

12. Mendeloff, "Regulatory Reform and OSHA Policy," p. 451.

toughest lesson of economic deregulation has been that overall efficiency may have to come at the expense of particular firms or districts.) In Congress, policy innovation is regularly the product of immediate opportunity, frustration, or fear—or some combination of the three.[13] Unless unusually coherent and persuasive, more detached "analysis" will finish a weak fourth. Proposals for creating economically efficient regulation simply do not speak to the themes that overseers generally wish to pursue.

Such immediate factors, arising episodically out of discrete situations, have tended to be the major impetus behind efforts within Congress itself to change either the institutional context of regulatory oversight or the powers of particular overseers. In 1957 sustained criticism of the independent regulatory commissions during the second Eisenhower term prompted Democrat House Speaker Sam Rayburn to demand the creation of the oversight subcommittee that John Dingell would later chair.[14] In 1971 Jamie Whitten, the conservative chairman of the House Appropriations subcommittee on agriculture, received jurisdiction over the EPA, the FDA, and the FTC, agencies to which liberals would judge him hostile. Thus in 1974 liberal Democrats sought to strip Whitten of his chairmanship, a move staved off when, in a compromise, he surrendered the EPA and the FTC.[15] Bills introduced in early 1983, during the upheaval at the EPA, would have turned the agency into a five-member bipartisan commission less subject to White House control.[16] In 1986, anxious to give Congress more formal power in the selection of the

13. But, as one recent study of policy innovation suggests, controversy may well generate research rather than impede it, as is often thought. See Nelson W. Polsby, *Political Innovation in America: The Politics of Policy Initiation* (New Haven and London: Yale University Press, 1984), p. 155.

14. Arthur Maass, *Congress and the Common Good* (New York: Basic Books, 1983), pp. 205–6. See also Bernard Schwartz, *The Professor and the Commissions* (New York: Knopf, 1959).

15. Alan Ehrenhalt, ed., *Politics in America: Members of Congress in Washington and at Home* (Washington, D.C.: Congressional Quarterly, 1983), pp. 832–33.

16. H.R. 1582 introduced by James H. Scheuer (D-New York) and S. 547 introduced by Daniel P. Moynihan (D-New York) and George J. Mitchell (D-Maine).

commissioner of Food and Drugs (and perhaps create additional channels for policing the policies of conservative presidents), Democrat Henry Waxman got the full Energy and Commerce Committee to endorse a change in the law to require Senate confirmation of future commissioners.[17] The Senate approved the same change in early 1988.[18] By the same token, as immediate needs or the symbolic value of proposed changes recede, the attention of Congress will likewise wane. The move to reorganize the EPA died after the scandal ended. The politics of the moment rather than detached reflection tend to guide the congressional search for better regulatory oversight.

Perhaps the most broadly significant recent change involved the Office of Management and Budget's oversight of regulatory rule making.[19] As noted earlier, a Reagan administration executive order gave the OMB's Office of Information and Regulatory Affairs (OIRA) an unprecedented warrant to promote cost-effectiveness in regulatory rule making.[20] But this new power displeased many in Congress who felt that OIRA had gone far beyond anything envisioned by the authors of the 1980 Paperwork Reduction Act that created it. This led critical overseers to suggest that OIRA reviews were unduly closed to outside scrutiny, partial to business, and an affront to congressional intent.

The battle reached a climax, if not a definite end, in 1986 with congressional threats to cut off all OIRA appropriations—and a counterthreat of a presidential veto by OMB Director James Miller. The move to withdraw funding continued even after the OMB altered its procedures to make its regulatory reviews more open to scrutiny. The controversy abated—though it was surely not permanently settled—when Congress passed a three-year reauthorization of OMB appropriations along with more explicit

17. H.R. 4754 introduced by Henry Waxman (D-California).

18. Michael Specter, "New Freedom for the FDA Commissioner?" *Washington Post*, Feb. 9, 1988, p. A21.

19. For a good summary of the controversy, see William Funk, "Paperwork Reduction Act Amendment," *Administrative Law News* 12 (Spring 1987): 3–4.

20. The executive order did not apply to independent regulatory commissions such as the CPSC or the FTC.

legislative language. The legislation also subjected future heads of OIRA to Senate confirmation. As is so often the case, tough, messy, and protracted negotiation between Congress and the executive branch proved unavoidable to thrashing out an arrangement that each side could live with—for the time being.[21]

Four Suggestions for Reformers

What direction, then, should reform take? I would offer four pieces of advice to congressional overseers, Congress watchers, and reform advocates. The emphasis here is not on endorsing or attacking particular oversight tools but on encouraging certain kinds of individual and collective vigilance. I believe that building critical sensitivities is at least as important as the advocacy of novel mechanisms.

1. *Keep discussion of particular oversight innovations politically and procedurally realistic.* Efforts to reform the oversight of social regulation face unavoidable political and institutional dilemmas. The more Congress, the White House, or the judiciary tries to exercise influence, the greater the chance for disagreement over what agencies ought to be doing and how. One institution wanting more or less or different regulation will often trigger a competing claim elsewhere in the political system. This conundrum, along with other partisan and political disagreements, must be confronted openly in discussing change, because it is unrealistic to expect reform to create apolitical harmony. Yet proponents of various ideas, especially politicians, have often sidestepped or understated it, preferring to criticize the status quo harshly and to defend novel mechanisms in heavily idealized terms. When advocates do address potential pitfalls, the focus is often more on methodological issues (how do we calculate a regulatory budget?) and on the difficulties posed by limited institutional

21. I believe it a safe guess that future presidents, regardless of party, will continue to find something like the current OMB role essential to advancing White House interests and priorities in regulatory policy. See James T. O'Reilly and Phyllis E. Brown, "In Search of Excellence: A Prescription for the Future of OMB Oversight of Rules," *Administrative Law Review* 39 (Fall 1987): 421–44.

resources (how would Congress find the time and staff to apply a generic legislative veto?) than on the central political challenges of disagreement and dispersed power.

2. *Reject, and combat when necessary, the rhetoric of runaway bureaucracy.* The easy rhetoric of bureaucratic imperialism and runaway agencies also hinders reform. Though the political attractions of such imagery are obvious, it badly oversimplifies and camouflages hard truths about regulatory governance: that conflicting ideologies and interests fundamentally shape the regulatory state, that the agencies in question typically have shown themselves highly solicitous of the signals transmitted within their respective policy networks, and that any reform faces its greatest difficulty in both adoption and implementation from within these very networks. But politicians and interest groups are likely to be of little help in setting matters straight, for they are the very players for whom the appeal of such position-taking behavior is most tempting. Independent opinion makers and various academic and journalistic commentators are free to unmask such loose talk for what it is and so contribute to a marginally more disciplined focus on the genuine problem of reconciling diverse interests.

3. *Focus prescriptive analysis on concrete, incremental political change along with, or even instead of, broad structural and procedural reforms.* Regulatory policy critics of a more academic bent might also consider whether the debate they have pursued ought to be sharpened in ways they have traditionally tended to avoid. If, as seems clear, some failings of regulatory programs may be traced largely to the supporting coalitions and key players involved in program oversight, analysts might do well to involve themselves more readily in a critical question: whether and how *particular networks* ought to be substantially altered. If chairman X or committee Y is largely responsible for keeping agency Z the way it is, then it makes sense for critics to highlight this linkage and ask whether and how it ought to continue. At present, such analysts prefer to play this game only in the most indirect ways. The legislated regulatory calendar would certainly upset existing political power relationships—that is, on one level, its very purpose. But despite the severe implications of proposed

reforms for the world of blood-and-guts politics, academic analysts too often discuss such "political factors" or "political realities" as distant, immutable context and without engaging them in any direct or detailed way. Given the relish with which critics in universities and policy research institutes attack regulatory statutes, policy outcomes, and the overall processes that generate them, their reluctance to investigate adjustments in specific political environments (that is, individual political fiefdoms) is striking.

But such an approach, a discussion in terms of targeted political incrementalism that would engage this context more directly, could breathe new life into consideration of policy reform. By examining the political dynamics of particular regulatory programs and exploring and advocating concrete ways in which these should be altered, the various critics of regulation might be more effective. It would not be easy; many in Congress would surely bristle at the intrusion. But that alone is no reason to avoid the effort. Some observers might also caution that such engagement could too readily politicize the community of analysts and scholars. Yet this community *already* engages in politics; its language, forums of discussion, and aura of detachment only disguise this fact. To argue for more or less or different oversight is an inherently political act, simply because one thereby aims to structure public power and collective choice along preferred lines. And by shifting the focus from broad reforms to narrow ones, one captures some advantages of incrementalism—reduced opposition and fewer unanticipated consequences.

This is not to say that broad generic reform is entirely undesirable—if one wants to start "trading off" among the costs imposed by a variety of regulatory programs it is unavoidable—but that narrower change of an explicitly "political" type ought also to have its place on the reform agenda. Such political reforms are not painless, nor are they panaceas. But they should be dealt with more often and more directly.

4. *Ensure greater sensitivity among overseers to the larger, perhaps unseen, ramifications of the demands they make on agencies.* It is also appropriate to explore, especially in an era of budget deficits and the resulting belt-tightening that will be required at agencies

of all kinds, to what extent various hidden zero-sum choices will be increasingly engineered by committee-level overseers pursuing narrow targets. How often does committee insistence that some problem be placed onto or elevated within the agency's agenda result in unseen action to deemphasize some other priority? The potential for such adjustments ought to be the subject of further investigation and debate, especially since the current need to embrace fiscal restraint may reduce the opportunity to create new programs while increasing the incentive for oversight entrepreneurs to tinker with existing ones. Said a former FDA chief counsel:

> Here's an agency with a certain number of employees and a certain number of dollars that could all be used to put into effect one *sentence* of the Food, Drug and Cosmetic Act. There should be a realization that you have to reduce resources for one purpose if you are going to increase them for another. But Congress never looks at it that way. There is never a hearing or news story to consider something like that. Congress should be willing to tell the agency what it should *stop* doing in order to do more of what Congress is currently concerned about.[22]

At present, such choices are doubtless largely a matter of executive finesse. The potential for such adjustments ought to be the subject of further inquiry.

How might one encourage greater congressional attention to this problem? Committees could adopt written rules to raise the question.[23] Or subcommittee chairmen can simply make a habit of raising the issue and seeing to it that their staffs do so. The

22. Personal interview.
23. The *Rules of the House of Representatives* appears to encourage a degree of foresight. Rule 10 stipulates that each standing committee "shall review and study any conditions or circumstances which may indicate the necessity or desirability of enacting new or additional legislation within the jurisdiction of that committee ... and shall on a continuing basis undertake futures research and forecasting on matters within the jurisdiction of that committee." However, there is little sign that either the House or its committees have interpreted this language to produce the specific kind of foresight I am urging. Indeed, "futures research and forecasting" that raises the priority of some issues for agencies without explicitly addressing the concomitant lowering of other priorities may only contribute to the problem.

important thing is not that a requirement be formalized—though this would have the virtue of explicitness—but that committees create an accepted custom of inquiry. Overseers ought to ask themselves and agency officials what, if anything, might be inadvertently sacrificed if the bureaucracy were to devote more attention to a particular congressional priority.

Two questions arise. Would subcommittees and individual overseers take their responsibility at all seriously? And might agencies use such inquiry as a weapon to avoid doing things they oppose? In Congress, one certainly cannot expect completely to override existing imperatives and incentives. The aim here is merely to make the problem of such unseen trade-offs an explicit and routine concern. Members of Congress want to make good public policy, and some would give serious thought to this problem. That alone would be an improvement. And, yes, lazy or deregulation-minded officials might attempt to make unwarranted excuses. But, of course, many policies invite a multitude of arguments—including frivolous ones. The possibility that players in the game of politics may sometimes make unjustified claims is hardly a reason to keep significant policy questions under wraps. After all, if an agency has arguments worth considering, Congress and the public should hear them.

These recommendations may seem modest, but I believe they are both plausible and directed at real, rather than imagined, failings. I intend them to help establish some sensible parameters for future debates over reform generally, not to push an ideology or redress the errors of a particular agency. Given the importance of the processes and policies in question, and the complexities of technology, cost, participation, and accountability to which they are subject, all attempts at thoughtful dissection ought to be welcome. This is mine.

Appendix
Note on
Research Strategy

This book is a commentary on the recent and potential congressional role in overseeing a certain kind of regulatory bureaucracy. It is based on a forthrightly old-fashioned and soft research approach—the examination of documents and discussions with persons who are variously knowledgeable. No rigorous attempt is made to formulate or to test hypotheses about that role, although I anticipate that this work should assist others in doing so. Rather, I set out simply to chart the landscape of regulatory oversight, hopeful that an alert observer could derive some reasonably coherent insight into what it is good for, and how (if at all) it might be rendered even better. From the beginning, it seemed to me that the best way to get at such concerns was to sift through as much recent experience as I could, especially since harder measures of behavior and response seemed elusive, useless, or, worst of all, potentially misleading.[1] I was less interested in knowing "how much" oversight there is than in a rather less accessible but to me more interesting question: What difference does oversight make?

As anyone familiar with them knows, Congress and regulatory

---

1. On this point, see the discussions in G. Calvin Mackenzie, *The Politics of Presidential Appointments* (New York: Free Press, 1981), pp. 278–84, and Nelson W. Polsby, *Political Innovation in America: The Politics of Policy Initiation* (New Haven and London: Yale University Press, 1984), p. 6.

agencies generate mountains of printed material, invaluable for probing the relevant terrain. Virtually everything said on the floor of either house or during official committee hearings is available for inspection—though sometimes slightly sanitized or amended. In addition, large numbers of committee reports provide argument and evidence on any number of matters that have attracted attention inside Congress. These and similar materials are rarely subjected to reasonably thorough scrutiny extending across multiple program areas. Taken together, a sensitive reading of hearings, reports, bills, and the like offers the best single guide to the role that Congress plays in an issue or an agency.

Yet the written record, whether for Congress or within an agency, leaves gaps. Much congressional power is wielded informally, even tacitly. And in many cases written records hint at relationships and motivations but do not address them overtly. This is hardly surprising. Members of Congress, staff, bureaucrats, and interest-group leaders often play the various instruments of politics with a determined subtlety. They will not refer aloud or in writing to alliances or to underlying incentives. Certainly to read only the published record at face value is to think that no political actor ever had a self-interested or conniving thought in his or her life.

To have any chance of getting beyond the bounds imposed by this artifice, one must either be behind the scenes or get access to those who are or have been. As a practical matter then, one must interview. My research assistant and I conducted over seventy for this book. Interviewees included present and former congressional staff, agency officials, and interest-group representatives. In nearly every case, these persons were guaranteed anonymity to assure candid responses. Indeed, many demanded such a guarantee before consenting to talk. Only one member of Congress was interviewed. This may seem a strange admission in a book about Congress. But legislative staff aides offer three important advantages over members to the researcher.[2] First,

2. For a good example of research reliant on staff responses, see Robert J. Art, "Congress and the Defense Budget: Enhancing Policy Oversight," *Political Science Quarterly* 100 (Summer 1985): 227–48.

they are as a rule more knowledgeable about all facets of the oversight process than are members. Several staff aides interviewed were, in effect, career overseers of regulatory bureaucracies. They constitute the front line of congressional relations with agencies of all kinds and are far more likely to know how issues played out over time. They will, among other things, have monitored the course of agency response to congressional oversight initiatives, something that members are less likely to have done. (Agency staff, obviously, are similarly informed.) Second, staff assistants are generally far more accessible than members, whose time is often tightly budgeted. Especially when Congress is not in session, staff aides offer a virtual gold mine of information about the recent course and past history of nearly any national issue. And finally, I believe that staff aides are, under the right circumstances, generally more inclined to candor regarding the delicacies of constituency and other political influences. In interviews I was especially anxious to get beyond a rehashing of public interest justifications previously served up for the record. Staff assistants seemed less likely to waste my time in this regard.

All interviews were relatively open-ended encounters (that is, no formal questionnaire was used), but in every case my research assistant and I had a distinct, focused set of events or practices about which we sought insight. Often, however, interviewees were either asked for or volunteered their impressions of broader matters, especially the general role of congressional oversight. As it turned out, my encouragement of such free analysis and speculation was fortunate, because it not only promoted rapport but also led some persons to raise issues (in one or two cases, even theoretical points) that proved useful to ponder.

But a word of caution is in order. I quickly found regulatory oversight to be a subject of considerable sensitivity in some quarters of both Congress and the bureaucracy, despite my persistent attempts to put people at ease by stressing the academic nature of my inquiry. Even staff aides may fear to unmask the extent of their contacts inside the bureaucracy. They also have strong incentives to overstate the significance of oversight efforts they may have initiated or participated in. By the same token, agency officials can be understandably reluctant to concede that they, or their bureaucracies, may have capitulated to outside pressure. Though it did not prove especially hard to get most persons contacted to consent to interviews, some were obviously a bit suspicious of the use to which their remarks might be put. (Was I supported by a conservative foundation or a liberal one?) Interviewees often seemed to see a curious professor as they would a reporter—that is, as but one more vehicle to help structure the scope of political conflict to their advantage. This is not surprising, and it need not doom any research effort. It does, however, amplify the need for circumspection and "hardheadedness" in anyone who would attempt to work in a similar vein.

I also employ a fair amount of journalistic material, ranging from such specialized organs as the *Congressional Quarterly Almanac* and the *Occupational Safety and Health Reporter* to general circulation newspapers like the *New York Times* and the *Washington Post*. Such resources, when used with due care, can be helpful in illustrating and fleshing out broader, more theoretically informed analyses than most working journalists would be likely to undertake.

Certain focal choices perhaps bear explanation. I include no separate chapter on the work of the General Accounting Office. While the GAO is certainly a precious oversight resource for Congress, I decided early in the research effort to concentrate primarily on committees, the institutions at the heart of legislative influence over agencies. Of course, committee overseers frequently use GAO products, routinely requesting studies and investigations on many topics. Such studies often provide useful fodder for congressional policy entrepreneurs anxious to find or highlight some perceived abuse or insufficiency. This is because the press regularly picks up, and plays up, the results of GAO investigations.[3]

3. Anne Motley Hallum, "The Politics of Oversight: Congress, the Media, and the U.S. General Accounting Office," paper delivered at the 1984 meeting of the Southern Political Science Association in Savannah, Georgia, November 1–3.

I do not discuss Congress's constituency service function because I concentrate on committee and chamberwide dynamics. Constituency service is undertaken by a member's personal staff, typically by persons assigned that explicit task. Furthermore, initial interviews, along with the appearance of an immensely rich and detailed study of constituency service, persuaded me that the main discernible effect of such client troubleshooting is to compel: (1) swift answers to inquiries and (2) a hard look at discrete cases.[4] Broad policies are, apparently, put at issue only rarely.

Finally, I do not examine third-order or spillover effects of congressional activity not directed explicitly at an agency's administrative and policy choices. For example, the congressional revenue committees may create tax incentives in, say, the timber industry—inducements with implications for the environment. Or government policy may depress gasoline prices below what they would otherwise be, leading indirectly to more driving and thus to more automotive injuries and fatalities. However real these effects may be, I exclude them from consideration here because overseers rarely deal with them and because there is no straightforward way to tease them out.

4. John R. Johannes, *To Serve the People: Congress and Constituency Service* (Lincoln: University of Nebraska Press, 1984), chap. 7.

Index

Acid rain, 174n.3
Adams, Brock, 127, 128
Adkinson, F. Keith, 80–81
Agencies, 153; delaying tactics by,
24, 41, 85–86; officials in, 50–51,
71, 115, 151, 167, 175n.6, 178;
political appointees to, 25, 35, 36,
65, 77–82, 98, 174; protection of,
154, 160, 172, 173; staff of, 96,
98, 110, 142
Air bags, 121–22, 123, 126–29,
143, 173
Air pollution: control, 20, 37–38,
61n.54, 66, 105–6, 157, 174n.3,
178. *See also* Clean Air Act
All-terrain vehicles (ATVs), 74, 75–
76
Angel, Arthur, 134
Antibiotics: in animal feed, 46, 55,
89, 99, 164, 173
Appropriations, 90–94, 103–4,
114–15, 196; for agencies, 12, 27,
118n.2, 173, 196; Labor-HEW,
109–10. *See also* Appropriations
under agencies, e.g. Consumer
Product Safety Commission,
appropriations
Appropriations committees, 13, 91,
92–94, 95, 99, 104, 109, 115.
See also House Appropriations

Committee; Senate Appropriations Committee
Asbestos, 61n.54, 73, 74–75, 151,
180–82
Assessment of programs, 18, 73,
154–55, 158–63, 192. *See also*
Cost-benefit analysis; Cost-effectiveness analysis
Auchter, Thorne, 63, 114
Authorization: of agencies, 2–3, 12,
185, 186
Authorization Committees, 8, 12,
13, 20, 140
Automobile industry, 37, 122–23,
127, 128, 129, 131, 132, 137n
Automobiles: emissions control, 20,
37, 106; used, 130–33. *See also*
Air bags; Seat belt-ignition
interlock

Bailey, Patricia, 132
Barnard, Doug, 75, 76
Barnes, James, 180–81
Benson, James, 53
Bingham, Eula, 61, 62n.56
Boland, Edward, 104, 107,
108
Braybrooke, David, 157
Breaux, John, 113
Bryner, Gary C., 189n.2